Cover Photograph
Carrot Raisin Cake (see "Healthy Five" Recipe Section)

BAKING without FAT

By George Mateljan, Health Valley Foods

Published by
Health Valley Foods
16100 Foothill Boulevard, Irwindale, CA 91706-7811

Printed in the United States of America

 Printed on Recycled Paper using Environmentally Safer Inks.

Also by George Mateljan:
Natural Foods Cookbook
Healthy Living Cuisine
Healthier Eating Guide & Cookbook
Cooking Without Fat

Baking Without Fat
© 1994 Health Valley Foods
16100 Foothill Blvd.
Irwindale, CA 91706-7811

ISBN 0-9633608-1-7

Library of Congress
catalog card number
93-077482

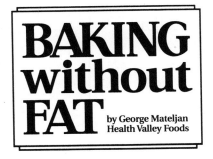

BAKING
without
FAT
by George Mateljan
Health Valley Foods

acknowledgments

The collaborative efforts of many dedicated and talented individuals made this book possible.

I especially want to acknowledge the enormous contributions made by Barbara Luboff, M.S., R.D., Director of Education at Health Valley. Barbara collaborated with me in creating all the recipes in this book, and acted as the leader of the team that developed and perfected them. She is not only extremely knowledgeable about nutrition, she is also very gifted creatively. This book literally would not exist without her.

Jim Burns edited and coordinated the book.

Wendy Crump was an important member of the team that developed the recipes. Her ideas and knowledge contributed greatly to this book.

John Convey patiently tested the recipes over and over, and provided valuable feedback in perfecting and refining them.

Cristina Aldana did the final testing of the recipes and helped ensure that all the directions are clear and accurate.

Ron Deering maintained all the data for the project and analyzed the nutritional content of the recipes.

Terry Taketa assisted me with the editorial content.

Bernard Landes provided his expertise on nutrition and health, and contributed to the editorial sections.

Harry Urist assumed the tremendous responsibility of checking and proofing the text and recipes.

Mike Clayton, Lessa Woods and Donna Mitnick did a wonderful job of designing and executing the graphic elements of this book, making it attractive and easy to read.

Gary Moats was the photographer who made the photos of our recipes so attractive, with the assistance of food stylist Robin Tucker.

My thanks to John Arbeznik, Charles Brockett, Dean Brynildsen, Rod Crossley and John Fulkerson for their valuable leadership and contributions.

dedication

This book is dedicated to Eli Khoury, Health Valley's Master Baker, and a baking scientist who possesses both outstanding technical knowledge and extraordinary artistry. Eli is an old friend of mine and one of the most talented baking professionals I have ever worked with. He has collaborated with me in creating our Health Valley Fat-Free product line. I am grateful for his enormous contributions to Health Valley and for his longtime friendship.

a message from the author

All my life, I've had a passion for food. Even as a child, I was fasci-nated by food preparation. By the time I was 5 years old, I already had my own kitchen tasks to perform during the holidays. My mother would measure out the ingredients and give them to me to mix together. When we made bread, I would watch in wonder as simple ingredients such as flour, water and yeast were transformed into something altogether different. It was magical to see the dough rise. And I've always loved the mouth-watering fragrance of baked goods. When the golden loaves of bread finally emerged hot from the oven, I felt a sense of pride and accomplishment that was the greatest reward I could ever imagine.

In 1970, I turned my passion for food into my life's work when I started a small company called Health Valley Foods. The company's original purpose was to prepare only good tasting foods made the healthy way. We have been consistent in maintaining those stan-dards for over 20 years without regard to profit or effort. It has never been my intention to build a financial empire. I have always received my greatest satisfaction from knowing that our Health Valley foods offer healthy benefits for our customers.

Even in the early years, I realized that it wasn't enough merely to prepare and distribute healthy foods. Our customers also need infor-mation on how to use our foods as part of a healthier way of eating that can contribute to the quality of their health and their lives. That's what motivated me to share my knowledge and experience about nutrition by writing my first cookbook in 1980.

Over the years, I've written four books on healthier cooking and eating. The most recent, *Cooking Without Fat,* has been by far the most popular. Even though the book has not been sold in book stores, and hasn't been promoted by any publishing company, it has sold over 500,000 copies.

I am very gratified by the response to the book. My feeling is that the book has been a success because it fulfills a need for health conscious people. *Cooking Without Fat* offers something no other book does—the secrets to preparing good tasting, convenient, nutritious and satisfying meals *without using any added fat or high-fat ingredients, and without any refined sugar, added salt, or white flour.*

A surprising number of people who purchased *Cooking Without Fat* took the time to call or write Health Valley to comment on it. Many people had a similar request—more recipes for *baking* without fat.

This book is in response to those requests.

Yours in Good Health,

George Mateljan

P.S. I just want to share one of the many letters I received asking for more recipes for baking without fat:

> *"A lot of us can't wait until your* Baking Without Fat *is released—I have three copies already spoken for.*
>
>  *"My husband and I have horrendous 'sweet teeth'—plus I <u>love</u> to cook and bake. It's good to know that pretty soon we can have our cake and eat it, too!! (As I write this, I'm draining two containers of yogurt so that tomorrow morning I can make the New York Cheesecake recipe from your* Cooking Without Fat. *It really is so good.)*
>
> *"Thanks again for all your wonderful and guilt-free food."*
>
> —Judith G. Lord, Exeter, R.I.

Table of Contents

**BAKING
without
FAT**

introduction

For me, baking has always been a wondrous act of creation. You start with the simplest of raw ingredients, and by adding your own care, you transform them into something that fills your home with wonderful aromas, and emerges hot from the oven to nourish your soul as well as satisfy your body.

It's easy to see why I have always loved to bake.

But I have an equally strong love for healthy foods, so it angered and upset me to find out how much fat is "hidden" in many traditional baking recipes.

My Personal Story About Carrot Cake

Carrot Cake is a dessert I had always loved. It tastes good and should be healthy because the key ingredient is carrots, one of nature's richest sources of the important antioxidant, beta carotene. And the combination of wheat flour and carrots produces a food rich in fiber, another important part of a healthy diet.

But what really makes me angry is the fact that the traditional recipe contains much more fat than it does carrots. The batter calls for a cup and a half of oil and four eggs. Add the frosting that is made with cream cheese and butter, and topped with nuts, and one serving of this "healthy" sounding cake can contain as much as 29 grams of fat!

That's about the same amount of fat found in a fast food quarter pound hamburger!

I found this to be intolerable. In fact, it made me so angry that I decided I had to do something about it. After all, I have dedicated my life to healthier eating. The reason I founded Health Valley in the first place was to prepare the kinds of good tasting, convenient and nutritious foods that I wanted for myself and my family, but that weren't being offered by commercial food companies. So from the beginning Health Valley has been committed to preparing the finest quality foods made the healthy way, without compromise. Our passion is to create healthy foods that truly contribute to a better quality of life. That's why I no longer bake with any fat. And when I became angry about all the hidden fat in carrot cake I made a commitment to offer you a Carrot Cake recipe made without any added fat or high-fat ingredients that still tastes delicious.

In fact, Carrot Cake is so symbolic of what this book is all about that we featured our own Fat-Free version of it in the photograph on the front cover. We also developed several other recipes with carrots because this vegetable is one of nature's richest sources of the important antioxidant, beta carotene.

To understand where all the extra fat and calories in the traditional recipe come from, here is a comparison of all the ingredients in the two recipes:

Recipe for Traditional Carrot Cake with Cream Cheese Frosting	Recipe for Carrot Raisin Cake with Creamy Vanilla Frosting from *Baking Without Fat*
ingredients: 2½ cups white flour ½ teaspoon salt 1 teaspoon cinnamon 2 cups white sugar 1 teaspoon vanilla 4 eggs 2 cups grated peeled carrots 1¼ cups vegetable oil 2 tablespoons unsalted margarine 1 cup chopped almonds	ingredients: 2½ cups and 2 tablespoons whole wheat pastry flour 1½ teaspoons baking soda 1½ teaspoons cream of tartar 1½ teaspoons cinnamon ¼ teaspoon ground nutmeg 1½ cups honey ⅓ cup frozen pineapple juice concentrate (defrosted) 2 teaspoons vanilla 2 egg whites, unbeaten 1½ cups grated peeled carrots 2 jars carrot baby food puree 1 cup raisins 2 egg whites, lightly beaten
Cream Cheese Frosting	**Creamy Vanilla Frosting**
ingredients: 8 ounces cream cheese 3 cups powdered sugar	ingredients: 1 cup nonfat yogurt cheese ½ cup and 2 tablespoons pure maple syrup 2 tablespoons nonfat dry milk solids 2 teaspoons vanilla
yield: 16 servings	yield: 16 servings

Here is a comparison of the fat and calories in the traditional carrot cake recipe and the one in this book:

Serving: (¹/₁₆ of recipe)	Fat (grams)	Calories from Fat	Calories
Traditional Carrot Cake	29g	49 percent	526
Carrot Raisin Cake From *Baking Without Fat*	**Fat-Free**	**Fat-Free**	**269**

How We Bake Without Fat in Our Kitchen

When I was growing up, the kitchen was always my favorite room in the whole house. Partly, it was because my mother spent so much time there creating such wonderful meals for our family. And also it was because the kitchen was such a warm and inviting place, filled with the wonderful aromas of simmering foods and baked goods.

Remembering those fond memories, I wanted the test kitchen here at Health Valley to be clean and efficient, but <u>not</u> sterile and cold. Today, our test kitchen is a warm and friendly place where people love to gather, just like the kitchen in which I grew up.

Unlike the test kitchens at commercial food companies, ours doesn't have special commercial grade equipment. Instead, we selected the same appliances found in most homes. We did this deliberately, so we could be sure that the recipes we developed in our kitchen would work just as well in yours.

We also selected ingredients that are readily available in most markets. Be assured that you won't have to change everything in your pantry.

For the sake of convenience, many recipes call for ingredients, such as crisp rice cereal, fat-free granola or fat-free cookies to use for crusts or toppings. When these kinds of ingredients were called for, we used Health Valley products, but you can use other brands.

There are two advantages to using Health Valley products:

First, since we developed the recipes using our own products, you can be sure you'll get the best results by using the same Health Valley products as ingredients.

Second, when you use Health Valley products, you are assured of getting foods made the healthy way with the world's finest natural ingredients, with no hidden fats in them.

The one thing you *won't need* is fat or oil. The only oil we used in our kitchen was to sharpen our knives.

The many kind comments of our customers inspire us in our work and let us know our efforts are worthwhile. Let me share another letter with you, and please keep those comments coming:

"First, I want to thank all of you and let you know I really appreciate all the hard work you are doing so we can all be healthier, happier people.

"One day I received a sample of your Fat-Free cookies in the mail. Those cookies changed my life. I sent for your Cooking Without Fat *book and started living Fat-Free. I have lost 40 pounds and feel great. Please keep up the good work, and I will tell everyone about your products and what they can do."*

–Viola Ledger, Fairfield, Ohio

You Can Use the Recipes in This Book with Confidence

You can do more than just enjoy these recipes without guilt, you can actually feel good about providing your body with many of the important nutrients you need to make a positive impact on your health.

And you can use these recipes with confidence knowing that there is no "hidden" fat. That means, all the recipes are made without any added fat, and they are also free from high-fat ingredients.

We're very proud of this book because it represents what Health Valley stands for—to provide good tasting, convenient foods that help you eat healthier, so you can look and feel your best.

Where to Start to Get the Most From This Book

Perhaps the greatest benefit this book has to offer you is enjoyment. I have always believed that the enjoyment of food is not only one of life's great pleasures, but that it also helps our bodies to assimilate nutrients better and helps our overall health when we truly relish what we eat. That's why we always kept your enjoyment in mind in developing these recipes.

There are so many wonderful recipes, you may not know where to start. Although there is no one "right" way to start, let me offer some suggestions regarding my own personal favorites.

My Favorite Quick (10-20 minute) Recipes

If you're looking for recipes that can be made quickly, I would start by recommending the Peach Blueberry Crisp. It takes only about 10 minutes to prepare and tastes delicious. Some other fast recipes include Honey Raisin Cookies, Blueberry Muffins and Coco Crispy Cookies, which each take only about 15 minutes to prepare. If you have only about 20 minutes and you want to make something delicious, try the Orange Cake or Raspberry Filled Bars.

My Favorite Special Occasion Recipes

If you're planning to entertain or want a recipe appropriate for a festive occasion, my recommendation would be to try the Coco Berry Cheesecake. It looks special, tastes special and never fails to cause "oohs" and "aahs" whenever I serve it to guests. I don't even bother to tell them it's made without fat because usually they find it hard to believe anyway. The recipe is also a wonderful source of calcium without the fat and calories associated with most dairy products, because it's made from nonfat yogurt. Some other special occasion recipes include Sachertorte and Black Forest Cake. Or if you're not a chocolate lover, Carrot Raisin Cake, Lemon Cream Cake or Banana Cream Cake can be the highlight of any dinner party.

My Favorite Recipes for Children

If you're looking for recipes that children will love, my suggestions would be to bake the Gingerbread, Frosted Coco Cupcakes, or Crispy Rice Treats. The Crispy Rice Treats are best right as they come from the oven and tend to absorb moisture if allowed to sit for very long. Of course, that's never a problem when we make them in our test kitchen, because they get eaten almost immediately.

My Favorite High Nutrition Recipes

One of my personal favorites is the Citrus Garden cake. I'm really proud of this cake because it tastes absolutely delicious and it's made with both fruits and vegetables! Citrus Garden cake not only has a refreshing citrus taste, it also includes the nutrition provided by carrots and zucchini.

Another recipe that I highly recommend is the Strawberry Angel Food Cake. The traditional angel food cake is very low in fat because it is often served with high-fat whipped cream. With our recipe, you serve it with a light, creamy topping that is made with no added fat.

My Favorite Wheat-Free Recipe

We are very proud of our sensational Honey Raisin Cookie, which is flourless and makes a delicious wheat-free treat. This is just one of the many recipes we developed especially for people who have special nutritional needs.

Let Me Know Which Recipes Are Your Favorites

There are so many recipes I love that I could go on for several more pages, but I'm afraid that might keep you from just going ahead and trying some of these recipes.

I'd like nothing better than for you to try several of these recipes and then write and tell me which are your favorites.

Let me share another of the letters that Health Valley has received recently:

"My friend and I bought your Fat-Free cook-book (Cooking Without Fat), *and we are enjoying the recipes very much. In seven weeks, I have lost 20 pounds.*

"We plan to make Thanksgiving dinner with your Cooking Without Fat *recipes for our families, and not tell them until the meal is over."*

—Linda R. Zan, Chicago, Ill.

*"Our passion is to create
healthy foods that truly
contribute to a better
quality of life."*

chapter one

Our Love for Baking

My love for baking is shared by many of the people at Health Valley. So when it came time to create this book, I didn't have to go outside the company to assemble a team to work on it because we already have all the dedicated, talented people right here. From the beginning, all of us realized that we were attempting to do something that had never been done before—namely to develop good tasting baking recipes without any added fat or refined sugar. We knew that it would require a team effort to accomplish our task because when you eliminate fat and sugar, you change the way flavor is carried across the palate. That meant we had to find other flavor carriers and we had to virtually rewrite the book on flavors.

I don't think we could have been successful unless everyone had a genuine love for baking, in addition to all the expertise and experience necessary.

That's why this book is a true labor of love. Everyone who worked on it went all out for you. We created recipes to provide you with both pleasure and important nutritional benefits.

Our Commitment

Health Valley is dedicated to being a positive force in helping people enjoy longer, richer, more fulfilling lives. And one of the ways we do this is by sharing our knowledge and experience with you. It has always been my personal belief that the solution to rising health problems is for each of us to take control of our own health, and actively prevent degenerative diseases, rather than attempting to treat the conditions once they have developed. My hope is that by sharing our knowledge, you will be able to eat better and live a healthier life. This is all part of Health Valley's vision to help make the world a better, healthier place.

Each member of our team was committed to producing a book that would help fulfill our company's vision by sharing our baking knowledge with you. The recipes in this book are the result of adapting Health Valley's expertise in creating over 100 good tasting, healthy Fat-Free foods to the equipment and ingredients in your kitchen. We recognize that you do not have access to specialized equipment specifically for Fat-Free baking and created techniques that work with the equipment found in most family kitchens.

Another part of our commitment was to offer you a whole new breakthrough method of baking that has <u>absolutely</u>:

- No added fat or high fat ingredients
- No cholesterol
- No white flour
- No refined sugar
- No added salt
- No artificial fat substitutes

But that's not all. The recipes in this book are more than just sweet treats, they're real foods that provide a variety of nutritional benefits that make them an important part of a healthier way of eating.

This is also **the first cookbook with recipes that are not just low in fat, but recipes that are Fat-Free.**

How We Created Good Tasting Baking Recipes Without Whole Eggs, Butter or Refined Sugar

Every experienced baker knows that there are some staple ingredients common to almost all baking recipes. Flour, sugar, eggs and butter are probably the four cornerstones of baking.

When we decided to write this book, we made a commitment to create recipes without three of these four basic ingredients: refined sugar, eggs and butter. Even flour was affected because we do <u>not</u> use any white flour, only whole wheat pastry flour for its natural nutrients and beneficial fiber.

Here's how we managed to fulfill our commitment to baking the healthy way and still providing you with full-flavored recipes:

The first ingredient we eliminated was egg yolks, where virtually all the egg's fat resides. Without the yolk, you lose a certain richness of flavor and the body that fat provides in baking, but by increasing the amount of spices and other flavorings, we created a bold taste without fat.

The next high-fat culprit we eliminated was butter. We found that different combinations of ingredients could substitute for the characteristics butter provides. For example, in some recipes, fruit purees provide the same moist mouthfeel as butter, but without the artery-clogging levels of fat.

One of the hardest ingredients to eliminate was refined sugar. We turned to alternative sweeteners that have distinctive flavors and nutritional benefits lacking in refined sugar. The list includes honey, maple syrup and fruit juice concentrates. Of course, unlike refined sugar, which adds no moisture to the recipe, the natural sweeteners we used all add some liquid to each recipe, and they do not have the same concentrated sweetness of refined sugar. For that reason, we had to make a number of adjustments to each recipe to achieve the precise balance of flavor, moisture and mouthfeel to provide all the taste satisfaction you expect from quality baked goods.

Our recipes are the result of the hundreds of small adjustments and refinements needed to achieve just the right balance without whole eggs, butter or refined sugar. That's why it's important that you understand and follow the recipe instructions even more carefully than you would in an ordinary cookbook, if you want to achieve the best results.

The Seven Exclusive Healthy Benefits in This Cookbook

This is *not* just another cookbook. It is really two books in one.

First, it's a book that contains over 100 recipes made without any added fat. But we didn't stop there. We went a step further. So secondly, it's a book created to provide you with recipes that have been developed to meet your personal nutritional needs.

For example, if you are sensitive to wheat or simply want to cut down on the amount of wheat products you eat, you'll find wheat-free recipes clearly indicated with a special symbol. If you are a strict vegetarian or have a sensitivity to dairy products, you'll find recipes that are completely free of dairy products, clearly indicated with a special symbol.

We know you want to eat healthier, and this is the only cookbook that offers you these seven healthy benefits:

1. <u>All</u> recipes are lower in fat and calories than comparable recipes made with fat. Some of the recipes have 50% fewer calories, and a few, such as Peach Tart, are as much as 56% lower in calories. **83 recipes are Fat-Free and will be indicated by this symbol.**

2. **You get 31 wheat-free recipes,** which are beneficial whether you are allergic to wheat or merely want to reduce the amount of wheat products you eat. Recipes that are wheat-free are indicated with this symbol.

3. **You get 48 recipes free of dairy products,** which are beneficial to people who are allergic to milk products and those who have lactose intolerance. Recipes that are free of dairy products are indicated with this symbol.

4. **You get 17 recipes that can help you fulfill the Healthy Five** recommendation of eating five servings of fruits and vegetables each day. Recipes that are especially good at helping you fulfill the Healthy Five recommendation are indicated by this symbol.

HEALTHY FIVE

5. **You get 45 recipes that appeal to children,** so they can receive the nutrition they need in baked goods they enjoy. Recipes that are especially good for children are indicated with this symbol.

GREAT FOR KIDS

6. You get recipes rich in antioxidants, the nutrients of the 1990s, including beta carotene, vitamins E and C. **Four recipes that provide over 500 IUs of beta carotene per serving are indicated with this symbol.**

BETA-CAROTENE

7. You get recipes with both soluble and insoluble fiber. We use whole wheat pastry flour as well as rolled oats, brown rice cereal and corn meal, which all contain beneficial fiber. The vast majority of recipes contain between 2 and 4 grams of fiber per serving. The main exceptions include the nonfat yogurt cheese, and the frostings, sauces and toppings, which are not meant to be served alone; and the cookies, where the serving size is smaller, so the average amount of fiber is 1 gram.

In addition to these seven nutritional benefits, you also get eight recipes that are rich in calcium. All of our cheesecake recipes are made with nonfat yogurt cheese, so they provide calcium without the fat found in regular dairy products. For example, one serving of the New York Lemon Cheesecake recipe supplies 30% of the RDA for calcium.

What Makes This Cookbook So Special

For many food companies, their most valuable assets are their "trade secrets"–the ingredients and techniques they use to make their products. They guard their trade secrets jealously and don't give them out because they don't want anyone else to be able to compete with them and cut into their profits.

At Health Valley, the most valuable thing we have is knowledge. But rather than trying to keep it to ourselves, we put our efforts into sharing it with others so they can benefit.

First of all, we want to share our baking without fat secrets with you. Use them in your own home to prepare better, healthier foods.

We also notice that other commercial food companies have used the information we published in our previous book, *Cooking Without Fat*, and applied it to making lower-fat products. Rather than being concerned about the competition, we are glad that we may have influenced other companies in a positive way. Our goal is to improve the food supply for everyone, and if that means helping other companies to make better food, we are pleased to do so. Some people might question why we would share our secrets in this book. The reason is simple–our company exists to build the health and well-being of our customers, rather than our bank balance.

Health Valley pioneered the concept of baking without fat and we continue to prepare a greater variety of Fat-Free cookies, muffins, crackers and fruit bars than any other company in the world. We are fortunate to have more first hand knowledge about baking without fat than any other company. Our experience developing Fat-Free products showed us that removing fat often causes the dough to be stickier than what most companies are used to, and this creates new problems for processing. For each Fat-Free product we produced, we tested many different possible product formulations, and found that sometimes we had to develop whole new kinds of equipment. In all, product development required testing hundreds of different fat-replacing systems and dozens of different processes.

We're very excited about the recipes because for the first time, we are sharing our secrets for baking without fat with you. This is our contribution to improving the way you eat by showing you how to cut down on fat, without giving up the flavor and enjoyment of the foods you love.

Because we love to bake, we were delighted to devote an entire book to the subject. Our goal was to transform the whole concept of what home-baked goods should be, the way we did with our Health Valley Fat-Free products – to help you live a healthier lifestyle.

"Health Valley is the most wonderful company in the world! I've been losing weight steadily since embarking on a low-fat diet and exercise regimen late last year, and your products are a big part of the reason! ... Companies like yours are the wave of the future."

Sheri Jordan, Williston Park, N.Y.

"What I've discovered is that there really is no model anywhere in the world for baking without fat."

chapter two

The Baking Without Fat Method

Baking Without Fat Is a Whole New Way of Baking

I have traveled extensively and studied the baking methods of many different countries and cultures. What I've discovered is that there really is no model anywhere in the world for baking without fat. Fat in the form of shortening or butter is used in baking everywhere. The noted food writer M.F.K. Fisher was quoted as saying, "The basis of French cuisine is butter, that of Italy, olive oil, of Germany, lard, and of Russia, sour cream."

In my own travels, I discovered this is definitely true. In fact, wherever I went, there was usually a great deal of pride and prestige in using the local butter or oil in baking.

For example, when I studied at Guiliano Bugialli's cooking school in Florence, Italy, I saw how much olive oil was used. Although olive oil is a healthier form of fat than those that are highly saturated, too much fat of any kind can cause health problems. In Italy, olive oil is used in a variety of baked goods, such as an apple cake called "Torta di Mele" that calls for two-thirds cup olive oil. And both butter and eggs are used in the traditional Italian Christmas bread, "Panettone."

At La Varenne Ecole de Cuisine in Paris, I watched the artistry of chefs who used copious amounts of butter with great pride as they prepared recipes, especially baked goods, such as madeleines, croissants and brioche. Both eggs and butter are required to make the French pastry, genoise. In this dish, butter goes into both the batter and the butter cream frosting. It seems the more butter you use the better!

And when I attended the Gourmet's Oxford, I saw chefs use not just cream, but double cream!

I also have seen the role fat plays in more exotic cuisines:

In Mexico, lard is very popular, while Indian cooking features a clarified butter called ghee. And both Indian and Thai cooking use coconut, which is high in saturated fat.

In Middle Eastern baking, sesame oil and seeds are staples. Sesame seeds are about 80 percent fat. That's why the Turkish baked confection halvah, made with sesame seeds and honey, is about 50 percent fat.

The Greeks bake a sinfully rich nut loaf, Ala Aphrodite Lianides, which contains butter, pecans, walnuts and almonds.

You may be shocked to find out that some cheesecake recipes not only contain cream cheese, which is high in fat, they also contain lard to keep the texture firm.

In fact, the more I learned about how much fat is hidden in baked goods, the more angry I became.

Everywhere I went I saw how fat was an important ingredient in baking. It is the main flavor carrier, and it changes the way in which flavors are perceived, slowing some flavor aspects, and altering the overall balance. Fat, in the form of shortening, helps determine the volume and texture of the finished product. Because fat can perform so many functions in baking, very few recipes work well if you simply cut out fat without finding other ways to compensate for it.

That meant we had to use our years of experience in creating over 100 Health Valley Fat-Free foods to develop a revolutionary new way of baking without fat that you can use in your kitchen.

Essentially, the revolutionary new method for Baking Without Fat that we developed involves *substitution*.

Substitution actually accomplishes two things:

1. It cuts down on fat, which is a benefit in itself.
2. By exchanging ingredients such as fruit for fat, you also increase the nutritional benefits of the recipe.

There is no one magical formula that works in every recipe. The artistry involved in creating these recipes came from finding just the right combination of ingredients to substitute for fat that resulted in the ideal flavor, texture and body.

We are proud of what we accomplished and we feel confident that you will enjoy the results of our efforts.

The Role of Fat in Baking

Fat performs many different functions in baking:

• Fat can act as a shortening and help determine how much air can be incorporated into the batter. In this way, fat can influence volume and lightness.

• Fat can add a creamy mouthfeel and affect the texture.

• Fat effects the way flavor is released in the mouth. Some flavoring agents are referred to as being "lipophilic" because they are normally found in a medium that consists of fat. Vanilla and chocolate are two examples of lipophilic flavoring agents. When the fat is removed from lipophilic flavoring agents, the flavors are released into the mouth and nasal cavity at a much quicker rate than when fat is present. As a result, an initial burst of flavor is perceived and then quickly dissipates. So the perceived flavor of a product can be dramatically changed when a Fat-Free product is developed, even though the same flavor composition is used.

For all these reasons, replacing fat in baking is not simple or easy, but it can be accomplished. That's because fat itself isn't a flavor, but it acts as a carrier for many flavor elements. Virtually all whole foods contain fat, often in minute amounts. However, fat doesn't occur alone in nature, so it seems logical that we should be able to bake without adding fat.

The sense of taste results from a complex interaction among the taste buds.

There are only four tastes that your tongue can sense: sweet, sour, salty and bitter.

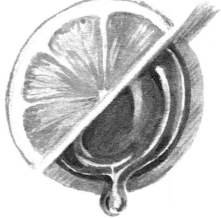

In nature, the ability to sense bitter and salty tastes are mainly protective functions, in that many poisonous substances have a bitter taste, and the ability to taste salt allows us to distinguish between fresh water and sea water.

Sweet and sour are really the only two tastes that serve us in sensing the foods we eat. The secret to creating delicious foods in baked goods without added fat lies in amplifying, enriching and balancing sweetness with other natural flavors, including spices and fruit flavors.

Naturally, foods made without any added fat are not going to taste exactly the same as foods that are high in fat. But many taste preferences are acquired rather than something we are born with.

For example, the first time most people taste coffee it seems quite bitter. Yet eventually, many of these same people grow to enjoy the taste. Flavors from items as varied as beer, wine, oysters, and raw fish are often called "acquired tastes."

What can we learn from this? To successfully cut down on fat, educate your palate to appreciate the natural flavors of foods without added fat.

The New Method of Baking Fat-Free by Substituting

Fat performs so many different functions in baking that there is no one ingredient you can use as a substitute that works in every recipe. And even when you find an ingredient that is able to perform the same function as fat in a particular recipe, it is never as simple as removing a specific amount of fat and replacing it with the same amount of the substitute.

For example, fat may be used primarily to add a creamy texture, but at the same time, it will act as a carrier for flavor or alter the way the flavor is perceived. Even when, for example, pureed banana works as a substitute for fat in providing a creamy mouthfeel, removing the fat can still require other changes that compensate for the loss of fat as a flavor carrier. In other words, in addition to making one change in the recipe, it might also be necessary to increase the level of some flavors and decrease the amount of others.

Another thing that can complicate the process of substitution is that some replacement ingredients may not be neutral tasting and can add flavors of their own that alter the overall taste of the recipe.

So substituting for fat is a complex procedure that requires skill and patience.

After hundreds of hours in the kitchen, we developed a whole new method for you that allows you to bake without fat in your own home and enjoy really good tasting recipes with the moist, tender texture you want. The secret is to substitute for fat using a variety of methods that vary according to the individual recipe. These methods include:

1. Substituting nonfat dairy products for full-fat ones
2. Substituting pureed fruit for fat
3. Substituting egg whites for whole eggs
4. Highlighting natural flavors to make up for the lack of fat
5. Investing in nonstick bakeware

By following our recipes, you'll be able to make baked goods that are tender, moist, sweet and enjoyable without any added fat.

Here are more details about the techniques we use:

1. We substitute nonfat dairy products for full-fat ones.

Full-fat dairy products–whole milk, cream, butter, sour cream and yogurt–are some of the biggest contributors of saturated fat in the American diet. By substituting nonfat dairy products, we can save a tremendous amount of fat and still get similar results.

For example, 1 cup of nonfat plain yogurt contains only .4 gram of fat, compared with 7.4 grams of fat in a cup of regular yogurt. That means you'll save 7 grams of fat with this substitution, and in most recipes, you won't even notice the difference.

Another important substitution in this book is using nonfat yogurt cheese, instead of sour cream or whipped cream.

You'll find the recipe for yogurt cheese on page 129. It's easy to make, and the resulting product makes a fat-free substitute that you can use to make cheesecake and other recipes. There is also fat-free sour cream that is now available commercially.

We also use both nonfat dry milk and skim evaporated milk in many recipes as a substitute for full-fat dairy products, such as milk and cream.

2. We substitute pureed fruit for fat.

In many baking recipes, mashed bananas or applesauce or other pureed fruit can provide both sweetness and the moist, creamy texture that fat provides. You can puree fruit yourself in a blender or food processor, or simply raid the baby food shelf at your local market for pureed fruit with no added sugar or fat.

How to Puree Fruits and Vegetables for Immediate Use

Throughout these recipes, we use fruit instead of fat as part of our baking method. We suggest that for convenience you use baby food or canned puree. But be aware that you can also create your own purees at home with very little effort. Also, foods that are minimally processed will retain the most vitamins, minerals and fiber.

A puree is simply a paste that is created by grinding either a fruit or vegetable through a food processor or a blender for between 10 and 20 seconds. Purees work best when the fruit or vegetable that you are using is either soft or stewed. Leave the skins on. If you puree berries remember to strain them to remove the seeds.

Using organic fruits and vegetables helps to insure that the food you are eating contains the minimum amount of pesticide or fumigant residues. It also helps to encourage farmers to save our precious topsoil, and to keep our water supply clean.

Here are the fruits we use frequently:

APPLES

To substitute for unsweetened applesauce, wash and quarter two firm, ripe apples. Remove stem, and core to remove seeds. Place apple pieces in a pan with just enough water to cover and simmer with lid off for 8-10 minutes, or until tender. Place half the cooked pieces in blender or food processor fitted with metal chopping blade and grind until no whole pieces are left, about 15 seconds. It will take less time in food processor. Repeat process with other half. Spoon into bowl. Makes about 1 cup.

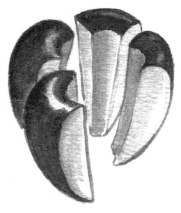

APRICOTS

To substitute for either apricot, or apricot with tapioca baby food puree, take four medium-size, ripe and soft apricots, wash and cut in half. Remove pit, any hard interior core and any blemishes in skin. Place apricot pieces in a pan with just enough water to cover and simmer with lid off for 5-8 minutes, or until tender. Place half apricots in the blender or food processor, and process for 10 seconds, or until no whole pieces are left. Repeat process with other half. Spoon into bowl. Makes about 1 cup.

CARROTS

To substitute for carrot baby food, take 6 medium-size ripe carrots, cut off the tops, the tap root and peel, or wash thoroughly. Cut into 1-inch sections. In a pot over medium high heat, put the carrots and enough water to cover, and bring to a boil. Reduce heat and cover for 10 minutes, or until carrots are tender. Pour carrots into a colander, and refresh with cold water. Place one-third of the carrots into a blender or a food processor and process for 15 seconds or until smooth. Repeat process until all carrots are pureed. Spoon into a bowl. Makes about 2 cups.

PRUNES

To substitute for prune baby food, take a dozen prunes, and slice open to remove pit, and stem, if there is one. If prunes are very dry and hard, steam suspended over boiling water in strainer for 5 minutes, or until soft. Grind for 15 seconds, or until no whole bits of fruit are left. Spoon into bowl. Makes about 1 cup.

PUMPKINS

To substitute for canned pumpkin puree, choose ripe pumpkin, around 6 pounds, wash and cut in half. Scoop out seeds and strings. In 375°F. oven, bake both halves hollow side down in baking pan or heat-resistant glass dish for 1½ to 2 hours, until tender. Remove from oven and cool. Using large spoon, scrape out meat, and grind in blender or food processor about 12 seconds, until smooth. Repeat process until all pulp is pureed. Spoon into bowl. Makes about 4 cups.

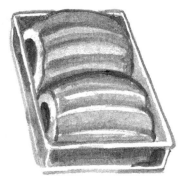

SWEET POTATOES

To substitute for sweet potato baby food, take one medium sweet potato, wash and cut off stringy ends. Cut into half-inch rounds, and boil in water in medium saucepan covered for 30 minutes, or until tender. Remove from heat. With fork, transfer half sweet potatoes into blender or food processor. Grind for 10 seconds, or until puree is relatively smooth. Repeat process with other half. Spoon into bowl. Makes about 2 cups.

3. We substitute egg whites for whole eggs.

In many baking recipes, we have been successful substituting two egg whites for each whole egg that is called for. Since all the fat is in the yolk, egg whites are virtually fat-free. For some recipes, such as custards, where the egg yolk provides viscosity and helps bind the ingredients together, we also add arrowroot to help it thicken. Substituting egg white for whole eggs not only cuts fat, it also eliminates the 300 mg of cholesterol found in each egg.

4. We Highlight Natural Flavors to Make Up for the Lack of Fat.

Because fat is a carrier for flavor, eliminating fat often causes baked goods to lose their rich flavor. Fat in baking also changes the way in which flavors are perceived by slowing some flavor aspects and altering the overall balance. There are a variety of ways we've discovered to compensate for the richness and balance of flavor that fat provides:

• We use a greater variety of spices and flavorings.

• We use a greater quantity of spices and flavorings than we would if we were baking with fat.

• We use different spices blended together.

• To achieve rich flavor without fat, we use complementary or contrasting spices and flavorings when baking without fat.

• We use sweeteners that add their own flavor.

• Instead of using white sugar, which adds sweetness without any flavor of its own, we sweeten baking recipes made without fat by using natural foods that also add flavor, such as fruit-juice-sweetened preserves, maple syrup and fruit juice concentrates.

5. We Invested in Nonstick Bakeware

Buying new cookware is an investment, but for the home cook who is actively committed to a Fat-Free lifestyle, upgrading one's pots and pans can be well worthwhile.

Cookware with high quality nonstick surfaces allow you to cook and bake without adding fat in the form of oil and butter to prevent sticking. And today's technology has resulted in nonstick surfaces that are much more practical and durable than the ones available even a few years ago.

For example, Farberware® offers a 20-year guarantee on its stainless steel "Millennium™" Permanent Never-Stick™ cookware with Excalibur™ surface. The new nonstick surfaces even allow you to use metal spatulas, tongs and whisks without damaging or marring them.

Remember that in cookware, as in most other things, you'll get what you pay for.

About Leavening

When you bake without fat, the ingredients may respond differently from what you may be accustomed to in conventional baking with shortening.

For example, fat counteracts the development of gluten in flour. Too much gluten development causes baked goods to develop tunnels, instead of remaining smooth and consistent. On top of that, whole grains, such as we use in our recipes, usually contain more gluten than refined flour. Because of the greater amount of gluten and the absence of fat, it is very important not to overmix the batter.

Another example is that you should use the cookie dough right after mixing it, rather than leaving it in the refrigerator the way you might with dough made with shortening. If you let cookie dough in recipes made without fat sit for too long before baking, it will become dry and hard.

We found that some of the best leavening agents to use when you're baking without fat include:

• Baking soda. People who are concerned about sodium intake should be aware that baking soda contains sodium.

• Cream of tartar. We have had success blending cream of tartar with baking soda, instead of using baking powder. Cream of tartar neutralizes the acidity in fruit juice, so combining it with baking soda allowed us to control the acid-alkaline balance that affects leavening in a batter.

• Egg whites. Virtually all the fat and cholesterol in an egg is found in the yolk. The whites are a fat-free ingredient that can act as a binder and, when beaten or whipped, can allow more air to be incorporated into baked goods to increase their volume and lightness.

• Baking powder without aluminum. Regular baking powder contains aluminum salts, a compound that health-conscious people try to avoid. We do not use baking powder of any kind in this book, but if you want to use it in your own recipes, we recommend the non-aluminum baking powders available in health food stores and markets.

How to Use Our Baking Without Fat Method in Your Own Recipes

Although you will find recipes for virtually all your favorite categories of baked goods in this book, you may have an old family recipe or a particular favorite you want to try and cut the fat from. You can try the same techniques we used in our Baking Without Fat method, but it isn't as simple as substituting fruit puree for fat, as an example. You may have to experiment to discover which of our techniques to use, as well as the right combinations and proportions to achieve good results.

What These Recipes Offer You

When we produce Health Valley Fat-Free baked goods, we use the special state-of-the-art ovens and other equipment that we have developed specifically for Fat-Free baking. We recognize that you don't have access to this kind of equipment at home, so we developed these recipes to work without the need for specialized equipment. In addition to being made without fat, the recipes in this book are also:

1. Good tasting.
2. Made the healthy way to provide a variety of nutritional benefits.
3. Easy to make using the equipment found in most kitchens, and ingredients that are easy to find in most stores.

There are a number of books that feature recipes showing you how to cut down on fat in cooking and baking. But many of them still use fat, because all they do is substitute vegetable oil for butter. This book is special because the recipes aren't just lower in fat, they're **made with absolutely no added fat whatsoever, so many of them are Fat-Free, and they're all made the healthy way.** And you can feel confident that there is no "hidden" fat in our recipes.

Natural Sweetness

The delicious all natural sweetness in these recipes comes from such nutritious ingredients as fruit and fruit juice concentrates, honey, maple syrup and molasses. Fruits are some of nature's best sources of fiber and essential vitamins and minerals, including the antioxidant nutrients–beta carotene and vitamin C.

Whole Grain Flours

The flours we use are all from whole grains. They provide fiber, the antioxidant vitamin E, and complex carbohydrates, your body's best source of energy.

When you enjoy these recipes, you have the assurance of knowing that you are not only cutting fat from your diet, you're also getting foods that provide a variety of special nutritional benefits.

Let me share a letter I received about our last cookbook:

"I sent for your Cooking Without Fat *a few months ago. My husband started cooking from your wonderful book and has lost 25 pounds.*

"Just want you to know how much we love your book and your products."

–Mrs. Don Hellebuyck, Utica, Minn.

"...help people to live
healthier and
eat better."

chapter three

Why You Should Bake Without Fat

Why You Should Cut Down on Fat

There is clear evidence that eating too much fat is the No. 1 nutritional hazard in our country today. I think companies that produce high-fat foods and disguise the fact by listing unreasonably small serving sizes are guilty of the worst kind of deception. These companies are cheating people out of their health for the sake of making a profit! I feel that food companies have an ethical responsibility to provide foods with real nutritional value, without gimmicks. That is why Health Valley is the leader in preparing Fat-Free and low-fat foods, and why we no longer make any foods that contain added fat. As far as we know, Health Valley is the **only** food company that prepares all its products without any added fat.

Health Valley has made this commitment because I am extremely passionate about cutting down on fat. In fact, people sometimes ask me whether I am on some kind of crusade and why I am so adamant about fat.

The answer is simple. Like many of you I've watched some of my own family, like my brother, suffer through the terrible consequences of degenerative diseases. And when I came to realize that many of these diseases could be prevented, I felt I had to spread the word and help people to live healthier and eat better. The best and most important way to start is by cutting down on fat.

Here are the comments of one of our valued customers who also happens to be a health care professional. Her letter was especially meaningful to me because her career, like mine, involves helping others to eat healthier:

"I work as a nutritionist specializing in weight loss and weight management. I can't tell you how helpful your line of Fat-Free products has been to

*my clients. They are always surprised at how
tasty the foods are and pleased with the variety.
Special favorites are the cookies, puffs, granola
and granola bars, crackers and soups. I love and
use them myself because they help me maintain
my 140 pound weight loss and still enjoy 'normal'
foods without feeling deprived.*

*"I feel very good about recommending your
products to my clients since I know they are also
low in sodium and calories, and are made with
the best quality ingredients. This is what I look
for in nutritious foods, and the convenience is a
plus for all us busy folk."*

—Roseanne Strull, Brookings, Ore.

The Benefits of Cutting Down on Fat

If there is one piece of advice I can give you, it is to cut down on the
amount of fat you eat.

Cutting down on fat is the healthiest dietary thing you can do for your
body, because it provides three important health benefits:

1. **It automatically cuts down on calories.**
2. **It reduces your risk of disease.**
3. **It allows you to eat more nutrient-dense foods.**

Since fat contains more than
twice as many calories as protein
and carbohydrates, cutting down
on fat automatically cuts down on
calories. Cutting down on fat can
help you achieve and maintain
your ideal weight without dieting.

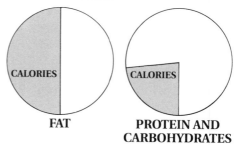

Eating too much fat increases your risk of developing heart disease
and some forms of cancer. Cutting down on the total amount of fat you
eat can help you stay healthier and live longer. In fact, the country's

leading health-promoting organizations, including the American Heart Association, the American Cancer Society and the U.S. Surgeon General have all published dietary guidelines that recommend reducing the total amount of fat in your diet to no more than 30% of calories. And many health authorities are recommending cutting down on fat even below 30% of calories, because there is also evidence that cutting fat to 15% of calories may not only prevent the conditions that contribute to cardiovascular heart disease, but can even reverse the condition if it already exists.

Finally, cutting down on fat can help you get more of the nutrients you need to look and feel your best. That's because the most nutrient-dense foods are those that are low in fat or virtually Fat-Free, including fruits, vegetables and grains. So when you cut down on foods that are high in fat, you can replace them with foods that provide greater amounts of essential nutrients.

It is gratifying beyond words to hear from our customers who have used our Fat-Free products and the healthy way of eating that we advocate to improve their health and their lives. Let me share one of these letters with you:

> *"I have never written to a company before, so I'm not sure where to begin, but I am so impressed with Health Valley Foods that I felt I should write to you!*
>
>  *"With the proper diet and exercise, I have been able to completely quit taking my diabetic pills, and I have lost a total of 223 pounds.*
>
> *"I am a new person! I have lots of energy and love my life.*
>
> *"I just want to thank you for your products and your cookbook because I attribute a lot of my success in weight loss, and now maintenance, to being able to have tasty, healthy foods like Health Valley's. I have no desire for 'junk food' and I don't feel deprived in the least!"*
>
> –Nanci Jones, Mansfield, Ohio

The Dangers of Hidden Fat

Since there is such a consensus on the benefits of cutting down on fat, it makes you wonder why most Americans still consume close to 40% of their calories from fat.

One of the main reasons is that many people are simply unaware of how much fat they are actually consuming because the majority of the fat in their diets comes from "hidden" fat.

Hidden fat is the fat that you don't see and don't expect to find in foods. Some foods, such as red meat, have visible fat that's relatively easy to remove. But they also have fat that is "marbled" throughout, which you really can't remove. Other foods, particularly many processed foods, are high in fat, and most people are unaware of just how much fat they contain.

The Importance of Baking Without Fat

Baked goods are among the leading examples of foods containing hidden fat. That's why it's so valuable to bake without fat.

Here is a chart showing you how much fat is hidden in traditional baking recipes, compared with the amount in comparable recipes in this book:

Dessert/1 Serving:	Traditional Recipe:	Baking Without Fat Recipe:
Carrot Raisin Cake	29 grams of Fat	Fat-Free
New York Lemon Cheesecake	33 grams of Fat	Fat-Free
Banana Date Cake	11 grams of Fat	Fat-Free
Peach Tart	24 grams of Fat	Fat-Free

One of the things that most inspired me when we were creating the recipes for this book was the comments customers made about the last cookbook. Let me share one of them with you:

46

"Your cookbook (Cooking Without Fat) *arrived. Two days later, your cheesecake recipe was prepared and served. We were absolutely astounded at the taste with practically no fat.*

"I belong to 'TOPS' (Take Off Pounds Sensibly). I took a slice of your cheesecake with me to a meeting, and everyone asked for the recipe. No one could believe it was so easy to make and so good.

"The bottom line—thank you for all your efforts to produce a dessert recipe that really tastes like one."

Susan Tameris, Virginia Beach, Vir.

When You Cut Fat in Baking You Automatically Cut Calories

Fat contains more than twice as many calories as protein and car-bohydrates. So when you cut down on fat in baking, you automatically cut calories. And by baking without fat, you can transform baked goods from sweet treats into foods that provide the nutritional quality your body needs. You can create snack foods that complement your meals, rather than "spoiling" them. Desserts that are high in fat and sugar pro-vide empty calories; when you consume them in place of more nutritious foods, you can rob your body of the nutrients you need to maintain good health. And when you eat foods with empty calories in addition to more nutritious foods, you end up taking in more calories than your body needs—and that can cause you to have a weight problem.

The alternative is not to give up the desserts and snacks you love, but to learn to make them the healthy way—without added fat, and with ingredients that provide the nutrients you need for good health. That's what this book teaches you to do.

Here is a chart with a few examples of how many calories you save by eating recipes in this book as compared to traditional versions of the same recipes made with fat:

Dessert/ 1 Serving:	Traditional Recipe:	Baking Without Fat Recipe:	You Save
Carrot Raisin Cake	526 Calories	218 Calories	308 Calories
New York Lemon Cheesecake	462 Calories	211 Calories	251 Calories
Banana Date Cake	288 Calories	220 Calories	68 Calories
Oatmeal Raisin Cookie	145 Calories	96 Calories	49 Calories
Peach Tart	442 Calories	159 Calories	283 Calories

Let me share the comments of one of our valued customers regarding the recipes in our last cookbook:

"I sent for your cookbook (Cooking Without Fat) *and changed my way of cooking and eating. In the process, I lost 31 pounds during the last six months.*

"I have tried many of the recipes in your book and they are really good. I serve them to guests and they enjoy them and have no idea that they are eating healthy food, until I tell them. Several of my friends have ordered your book after tasting the food and seeing the results I have been enjoying a no added fat diet (not really a diet, but a new healthy way of eating)."

– William L. Stone, Seal Beach, Calif.

What "Fat-Free" Means

The definition of "Fat-Free," according to the U.S. Food and Drug Administration, which regulates food labels, is that the food contains less than a half gram of fat per serving. At the same time, the FDA has established exactly how much a serving is for each type of food.

According to government regulations, any food product that qualifies as Fat-Free must round the amount of fat down to zero on the nutritional panel.

Using the government's definition, many of the recipes in this book are Fat-Free. We show the amount of fat in a serving of our Fat-Free recipes as zero in accordance with the label regulations. But be aware that virtually all natural foods contain some fatty acids. Therefore, Fat-Free does <u>not</u> mean that a food is completely free of all fat, but that the amount is so small that it is negligible.

Is It Healthy to Eat Fat-Free Foods

You do <u>not</u> need to eat any added fat in order to be healthy. There has never been a single reported case of fat deficiency among healthy people who eat a balanced diet. And there is no RDA for fat because your body can make most of what it needs, except for the "essential" fatty acids, linoleic acid and linolenic acid, which must come from the foods you eat. To maintain good health, your body only needs 3% of your total calories to come from essential fatty acids. The actual amount of linolenic acid the body needs could be as low as 0.1 percent of calories. That's about as much as you get in an ounce of oat meal. You can easily get this amount even from a very low-fat diet, because virtually all natural foods contain some fatty acids. Healthy adults should not be afraid of a fat deficiency when eating low-fat and Fat-Free foods, such as the recipes in this cookbook or Health Valley Fat-Free products.

Growing children have a greater need for fat in their diets than adults do, but the fat should come from natural foods, rather than from processed foods or added fat.

"...choose organically grown grains whenever they are available."

chapter four

Shopping Tips for Baking Without Fat

Everything You Need for These Recipes is Easy to Find.

When we were creating the recipes for this book, we made a conscious effort to use ingredients that are widely available in food stores all across the country. There are only a few ingredients that you may have to go to a natural foods store to find because they are not as widely distributed in supermarkets.

The ingredients you'll need that are not always available in supermarkets include:

Whole wheat pastry flour. This is a staple item in this book. It provides the nutritional benefits of whole wheat flour, but results in baked goods with a lighter texture than using regular whole wheat flour. If your supermarket doesn't carry it, a natural foods store definitely will.

Arrowroot. This is a natural thickener we use instead of cornstarch or thickening agents with fat, such as cream or egg yolks. You can find arrowroot in some supermarkets, but it is often in smaller sizes at a higher price than in natural food stores.

Coconut extract. This ingredient provides the distinctive flavor of coconut, without the saturated fat found in whole coconut. There are artificial versions of this product available in most supermarkets, but we recommend natural coconut extract. Again, if your supermarket doesn't carry it, go to a natural foods store.

Health Valley Brown Rice Lites® Cereal. Although it isn't essential to use the Health Valley version of puffed brown rice in these recipes, it is the brand we used in developing them, so you'll be certain of getting the best results by making the effort to find it. If your supermarket doesn't carry it, your natural foods store will, or may be willing to order it for you upon request.

Other than these few ingredients, you should be able to find everything you need to bake without fat at your local market.

Should You Use Nuts in the Recipes?

Many traditional baking and dessert recipes include nuts. For example, walnuts are a regular ingredient in banana bread and oatmeal cookies, and slivered almonds are a popular topping for puddings and custards.

Nuts and seeds fall into the category of foods that are quite nutritious, but are also very high in fat. With the exception of chestnuts, virtually all varieties of nuts get from 70 to 97 percent of their calories from fat. Because the whole reason for creating this book is to show you how to bake without fat, we didn't feel it was consistent to use high-fat ingredients such as nuts.

However, if you are not as concerned about the extra calories and fat, and you use them in moderation, nuts can add a very nice flavor accent to many of these recipes. The chart below shows you the fat and calories in nuts:

Nuts

Variety and Serving Size	Calories	Fat (grams)	Calories from Fat
Almonds, 1 oz.	165	15g	82 percent
Cashews, dry roasted, 1 oz.	165	13g	71 percent
Hazelnuts, 1 oz.	180	18g	90 percent
Macadamia, oil roasted, 1 oz.	205	22g	97 percent
Peanuts, oil roasted, 1 oz.	165	14g	76 percent
Pecans, 1 oz.	190	19g	90 percent
Pine nuts, 1 oz.	161	17.3g	96 percent
Pistachios, 1 oz.	165	14g	76 percent
Sesame Seeds, 1 tbsp.	45	4g	80 percent
Sunflower Seeds, 1 oz.	160	14g	79 percent
Walnuts, 1 oz.	170	16g	85 percent

Should You Use Unsweetened Cocoa Powder in These Recipes?

Chocolate is often considered a taboo ingredient among health-minded people because it contains sugar, fat and caffeine. However you can find unsweetened cocoa powder, which offers the taste of chocolate without the sugar, and with so little fat and caffeine that many people feel the amounts of each are negligible, so they don't pose much risk.

To create our Health Valley products, such as our Healthy Chips® Cookies, we use a special dark Dutch cocoa powder that contains no fat, no sugar and only minimal amounts of caffeine. Although this cocoa powder is only available to manufacturers and not to the public, we feel that it will be in the near future.

In the meantime, if you are concerned about using cocoa powder, you have the option of substituting carob powder in these recipes.

The Importance of Using Pure Maple Syrup in These Recipes.

You'll find that we only use natural sweeteners in this book. One of them is real maple syrup, which should *not* be confused with many of the commercial pancake syrups that are maple-style, but not pure maple syrup.

Pure maple syrup is the choicest of all syrups and is collected from a variety of maple trees without doing harm to them.

The sugar maple *(Acer saccharum)* tree is the one that provides the sweetest sap. The best months for collecting it are late February, March, and early April. Once it has been collected, the clear maple sap is boiled to reduce the amount of water and create a natural syrup.

It is important to use pure maple syrup where it is called for in these recipes, rather than commercial pancake syrup, which is usually just dissolved sugar with artificial flavorings added. Using one of these products will not provide the recipe results you desire.

Shopping for Whole Foods with the Lowest Fat

Most unprocessed, whole foods are lower in fat than the processed versions of the same foods. But some whole foods are better low-fat choices than others. Here are some charts with ingredients commonly used in baking to consult before buying:

Dairy & Eggs

LESS THAN 15% OF CALORIES FROM FAT

Food and Serving Size	Calories	Fat (grams)	Calories from Fat
Health Valley Fat-Free			
Soy Moo® soy milk, 1 cup	110	0.0g	0 percent
Cottage Cheese, nonfat, ½ cup	90	0.4g	4 percent
Egg whites, 1 egg	16	0.0g	0 percent
Milk, nonfat, 1 cup	85	0.4g	5 percent
Milk solids, nonfat, 1 cup	80	0.0g	0 percent
Yogurt, nonfat, 1 cup	127	0.4g	3 percent

16% TO 30% OF CALORIES FROM FAT

Food and Serving Size	Calories	Fat (grams)	Calories from Fat
Buttermilk, 1 cup	100	2.0g	19 percent
Cottage Cheese, low-fat, ½ cup	104	2.2g	19 percent
Milk, 1% fat, 1 cup	100	2.6g	23 percent
Yogurt, low-fat, 1 cup	145	3.5g	22 percent

GREATER THAN 30% OF CALORIES FROM FAT

Food and Serving Size	Calories	Fat (grams)	Calories from Fat
Cream Cheese, 1 oz.	100	9.9g	89 percent
Eggs, whole, each	80	5.6g	63 percent
Heavy Cream, 1 oz.	103	11.2g	98 percent
Ice Cream, premium, ½ cup	175	12g	61 percent
Milk, whole, 1 cup	150	8g	49 percent
Sour Cream, ¼ cup	123	12g	88 percent
Soy Milk, 1 cup	140	5g	32 percent

Fruits

LESS THAN 15% OF CALORIES FROM FAT

Food and Serving Size	Calories	Fat (grams)	Calories from Fat
Apple, 1 medium	80	0.5g	6 percent
Apricots, 2 small	50	0.3g	6 percent
Banana, 1 medium	105	0.6g	5 percent
Cantaloupe, 1 cup	95	0.4g	4 percent
Dates, ½ cup	115	0.4g	1 percent
Figs, 2 dried	238	0.2g	8 percent
Grapefruit, ½ medium	40	0.1g	2 percent
Grapes, 12	35	0.3g	8 percent
Kiwi, 1	45	0.0g	0 percent
Orange, 1 medium	60	0.2g	2 percent
Peaches, 1 medium	35	0.1g	2 percent
Pear, 1 medium	120	0.7g	5 percent
Plums, 1 medium	35	0.0g	0 percent
Prunes, ½ cup dried	115	0.4g	2 percent
Raisins, ½ cup	80	0.4g	3 percent
Tangerines, 1 medium	35	0.0g	0 percent

16% TO 30% OF CALORIES FROM FAT

Food and Serving Size	Calories	Fat (grams)	Calories from Fat
Blackberries, 1 cup	75	0.6g	12 percent
Blueberries, 1 cup	80	1.0g	11 percent
Cherries, 10	50	0.8g	18 percent
Nectarines, 1 medium	65	0.6g	13 percent
Pineapple, fresh, 1 cup	75	0.7g	12 percent
Raspberries, 1 cup	60	0.7g	15 percent
Strawberries, 1 cup	45	0.6g	20 percent
Watermelon, 1 cup	50	1.0g	18 percent

GREATER THAN 30% OF CALORIES FROM FAT

Food and Serving Size	Calories	Fat (grams)	Calories from Fat
Avocado, 1 medium	305	30.0g	88 percent

All fruits are excellent choices for cutting fat in your diet. Only avocados should be used sparingly to avoid high fat intake.

Vegetables

LESS THAN 15% OF CALORIES FROM FAT

Food and Serving Size	Calories	Fat (grams)	Calories from Fat
Broccoli, cooked, 1 cup	45	0.4g	1 percent
Carrot, raw, 1 medium	30	0.1g	7 percent
Cauliflower, 1 cup	30	0.2g	4 percent
Corn, cooked, 1 cup	135	1.0g	8 percent
Potatoes, 1 large	220	0.0g	0 percent
Sweet Potatoes, baked, 1 med.	115	0.1g	1 percent
Zucchini, 1 cup	18	0.0g	0 percent

16% TO 30% OF CALORIES FROM FAT

Food and Serving Size	Calories	Fat (grams)	Calories from Fat
Summer Squash, 1 cup	35	0.6g	15 percent

All vegetables are excellent choices for cutting fat in your diet.

Grains

LESS THAN 15% OF CALORIES FROM FAT

Food and Serving Size	Calories	Fat (grams)	Calories from Fat
Flours			
Amaranth, 2 oz.	190	1.0g	5 percent
Brown rice, 2 oz.	200	1.0g	5 percent
Corn meal, 2 oz.	216	2.4g	10 percent
Rolled oats, 2 oz.	200	1.0g	5 percent
Whole wheat, 2 oz.	200	1.0g	5 percent
Whole wheat pastry, 2 oz.	215	0.9g	4 percent

Sweeteners

LESS THAN 15% OF CALORIES FROM FAT

Food and Serving Size	Calories	Fat (grams)	Calories from Fat
Orange Juice (frozen concentrate), 6 oz.	80	0g	0 percent
Fruit Preserves (juice sweetened) 1 tsp	14	0g	0 percent
Honey, 1 Tbsp	64	0g	0 percent
Maple Syrup, 1 Tbsp	50	0g	0 percent

Nuts & Seeds

LESS THAN 15% OF CALORIES FROM FAT

Food and Serving Size	Calories	Fat (grams)	Calories from Fat
Chestnuts, roasted, 1 oz.	69	1.0g	12 percent
Water Chestnuts, raw, 1 oz.	16.5	0.02g	1 percent

GREATER THAN 30% OF CALORIES FROM FAT

Food and Serving Size	Calories	Fat (grams)	Calories from Fat
Almonds, 1 oz.	165	15g	82 percent
Cashews, dry roasted, 1 oz.	165	13g	71 percent
Hazelnuts, 1 oz.	180	18g	90 percent
Macadamia, oil roasted, 1 oz.	205	22g	97 percent
Peanuts, oil roasted, 1 oz.	165	14g	76 percent
Pecans, 1 oz.	190	19g	90 percent
Pine nuts, 1 oz.	161	17.3g	96 percent
Pistachios, 1 oz.	165	14g	76 percent
Sesame Seeds, 1 Tbsp	45	4g	80 percent
Sunflower Seeds, 1 oz.	160	14g	79 percent
Walnuts, 1 oz.	170	16g	85 percent

Nuts provide a variety of beneficial nutrients, but should be used sparingly to avoid high fat intake.

Cereals

LESS THAN 15% OF CALORIES FROM FAT

Food and Serving Size	Calories	Fat (grams)	Calories from Fat
Health Valley Fat-Free Date Almond-Flavor Granola, 1 oz.	90	0.0g	0 percent
Health Valley Brown Rice Fruit Lites® Cereal , 1 oz.	100	0.0g	0 percent

16% TO 30% OF CALORIES FROM FAT

Food and Serving Size	Calories	Fat (grams)	Calories from Fat
Granola, Low-Fat, 1 oz.	106	2.0g	17 percent

GREATER THAN 30% OF CALORIES FROM FAT

Food and Serving Size	Calories	Fat (grams)	Calories from Fat
Granola, regular, 1 oz.	130	6.0g	41 percent

Although all whole grains are low in fat, when they are processed into ready-to-eat commercial cereals, fat is sometimes added. That's why it is best to check the nutritional panel on cereal for fat before purchasing them. Health Valley never adds fat to any of its cereals.

A Complete Shopping List for Baking Without Fat

To make it even more convenient for you to bake without fat, we've put together this list of ingredients that can help you achieve the taste, texture and nutritional results you want.

Don't be intimidated by the length of the list, because it isn't necessary to purchase everything at one time. This is just to give you an idea of what ingredients are used in this cookbook.

Some of the items are probably already in your kitchen. In other cases, such as pureed fruit, you have the option of making your own by using fresh fruit from your own garden, or taking advantage of the convenience of already-prepared versions in your market.

The items are grouped according to their function in baking without fat, so in many categories, it isn't necessary to purchase every item on your first shopping trip.

Flours/Grains:

We use whole wheat pastry flour for baking, and we recommend choosing organically grown grains whenever they are available.

Whole wheat pastry flour offers the beneficial fiber and other nutrients missing from white flour, yet it has the lighter texture and lower gluten content necessary for baking. Foods grown without chemical fertilizers, herbicides and pesticides help preserve our nation's pure water supplies and our topsoil.

crisp brown rice cereal
corn meal
rolled oats (oatmeal)
whole wheat pastry flour
  (made from whole wheat, but lower
  gluten for "lighter" baking)

Leavening:

arrowroot
baking soda
cream of tartar
egg whites

Sweeteners:

frozen pure fruit juice concentrates
  with no added sugar
fruit-juice-sweetened preserves
honey
pure maple syrup
molasses

Fruit/Vegetable Purees:

canned fruit, unsweetened in its
    own juice
canned pumpkin
canned tomato sauce
dried fruits: apples, apricots, dates,
    pineapple, papaya and raisins
fresh fruits
fresh vegetables
frozen fruit with no sugar added
frozen pure fruit juice concentrate
strained baby food fruit puree
strained baby food vegetable puree
unsweetened applesauce

Dairy Products:

eggs (use whites only)
nonfat dry milk solids
nonfat plain yogurt
skimmed evaporated milk

Spices/Extracts/Flavorings:

allspice
almond extract
cinnamon
citrus peel (grated)
cloves
coconut extract
ginger, fresh and powdered
lemon extract
nutmeg
orange extract
vanilla

The Benefits of Using
Health Valley Fat-Free Products in Baking Without Fat

Along with creating recipes without fat that taste good and are nutritious, we were also conscious of your need for convenience. That's why we incorporate some prepared foods, such as fat-free cookies, to make pie crust, to save the time and trouble of sifting, mixing and rolling dough.

For example, a quick and convenient way to create pie crusts without fat is to grind up Health Valley Fat-Free Granola and combine it with frozen apple juice concentrate, honey and egg whites to create a delicious press-in crust. Another example, is crumbling Health Valley Fat-Free cookies over the top of fruit cobblers and puddings.

Here are the Health Valley products that are especially beneficial for use as ingredients in the recipes in this book:

- Health Valley Fat-Free Date Almond-Flavor Granola
- Health Valley Brown Rice Fruit Lites® Cereal
- Health Valley Fat-Free Soy Moo® soy milk (an ideal non-dairy substitute for skimmed evaporated milk, it also lends a delicate caramel flavor to recipes, such as rice pudding)

Although you can use any brand of fat-free or low-fat products, we recommend using our Health Valley Fat-Free foods. That way, you have the assurance of knowing that the recipe will turn out just the way it was intended, because we used Health Valley products to develop these recipes. You'll also be enjoying a Fat-Free product that's made the healthy way. That means there's no white flour, no refined sugar, no excess sodium and no preservatives or artificial ingredients used.

When you buy Health Valley Fat-Free products, you'll also be helping us provide support for organic farmers who grow foods without chemical fertilizers, herbicides or pesticides. Health Valley uses more organic ingredients than any food company in the world–more than 50 millions pounds a year. That's because growing foods without chemicals helps protect our nation's precious supplies of pure water and fertile topsoil better. We also believe that foods grown without chemicals simply taste better.

"These recipes are not an indulgence, but part of a healthier way of eating."

chapter five

Seven Special Nutritional Benefits to Meet Your Needs

In creating the recipes for this book, we made it our goal to be certain that they not only taste good, but that they also meet your individual nutritional needs.

Most baked goods, such as cakes and cookies, have traditionally been looked upon an indulgence. That's because they've tasted good, but provided mostly "empty" calories with very little nutritional value.

The revolutionary way of baking we developed means that these recipes are not an indulgence, but part of a healthier way of eating. And because we recognize that you are an individual with your own special needs and preferences, we've created recipes to meet your needs and desires.

Here are more details about seven special benefits you'll find in this book:

1. Our Recipes Are Lower in Calories Than Comparable Recipes Made with Fat.

Fat contains more than twice as many calories as protein and carbohydrates. So when you cut down on fat, you automatically cut down on calories as well.

That means, you won't be as likely to be wearing that cheesecake on your hips a few days after it passes your lips.

One of the best things about these recipes is that you can finally enjoy baked goods and desserts totally without guilt. Since they're all made without any added fat or high-fat ingredients, they are lower in calories than comparable foods made with fat.

And if you're trying to control your weight, these recipes are especially valuable. Because by now you know that "diets" don't work. The only way to really achieve and maintain your ideal weight is by cutting down on fat as your regular way of eating. That means you have to be able to enjoy the foods you eat each day and not "diet" or feel deprived. After all, it isn't realistic for most of us to think we're going to do without sweets for the rest of our lives. So the recipes in this book allow you to prepare sweet, satisfying desserts and baked goods that are also lower in calories with very little fat.

Since all the recipes in this book are made without any added fat or high-fat ingredients, they are all lower in calories than comparable recipes made with fat. 83 recipes actually qualify to be called "Fat-Free" because they fulfill U.S. government labeling requirements that require a serving contain less than 0.5 grams of fat to use that term. Look for this symbol, which identifies recipes that qualify as "Fat-Free."

**FAT-
FREE**

To give you an idea of how the recipes in this book compare with traditional versions made with fat, here are a few comparisons:

Recipe (1 serving)	Calories	Fat (Grams)	Calories from Fat
Traditional Peach Pie	442	24g	48 percent
Baking Without Fat recipe	**185**	Fat-Free	Fat-Free
Savings:	257		
Traditional Carrot Cake	526	29g	49 percent
Baking Without Fat recipe	**269**	Fat-Free	Fat-Free
Savings:	257		
Traditional Cheesecake	462	33g	64 percent
Baking Without Fat recipe	**261**	Fat-Free	Fat-Free
Savings:	201		
Traditional Oatmeal Raisin Cookie (1 cookie)	145	6g	37 percent
Baking Without Fat recipe	**80**	Fat-Free	Fat-Free
Savings:	65		

2. Look for Wheat-Free Recipes.

If you are allergic to wheat or want to cut down on wheat, we have good news for you. This book contains recipes specifically created without wheat.

Wheat is one of the most common causes of food allergies, and may be responsible for as much as 50 percent of all the cases treated by allergists. One reason may be that we have become so dependent upon wheat in our diet, to the exclusion of other grains. Eating too much of any food, no matter how nutritious, can lead to sensitivities and allergies. That's why it's wise to include a variety of different grain sources in your diet, even if you're not allergic to wheat or any specific grain.

The Wheat-Free recipes in this book aren't just for people who have problems with wheat. Different grains contain different kinds of fiber and offer a different balance of nutrients. That's why you'll find so many different grain flours used in this book. The recipes are not just free of added fat, they are also recipes you can enjoy as part of a healthier way of eating and living.

Each Wheat-Free recipe is marked with this symbol so you can tell at a glance that it's Wheat-Free. **WHEAT FREE**

Please note that there is a difference between being sensitive to wheat and being sensitive to gluten. As you probably know, gluten is the vegetable protein found in wheat, rye, barley and oats that, among other things, has the ability to trap air in dough, enabling it to rise. That's why flours with gluten are such an integral part of so many baking recipes. If you are sensitive to gluten, you should avoid these Wheat-Free recipes because they are not gluten-free. There are flours that are free from gluten.

Beware of "Hidden" Wheat

If you're wheat sensitive, there are a number of foods you should avoid, beyond the obvious ones such as bread and wheat-based cereals. Many gravies and sauces are thickened with wheat flour, and products, such as packaged puddings, can contain flour. Certain meat products, such as sausages, often contain flour. And when you purchase prepared foods, look for flavor enhancing ingredients, such as hydrolyzed vegetable protein (HOP) and monosodium glutamate (MSG), because they often contain wheat and/or gluten. Even soy sauce is made from soybeans, water and <u>wheat</u>.

"My son has severe allergic reactions to a number of foods. Your wheat-free cookies enable him to have a snack from a box like everyone else (important for pre-schoolers), and also makes it so that if I don't have time to bake cookies one week, he can still have a snack."

"Thank you for making life a little bit more 'normal.'"

– Gina Hagler, Rockville, Maryland

3. Look for Recipes That Are Free from Dairy Products.

If you are allergic to dairy products or if you are lactose intolerant, we have created recipes for you in this book.

Dairy products are one of the most common causes of food allergies. An allergy to dairy products is caused by a reaction to the protein in milk and its byproducts.

Other people have sensitivities to dairy products caused by a difficulty digesting the lactose they contain. Certain ethnic groups, especially Native Americans, Asians, Africans, and some Mediterranean groups, lose the ability to digest lactose when they become adults.

In response to these concerns, we have developed a number of recipes in this book that are completely free from dairy products.

Each Dairy-Free recipe is marked with this symbol so you can tell at a glance that it's Dairy-Free.

DAIRY FREE

Even if you do not have a problem with dairy products, it is a good idea to eat a variety of foods and not become dependent upon a limited number, because that can contribute to developing food allergies.

The greatest reward Health Valley gets is the gratitude of its customers. Let us share an example with you:

"Thank you! Thank you! Thank you! This cookbook is exactly what I have been looking for."

–Shirlee Englese, Elk Grove Village, Illinois

Facts About Food Allergies

The word "allergy" was originally coined by an Austrian pediatrician who combined the Greek words "alios" which means "other," with the word "ergon," which means "work" or "action." So the word "allergy" indicates that an "other action," or essentially a "reaction" is caused.

This is an accurate description of what occurs when you have an allergy. Essentially, an allergic reaction occurs when the body's defense mechanisms are faced with an incoming allergen. Chemicals, such as histamines, are released, producing symptoms that include a rash, swelling, sneezing, wheezing, abdominal cramps, vomiting and even fainting. Exactly what causes one person to be allergic to a substance while someone else is not bothered by that same substance is not known.

However, we do know that the more you are exposed to a substance, the more likely you are to develop a sensitivity to it. So corn sensitivities are more common in Mexico, rice sensitivities in Asia, and rye sensitivities in northern European countries, especially Sweden. It may be that food allergies are the body's way of forcing us to develop more variety in our diets. We know that it is healthier to eat a variety of foods rather than to depend on a few of the same ones to supply the nutrients we need.

It should come as no surprise that many Americans are sensitive to wheat, since we eat it with almost every meal. In fact, wheat in one form or another probably makes up 25% of the daily calorie intake of the average American. And some allergists believe that wheat is responsible for anywhere from 30 to 50 percent of the allergies that they treat.

In addition to allergies, people can develop sensitivities to certain foods. For example, there are some people who are allergic to the protein in dairy products, while there are other people who are sensitive to dairy products because they have difficulty digesting the lactose in dairy foods. These are two separate reactions.

4. Our Recipes Can Help You Fulfill the "Healthy Five" Recommendation.

Fresh fruits and vegetables are some of the healthiest foods you can eat, because they're naturally low in fat, and rich sources of important vitamins, minerals and fiber. That's why the National Cancer Institute recommends that all Americans eat at least five servings a day of fruits and vegetables, in order to help protect against cancer and a wide range of other diseases. Unfortunately, only about 23% of Americans get their five servings each day.

Each Healthy Five recipe is marked with this symbol so you can tell at a glance that it's one of our unique Healthy Five recipes.

Unless you're a vegetarian, you may not know if you're getting your "Healthy Five."

First of all, just how much is a "serving" of a fruit or vegetable, and which foods should you count?

All fruits, melons, and berries count, and so do 100% fruit and vegetable juices. Leafy vegetables (like lettuce), root vegetables (like carrots), and legumes (such as lentils) all count. Potatoes count, except potato chips and french fries, which provide most of their calories from fat. Air popped popcorn is good food, but is classified as a grain rather than a fruit or vegetable. Orange marmalade and other sweet fruit preserves don't count because they are usually half sugar and are eaten in quantities that are too small to provide much benefit. Fruit-flavored yogurts don't count as fruits, since they contain only a little fruit. Breads, cereals, rice, pasta, and other grains do not count as part of the Healthy Five, but they should definitely be part of your healthy diet. In fact, in addition to your five servings of fruits and vegetables, experts recommend 6 to 11 servings of grains a day.

Servings don't need to be huge. Allow a cup of raw leafy vegetables, such as lettuce. Figure half a cup of cooked fruits and vegetables, including tomato sauces; one-quarter cup of dried fruit, one raw carrot, one whole fruit, such as an apple, orange or pear; or 6 ounces of juice. With smaller fruit, such as apricots or berries, eat at least a half a cup. For larger fruit, such as melons, judge by the size. If a cantaloupe is small, half might be a serving, but if it's a large one, one-third might be enough.

Because both fruits and vegetables are so important, we made it a point to include them both in these recipes.

It may surprise you to see vegetables, including cruciferous vegetables such as broccoli, in baking recipes. And your initial reaction might be to pass up this recipe section entirely. We hope you won't because these are some of the most innovative recipes in the book. If you'll keep an open mind and try them, you'll discover that there is now an exciting new way to create foods that really taste good, and that you know you should be eating for good health. These recipes are a revolutionary way to eat healthy, and they are the desserts of the future.

5. Look for Recipes That Appeal to Children.

We are especially proud of the fact that so many of the recipes in this book give you what you need for children – namely foods that appeal to children's tastes that also provide the nutrients they need. As every parent knows, children don't always like the foods that are best for them, including vegetables like broccoli, beets and carrots. This is the first book that contains recipes that include these vegetables, along with nutritious fruits in recipes that children will be happy to eat.

Nutritional research has provided increasing evidence that getting the proper nutrition during formative years can have a life-long effect on health. For example, it is now accepted that building a strong bone structure during adolescence and earlier helps prevent the development of osteoporosis later in life. That's why it is important for children to get sufficient amounts of the mineral calcium in their diets.

Unfortunately, many young people today are attracted to "junk" foods that provide too many of their calories from refined sugar and fat, and that are deficient in the important vitamins, minerals and fiber that children and adolescents need for good health.

We made a special effort to create recipes for this book that appeal to children and are made with ingredients they might not otherwise eat.

GREAT FOR KIDS

To make it easier for you to know which recipes children like best, we've identified them for you. Look for this special symbol.

6. Look for Recipes That Are Good Sources of Antioxidants.

Among the most important nutrients of the 1990's are the "antioxidants." These nutrients include beta carotene, vitamin C and vitamin E.

The reason these nutrients are getting so much attention is because of their potential to prevent both degenerative diseases and lessen the effects of aging.

Nutritional scientists believe that antioxidants may play an important role in reducing the damage done by "free radicals."

Free radicals are chemicals produced during normal reactions in the body. They are highly unstable molecules that are lacking in an electron and harm other molecules by "stealing" away electrons, resulting in oxidative damage. Sometimes this can include damaging DNA, the cellular material that contains the genetic code. When that occurs, a cell may not replicate itself precisely, making the new cell less efficient and giving it a reduced life span. Unless they are neutralized, free radicals can have a snowball effect. One free radical strips electrons from the next molecule, which then steals from the next, and so on. Ultimately, cells and tissues are damaged, and the result can be disease, such as cancer, or premature aging.

Antioxidants are nutrients in foods that are able to "donate" an extra electron, thereby neutralizing free radicals safely.

Today, most of us live in an environment that is hostile to our bodies. Air and water pollution, ultraviolet rays from sunlight, pesticides and additives can all generate free radicals. That's why we may need higher levels of antioxidants.

Many of the recipes in this book are rich sources of antioxidants, especially beta carotene. Beta carotene is found in leafy green and orange fruits and vegetables, including carrots, pumpkins, sweet potatoes and broccoli. That's why we made a special effort to include these ingredients in many recipes. Look for the special symbol at the top of each recipe that indicates it is a good source of beta carotene.

**BETA-
CAROTENE**

The recipes in this book also supply the other antioxidants, vitamins C and E.

Vitamin C is found in many fruits and vegetables, such as citrus fruits and juices, broccoli, and strawberries, all of which can be found in recipes in this book.

Some of the richest natural sources of vitamin E are whole grains. The vitamin E in grains is located in the germ portion, which is removed, along with the fiber-rich bran, to make white flour. That's why whole grain flour is more naturally nutritious than white flour. The recipes in this book call for whole grain flour only, so you get both the beneficial fiber and vitamin E.

7. The Recipes in This Book Are Rich in Fiber.

One of the most important parts of a healthy diet consists of food components that your body can't digest, and that provide no energy at all. We're referring to fiber.

Fiber is found only in foods from plant sources, including fruits, vegetables and whole grains. It is the part of the plant that isn't digested, so it provides no calories. But it does perform some very valuable functions in digestion and health.

Insoluble fiber, such as the kind found in wheat bran, provides bulk or roughage. It helps satisfy your appetite without adding calories. It also helps maintain a healthy digestive system and may help prevent cancers of the stomach, colon and rectum.

Soluble fiber, such as the kind found in oat bran, has been shown to help lower cholesterol, for a healthier cardiovascular system.

The recipes in this book are different from other low-fat recipes because they feature high-fiber ingredients, such as whole grains, fruits, vegetables and their purees, which are rich sources of both soluble and insoluble fiber.

Recipes made with white flour are lower in fiber because the fiber-rich bran layers are removed in milling white flour, leaving mostly starch.

We're proud to list the amount of fiber in every recipe.

"We were committed to recipes made without any added fat."

chapter six

Recipes

The Nutritional Standards We Set for These Recipes

As we have said previously, our goal in developing the recipes went beyond merely reducing the amount of fat. We were committed to perfecting recipes made *without any added fat,* that also provide beneficial fiber and nutrients, such as beta carotene and vitamin C. We were equally concerned about fulfilling the special dietary needs of people who are sensitive to dairy products and to wheat, and deliberately created *recipes that are wheat-free* and *recipes that are dairy-free.*

Here are the nutritional standards we maintained for the recipes:

- They contain no added fat or high-fat ingredients, so *all recipes are under 1.5 grams of fat per serving*
- They contain *no refined sugar,* and are sweetened with nutritious ingredients, including fruit juice, pureed fruit, honey and maple syrup
- They contain *no white flour,* just whole grain flours, such as whole wheat pastry flour, rolled oats, crisp brown rice and corn meal

Here is a breakdown of the recipes by the amount of fat per serving, and by special nutritional attributes:

- 83 recipes qualify as **"fat-free,"** meaning that they contain under 0.5 grams of fat per serving
- 21 recipes qualify as **"no fat added,"** meaning that no fat or oils have been added, but the ingredients used, such as rolled oats, naturally contain enough fat so that a serving contains more than 0.5 grams of fat.
- 48 recipes are **dairy-free**
- 31 recipes are **wheat-free**
- 4 recipes are **rich in beta carotene** (at least 500 IUs per serving)
- 17 qualify as **"healthy five"** recipes
- 45 recipes are **great for kids**

About the Recipes

- Recipes made without fat respond differently than similar recipes made with shortening. For example, overmixing can cause tunnels to develop in cake batter. That is why it is especially important to follow the recipe instructions carefully.

- Using the precise size of the pan or bakeware specified is important to the success of these recipes. We have found that high quality non-stick bakeware is a worthwhile investment because when you bake without fat, there is a greater tendency for the ingredients to stick.

- In recipes that call for egg whites, we do <u>not</u> recommend using egg substitutes because the egg whites are used to allow air to be incorporated into the batter, which helps give the finished product a fluffier, tender texture.

- Specific nutritional information is provided for each recipe. For people with special dietary needs, consult your physician, registered dietitian, or other health care professional. Food exchanges have also been included for your reference.

- The nutritional content of these recipes was calculated without garnishes or optional ingredients. Values were rounded in accordance with U.S. Food and Drug Administration nutritional labeling rules.

- Serving suggestions were not included in the nutritional information.

How to Read the Recipes

Each recipe occupies two facing pages. On the left hand page, you will find general information about the recipe and the key or featured ingredient that was used to develop it. There is a per-serving nutritional analysis and, in some cases, a serving suggestion.

Please note that the nutritional analysis is accurate for the recipe only and not for the recipe and the serving suggestion combined.

For example, one slice of our Carrot Pineapple Cake qualifies as Fat-Free and has 197 calories, as we note in the nutritional analysis. If you filled and glazed the cake with Creamy Maple Sauce or fruit-juice-sweetened preserves for a different presentation, the nutritional analysis would change.

On the right hand page is the recipe itself, with the ingredients, and the directions all clearly indicated. For your convenience, ingredients are listed in the order they are to be used.

It will simplify things for you and eliminate errors if you read both pages carefully before you begin to bake.

In the ingredients section of the recipes, the word "and" does not mean the same thing as the symbol "+". The word "and" merely indicates the total amount of an ingredient required, while the symbol "+" indicates that the same ingredient will be used in two separate steps within the recipe.

For example, "1 cup and 2½ teaspoons whole wheat pastry flour" indicates that all of this measurement is to be added at the same time. "¾ teaspoon + ½ teaspoon baking soda" indicates that the baking soda will be used twice within the recipe.

Recipes That Meet Your Individual Needs

This book is not just another cookbook because it has been developed to meet your personal nutritional needs. You will find recipes you can use even if you're allergic or sensitive to dairy products or to wheat; recipes that are especially good for children; recipes that are rich in specific nutrients, such as beta carotene; and recipes that are especially beneficial in helping you fulfill the recommendation that you eat five servings of fruits and vegetables each day.

To make it quick and easy for you to identify which recipes provide these special benefits, we've created symbols that you'll find in the upper right hand corner above each recipe description. Here are what the symbols look like and what they signify:

FAT-FREE   WHEAT FREE   DAIRY FREE   HEALTHY FIVE   GREAT FOR KIDS   BETA-CAROTENE

How to Read the Nutrition Information

Since the publication of our previous book, *Cooking Without Fat,* the Federal government has passed the Nutrition Labeling Education Act (NLEA), which changes the way nutrition is to be reported on food packages.

Among other things, the NLEA establishes what a serving size is for various categories of food products and also establishes the way numbers are to be expressed on packages. The purpose of the new food labeling law is to establish more uniformity in the way all manufacturers list nutrition and portion sizes, leading to more useful information about foods for consumers. The government wants consumers to be able to compare products more easily and be able to make more informed food choices.

Because the government is focusing so much attention on the new labeling law, we have decided to use its guidelines in presenting the nutrition figures in this book. We feel that eventually most people will be familiar with nutrition information in the form mandated by the NLEA, and that by conforming to the law, we will make it easier for you to evaluate the nutritional qualities of these recipes.

Unlike our previous book, where we listed the specific amount of each nutrient in a serving for each recipe, this book follows the labeling law by rounding the numbers.

Here are the NLEA guidelines we followed:

Protein and Total Carbohydrate: If there is less than 0.5 gram in a serving, the amount is expressed as zero.

Between 0.5 and 1 gram, the amount is expressed as "contains less than 1 g".

If there is more than 1 gram, the amount is rounded to the nearest 1 gram increment.

Total Fat: If there is less than 0.5 gram of fat in a serving, the amount is expressed as zero.

Between 0.5 gram and 5 grams of fat, the amount is rounded to the nearest 0.5 increment.

If there are more than 5 grams of fat, the amount is rounded to the nearest 1 gram increment.

Calories from Fat: If there are fewer than 5 calories in a serving, the amount is expressed as zero.

Between 5 calories and 50 calories, the amount is rounded to the nearest 5 calorie increment.

If there are more than 50 calories from fat, the amount is rounded to the nearest 10 calorie increment.

Cholesterol: If there are fewer than 2 milligrams of cholesterol in a serving, the amount is expressed as zero.

Between 2 milligrams and 5 milligrams, the amount is listed as "less than 5 mg".

If there are more than 5 milligrams, the amount is rounded to the nearest 5 milligram increment.

Sodium: If there are fewer than 5 milligrams of sodium, the amount is expressed as zero.

Between 5 milligrams and 140 milligrams, the amount is rounded to the nearest 5 milligram increment.

If there are more than 140 milligrams, the amount is rounded to the nearest 10 milligram increment.

Dietary Fiber: If there is less than 0.5 gram of fiber the amount is expressed as zero.

If there is less than 1 gram of fiber, the amount is expressed as "contains less than 1 g".

If there is more than 1 gram, the amount is rounded to the nearest 1 gram increment.

The only place where we did not follow these labeling requirements is with calories, where we listed the specific number of calories in a serving without rounding the numbers.

If you own a copy of our previous book, *Cooking Without Fat,* you should know that the first edition was written before the current labeling laws. The way we expressed the numbers was different from the way it has been done here.

The Right Equipment

To achieve the best success with these recipes, it is important to use the specific size of baking dish, pan or sheet that is called for.

Here is a list of the various sizes and quantities of equipment that are specified in the book:

– two 9x1½-inch nonstick round baking pans
– one 10½x15½x1-inch nonstick cookie sheet
– one 10-inch nonstick fluted tube pan
– one 8x11x2-inch ovenproof glass baking dish
– one 9x13-inch nonstick baking dish
– one 9-inch nonstick springform pan
– one 8-inch square ovenproof glass baking dish
– one 9-inch ovenproof glass pie dish
– one nonstick muffin pan
– one 1-quart trifle dish
– one 3-quart trifle dish
– one 1½-quart souffle dish
– 10 8-ounce ovenproof glass custard cups

Be sure to check the recipe to see what size you need *before* you actually start cooking, because our experience has shown that merely changing the size or shape of the baking vessel can drastically affect the moisture and texture of the finished product.

If you are unable to invest in nonstick cookware, we suggest that you use nonfat vegetable spray for all of our recipes, except for those based on meringues.

General Tips from the Test Kitchen

As you will soon find out for yourself, nonfat baking is substantially different from traditional baking, and some of the things that home bakers take for granted won't apply.

For example, the texture of nonfat cookies will be chewy instead of crisp. A slightly elastic consistency is normal—don't be alarmed and think that you have done something wrong.

And when you make one of the recipes, it's best to enjoy the results within two to three days. Of course, just how long any baked goods will keep depends upon what it is: Crispy Rice Treats taste best fresh from the oven, while the trifles taste better if they are made the day before and allowed to sit in the refrigerator until the flavors can meld. The recipes for bars will last for a week in the refrigerator and can also be frozen.

Other Tips from the Test Kitchen

Nonfat baking produces a lot of leftover egg yolks. Thirteen to 14 equal 1 cup. For example, in the strawberry angel food cake, we call for 10 egg whites. What can you do with the yolks?

In traditional baking, egg yolks are saved for such egg yolk sauces as mayonnaise or hollandaise, or for making custards, puddings or zabaglione.

The only recommendations we can make is that some people use egg yolks as a hair rinse to add luster. Or you can occasionally feed some of the leftover yolks to your pet to increase the shine in his or her coat. But remember, high-fat diets will produce the same sorts of health risks for pets as for their owners.

Applying Frostings

We've worked hard to create frostings without fat, and hope that you will take advantage of them. Specific instructions for each frosting are given in individual recipes, but here are a few pointers:

• let the cake cool before you begin frosting it.

• use a flat plate a few inches larger than the cake.

- place a few sheets of wax paper on the plate first and pull them out from under the frosted cake when finished. This will keep the plate looking pretty.

- begin by spooning frosting into center of cake, then working out and onto the sides.

- to apply a thin frosting or glaze, spoon on top of center of cake and allow to run down the sides.

How to Make Your Own Yogurt

In order to make yogurt cheese, you need a brand of yogurt that does not add gelatin. We have found Dannon® nonfat plain yogurt works well.

Another alternative is to make your own yogurt. That way, you know the yogurt is fresh, with all the beneficial active culture.

Making yogurt successfully really isn't difficult if you follow the simple instructions carefully. The yeast culture that is responsible for activating milk into yogurt is a living organism that is sensitive to temperatures. You need to maintain a constant temperature by using an insulated picnic cooler or an oven preheated to 105°F. It's also important to know that the yogurt culture doesn't respond well to being jostled while growing. You should place your equipment where you can leave it undisturbed. If you use one of the many electric devices for quick yogurt making, follow the directions carefully.

ingredients: 1 quart nonfat milk

⅓ cup nonfat dry milk powder

2 tablespoons plain nonfat yogurt or a package of yogurt culture

directions: Combine ⅓ cup milk with milk powder. Pour into large saucepan, and add remaining milk, stirring thoroughly to combine.

Heat mixture over low heat until temperature is 190°F. Use candy thermometer put into mixture to determine temperature. Cover and reduce heat to 110°F. Leave thermometer in saucepan.

Blend yogurt with 2 tablespoons warm milk mixture, or mix packaged yogurt culture according to instructions, and add to saucepan.

Pour mixture into sterilized, warm glass jar, cover tightly and keep on a warming tray or in warm, draft-free place for 6-8 hours. Temperature must remain between 105°F.-110°F. Or use electric yogurt maker and follow manufacturer's instructions.

Refrigerate when mixture has yogurt consistency. It will keep in refrigerator for 1 week.

yield: 1 quart

"Healthy Five" Recipes

I n developing these recipes, we not only wanted to create good tasting baked goods made without any added fat, we also wanted to incorporate ingredients that are naturally rich in the nutrients you need to look and feel your best. We decided that one of the ways to accomplish this goal was to create recipes specifically to help you fulfill the recommendation that you eat at least five servings of fruits and vegetables each day. All the recipes in this section feature fruits, along with vegetables. Because they are especially good recipes for meeting your Five-a-Day requirement, we call them *"Healthy Five"* recipes.

The first reactions many people have to including vegetables in baking are surprise and apprehension. But when you think about it, you've already been enjoying baked goods made with vegetables for years. Such old favorites as carrot cake, pumpkin pie and zucchini bread are some familiar baked goods that feature vegetables.

We simply took this concept a step further and found ways to expand the use of ingredients such as carrots, pumpkins and zucchini, along with a few others, such as sweet potatoes.

We urge you to keep an open mind and not prejudge any of these recipes before you try them. We believe you'll be pleasantly surprised by how well the combinaton of fruits and vegetables work.

We think you'll really enjoy the recipes in this section, and we can absolutely guarantee that when you do, you'll be getting nutritional benefits that go well beyond what you've ever enjoyed from baked goods before.

One of the secrets we learned in our test kitchen is not to tell people ahead of time that there are vegetables in the recipe. When we would ask Health Valley employees if they wanted to sample a piece of cake with vegetables in it, many times they politely declined. If we simply asked if they wanted to taste a new cake recipe, we were almost never turned down. Only after they told us how much they liked the recipe did we reveal the "surprise" ingredients. If you have children or someone in your household who doesn't like vegetables, we suggest you refrain from announcing the ingredients and simply let them enjoy the good taste.

This is a recipe that's great for providing essential nutrients that children need in a form that they'll eat. Raisins are a good source of iron, a mineral that everyone, especially children, needs.

The other key ingredient is carrots, which are one of nature's richest sources of vitamin A in the form of beta carotene. There are advantages that beta carotene offers over vitamin A. Since the body only converts beta carotene into vitamin A as it is needed, there isn't the danger of toxicity as there is if you ingest too much pre-formed vitamin A. There is also evidence that a diet that contains food rich in beta carotene may provide protection against coronary disease and some forms of cancer.

Carrots, which are available year-round, should be firm, straight and bright orange in color, with no splits in the sides. Avoid those that have green or yellow areas or wilted tops. Since they are root vegetables, carrots will store for a long time in the refrigerator. If you buy them with the tops still on, remove the tops and then store the carrots in the same bag in which they were purchased, and remember to keep it sealed.

Serving Suggestion:

There are a couple of ways to dress up this cake. One is by filling and glazing it with melted fruit-juice-sweetened preserves, using one-quarter cup per layer. Raspberry or apricot preserves, or orange marmalade would all be good choices.

Or, try frosting it with our Creamy Vanilla Frosting (see page 167) for added flavor and a beautiful appearance.

FAT-FREE   DAIRY FREE   GREAT FOR KIDS

BETA-CAROTENE   HEALTHY FIVE

Special Equipment

2 9-inch round nonstick baking pans

Temperature and Time

Bake at 325°F. for 40-45 minutes

Yield

16 servings

Nutrition per Serving

Calories: 218
Carbohydrates: 52 grams
Protein: 4 grams
Fat: Fat-Free*
Cholesterol: 0 milligrams
Sodium: 140 milligrams
Dietary Fiber: 4 grams

*All foods contain some fat. Less than .5 gram of fat per serving is nutritionally insignificant and considered to be "Fat-Free."

carrot raisin cake

ingredients:

2½ cups and 2 tablespoons
   whole wheat pastry flour

1½ teaspoons baking soda

1½ teaspoons cream of tartar

1½ teaspoons cinnamon

¼ teaspoon ground nutmeg

1½ cups honey

⅓ cup frozen pineapple juice
   concentrate (defrosted)

2 teaspoons vanilla

2 egg whites, unbeaten

1½ cups grated peeled carrots

2 jars (4 ounces each) carrot
   baby food puree

1 cup raisins

2 egg whites, lightly beaten

directions:

Preheat oven to 325°F. In large mixing bowl, combine flour, baking soda, cream of tartar, cinnamon and nutmeg. Set aside.

In medium bowl, mix honey, juice concentrate, vanilla, 2 unbeaten egg whites, grated peeled carrots and carrot puree. Stir into flour mixture and mix until just blended. Stir in raisins. Gently stir in 2 lightly beaten egg whites. ***Do not overmix.***

Spoon batter into 2 9-inch round nonstick baking pans. Bake at 325°F. for 40-45 minutes or until toothpick inserted in center comes out clean. Cool on wire racks for 20-30 minutes, and remove cakes from pans.

The word "aloha" is very versatile in that it can mean both "hello" and "goodbye," and it also describes a special attitude or spirit that is unique to Hawaii.

We gave this cake the name "aloha" because the flavors remind us of Hawaii and because it, too, is very versatile.

It offers a taste of Hawaii because it combines fruits associated with the island, including pineapple and bananas, together with the flavors of coconut extract and fresh ginger.

This is a versatile cake you can enjoy for any number of occasions from an outdoor summer barbecue to a family dinner at home. And the colorful marmalade drizzle makes it festive enough to serve at a more formal dinner party.

We use coconut extract in this recipe, which is a flavor essence, rather than an oil, and contains no fat.

If you're looking for a delicious Fat-Free cake you can enjoy anytime, say "Aloha" to this cake.

FAT-FREE   DAIRY FREE   HEALTHY FIVE

Special Equipment

10-inch nonstick fluted tube pan

Temperature and Time

Bake at 325°F. for 50-55 minutes

Yield

16 servings

Nutrition per Serving

Calories: 215
Carbohydrates: 52 grams
Protein: 4 grams
Fat: Fat-Free*
Cholesterol: 0 milligrams
Sodium: 200 milligrams
Dietary Fiber: 4 grams

*All foods contain some fat. Less than .5 gram of fat per serving is nutritionally insignificant and considered to be "Fat-Free."

aloha cake

ingredients:

2⅓ cups whole wheat pastry flour

¾ teaspoon + 1½ teaspoons baking soda

1 teaspoon cream of tartar

1 cup honey

⅓ cup pure maple syrup

1 teaspoon vanilla

1½ teaspoons coconut extract

1 tablespoon finely grated fresh ginger

2 teaspoons finely grated orange peel

1 can (8 ounces) juice-packed crushed pineapple, drained

2 egg whites, unbeaten

2 jars (4 ounces each) sweet potato baby food puree

2 large ripe bananas, sliced

¾ cup chopped dates

2 egg whites, lightly beaten

⅓ cup fruit-juice-sweetened orange marmalade, melted or 1 recipe Pineapple Glaze (see page 177)

directions:

Preheat oven to 325°F. In large mixing bowl, combine flour, ¾ teaspoon baking soda and cream of tartar. Set aside.

In medium bowl, mix honey, maple syrup, vanilla and coconut extracts, ginger, orange peel, pineapple and 2 unbeaten egg whites. Stir into flour mixture until just blended.

In blender, process sweet potato puree and banana for 1 minute; add dates and 1½ teaspoons of baking soda, continue to process until dates are pureed, approximately 2 minutes; stir into flour mixture. Gently stir in 2 lightly beaten egg whites. Do not overmix.

Spoon batter into 10-inch nonstick fluted tube pan. Bake at 325°F. for 50-55 minutes, or until toothpick inserted in center comes out clean. Cool on wire rack for 30 minutes, and remove cake from pan. Drizzle melted marmalade over top of cake; allow marmalade to drip over side of cake.

FAT-FREE · DAIRY FREE · HEALTHY FIVE

Carrot cake is actually the recipe that opened my eyes to the amount of "hidden" fat in baked goods. I always loved carrot cake because I considered it to be something that is healthy and tastes good. But the traditional recipe calls for a cup and a half of oil, plus four eggs, along with cream cheese, butter and nuts for the frosting and topping. As a result, a serving of traditional carrot cake can contain as much as 29 grams of fat!

We developed this recipe because we love the taste of carrot cake and wanted to be able to enjoy it without the fat and refined sugar. Carrots are combined with pineapple to create a sweet, moist, satisfying cake that is Fat-Free. It's also a wonderful source of beta carotene, the nutrient health-conscious people want to include in their diets.

Serving Suggestion:

You may want to fill and glaze this cake. Use one-quarter cup of melted fruit-juice-sweetened apricot preserves or orange marmalade per layer. Or try our Creamy Maple Sauce (see page 159).

Special Equipment

2 9-inch round nonstick baking pans

Temperature and Time

Bake at 325°F. for 40-45 minutes

Yield

15 servings

Nutrition per Serving

Calories: 199
Carbohydrates: 47 grams
Protein: 4 grams
Fat: Fat-Free*
Cholesterol: 0 milligrams
Sodium: 140 milligrams
Dietary Fiber: 3 grams

All foods contain some fat. Less than .5 gram of fat per serving is nutritionally insignificant and considered to be "Fat-Free."

carrot pineapple cake

ingredients:

2½ cups whole wheat pastry flour

1½ teaspoons baking soda

1½ teaspoons cream of tartar

1½ teaspoons cinnamon

¼ teaspoon ground nutmeg

1¼ cups honey

⅓ cup frozen pineapple juice concentrate (defrosted)

2 teaspoons vanilla

2 egg whites, unbeaten

1 can (8 ounces) juice-packed crushed pineapple, drained

2 jars (4 ounces each) carrot baby food puree

1 cup raisins

2 egg whites, lightly beaten

directions:

Preheat oven to 325°F. In large mixing bowl, combine flour, baking soda, cream of tartar, cinnamon and nutmeg. Set aside.

In medium bowl, mix honey, juice concentrate, vanilla, 2 unbeaten egg whites, pineapple and carrot puree. Stir into flour mixture and mix until just blended. Stir in raisins. Gently stir in 2 lightly beaten egg whites. ***Do not overmix.***

Spoon batter into 2 9x1½-inch nonstick round baking pans. Bake at 325°F. for 40-45 minutes, or until toothpick inserted in center comes out clean. ***Watch carefully to avoid overbrowning.*** Cool on wire racks for 20-30 minutes, and remove cakes from pans.

This is a recipe that combines the clean, refreshing taste of lemon with two vegetables that are old favorites in baking–carrots and zucchini. Even though carrots are a vegetable, they are naturally high in sugar so they provide a wonderful sweetness that works well in baking. In addition, carrots are one of nature's richest sources of beta carotene, the antioxidant that is being hailed as "the nutrient of the 1990's." This recipe is a delicious way to make sure you get the beta carotene you need in an enjoyable form.

If you're the adventurous type, you can make this recipe with grated broccoli stalks instead of the zucchini. Believe it or not, it works quite well. As long as the broccoli you use is very fresh, you don't even taste it in the finished recipe, but you do get the nutritional benefits of eating a cruciferous vegetable. In our test kitchen, we've made the recipe both ways, but we feature zucchini because it's a more familiar ingredient for baking in recipes, such as zucchini bread. If you decide to make the recipe with broccoli, be sure and add a bit more sweetener than as noted in the recipe.

Serving Suggestion:

Serve this cake frosted with Creamy Orange Frosting (see page 163).

FAT-FREE   DAIRY-FREE   GREAT FOR KIDS

BETA-CAROTENE   HEALTHY FIVE

Special Equipment

10-inch nonstick fluted pan

Temperature and Time

Bake at 325°F. for 1 hour

Yield

15 servings

Nutrition per Serving

Calories: 219
Carbohydrates: 52 grams
Protein: 4 grams
Fat: Fat-Free*
Cholesterol: 0 milligrams
Sodium: 140 milligrams
Dietary Fiber: 4 grams

*All foods contain some fat. Less than .5 gram of fat per serving is nutritionally insignificant and considered to be "Fat-Free."

citrus garden cake

ingredients:

¾ cup grated zucchini

2½ cups whole wheat pastry flour

1½ teaspoons baking soda

1½ teaspoons cream of tartar

1½ cups honey

½ cup frozen orange juice concentrate (defrosted)

2 teaspoons vanilla

1 tablespoon finely grated orange peel

2 egg whites, unbeaten

¾ cup grated peeled carrots

2 jars (4 ounces each) carrot baby food puree

½ cup raisins

½ cup chopped dates

2 egg whites, lightly beaten

directions:

Preheat oven to 325°F. Set grated zucchini between paper towels and press to remove excess moisture.

In large mixing bowl, combine flour, baking soda and cream of tartar. Set aside.

In medium bowl, mix honey, juice concentrate, vanilla, orange peel, 2 unbeaten egg whites, carrots, zucchini, carrot puree, raisins and dates. Stir into flour mixture until just blended. Gently stir in 2 lightly beaten egg whites. ***Do not overmix.*** Let batter set 5 minutes to thicken.

Spoon batter into 10-inch nonstick fluted tube pan. Bake at 325°F. for 1 hour, or until toothpick inserted in center comes out clean. Cool on wire rack for 30 minutes, and remove cake from pan.

DAIRY FREE **HEALTHY FIVE**

O nce you've sampled the traditional varieties of carrot cake, try this one. In it,
we've combined the two most-used vegetables
in cakes–carrots and zucchini–to create a
unique taste.

We're very proud of this recipe because it
satisfies even the most avid chocolate lover
and it is also a wonderfully nutritious cake that
provides beta carotene, the important and
beneficial antioxidant. This is another of the
recipes that combine both fruits and vegetables in a surprisingly delicious combination. It
also gives you the choice of using either
unsweetened cocoa powder, if you're a
chocolate lover, or carob powder. Although
unsweetened cocoa powder and carob powder
aren't related, they can be substituted for each
other, with a one-to-one ratio.

Serving Suggestion:

You can dress this vegetable cake up by
frosting with Coco Frosting (see page 151), or
by glazing with fruit-juice-sweetened orange
marmalade. And don't forget that this cake
tastes great by itself for breakfast or for a snack.

Special Equipment
10-inch nonstick fluted tube pan

Temperature and Time
Bake at 325°F. for 50-60 minutes

Yield
16 servings

Nutrition per Serving
Calories: 198
Carbohydrates: 47 grams
Protein: 4 grams
Fat: .5 gram
Calories from Fat: 2%
Cholesterol: 0 milligrams
Sodium: 140 milligrams
Dietary Fiber: 3 grams

coco garden cake

ingredients:

¾ cup coarsely grated zucchini

2½ cups whole wheat pastry flour

1½ teaspoons baking soda

1½ teaspoons cream of tartar

½ cup unsweetened cocoa powder
  or carob powder

2 teaspoons cinnamon

½ teaspoon ground nutmeg

½ teaspoon ground allspice

1½ cups honey

½ cup frozen apple juice concentrate
  (defrosted)

2 teaspoons vanilla

2 teaspoons finely grated lemon peel

2 egg whites, unbeaten

¾ cup unsweetened applesauce

¾ cup grated, peeled carrots

2 egg whites, lightly beaten

directions:

Preheat oven to 325°F. Set grated zucchini between paper towels and press to remove excess moisture.

In large bowl, sift flour, baking soda, cream of tartar, cocoa or carob powder, cinnamon, nutmeg and allspice; mix well.

In medium bowl, combine honey, juice concentrate, vanilla, lemon peel, 2 unbeaten egg whites, applesauce and grated carrots; stir into flour mixture. Stir in well drained grated zucchini. Gently mix in lightly beaten egg whites.

Pour batter into 10-inch nonstick fluted tube pan, and bake at 325°F. for 50-60 minutes. Cool 30 minutes and remove cake from pan.

One of the most common food allergies or sensitivities is to wheat. That's why we were determined to create a really moist, good-tasting muffin recipe made without wheat or fat. After making many trips to the oven, we perfected this recipe. The key is the combination of carrots, applesauce and raisins, which gives these muffins both a satisfying sweet taste, without refined sugar, and the moist tender texture any really good muffin must have.

We use fresh carrots in this recipe, which are available year-round. When buying them, look for those that are firm, straight and bright orange in color, with no splits in the sides. Avoid those that have green or yellow areas or wilted tops. If you buy carrots with the green tops still attached, be sure to remove the tops before storing them in the refrigerator, or the tops will draw the moisture out of the carrots, causing them to age prematurely.

DAIRY FREE   WHEAT FREE   GREAT FOR KIDS

BETA-CAROTENE   HEALTHY FIVE

Special Equipment
nonstick muffin pan

Temperature and Time
Bake at 350°F. for 25 minutes

Yield
12 large muffins

Nutrition per Serving
Calories: 171
Carbohydrates: 35 grams
Protein: 5 grams
Fat: 1.5 grams
Calories from Fat: 8%
Cholesterol: 0 milligrams
Sodium: 100 milligrams
Dietary Fiber: 1 gram

harvest muffins

ingredients:

1¼ cups rolled oats

1¾ cups oat flour (2⅓ cups
   rolled oats processed in blender
   about 2-3 minutes
   until finely ground)

¾ teaspoon baking soda

¾ teaspoon cream of tartar

1½ teaspoons cinnamon

⅛ teaspoon ground nutmeg

⅓ cup honey

2 teaspoons vanilla

½ cup unsweetened applesauce

1 jar (4 ounces) carrot baby food
   puree

1 cup grated peeled carrots

⅓ cup frozen apple juice concentrate
   (defrosted)

½ cup water

½ cup raisins

3 egg whites, lightly beaten

directions:

Preheat oven to 350°F. In large bowl, combine oats with oat flour, baking soda, cream of tartar, cinnamon and nutmeg; mix well. Set aside.

In medium bowl, mix together honey, vanilla, applesauce, carrot puree, grated carrots, juice concentrate and water; pour into oat mixture. Stir to blend. Stir in raisins. Gently mix in egg whites. ***Do not overmix.***

Using nonstick muffin pan, fill each muffin cup with batter.

Bake at 350°F. for 25 minutes, or until toothpick inserted in center comes out clean. Cool on wire rack for 10 minutes, and remove muffins from pan.

A ll of our cakes are delicious served the day they are made, or eaten within two days. We suggest that any leftovers be frozen in air-tight containers. You can then reheat them in a microwave oven for 30 seconds before serving.

The key ingredient in this recipe is pumpkin, which is a wonderful source of beta carotene. According to the National Cancer Institute, beta carotene helps to prevent a myriad of cancers–lung, stomach, bladder, esophagus and throat.

In general, vegetables and fruits that are orange in color are good sources of beta carotene. For example, carrots, apricots, peaches, sweet potatoes and cantaloupes are all good sources of this antioxidant nutrient.

Pumpkin is also loaded with fiber, which, among its many health benefits, can even help you to curb your appetite.

DAIRY FREE **HEALTHY FIVE**

Special Equipment
10-inch nonstick fluted pan

Temperature and Time
Bake at 325°F. for 1 hour and 5 minutes

Yield
16 servings

Nutrition per Serving
Calories: 199
Carbohydrates: 47 grams
Protein: 4 grams
Fat: .5 gram
Calories from Fat: 2%
Cholesterol: 0 milligrams
Sodium: 170 milligrams
Dietary Fiber: 2 grams

pumpkin delight cake

ingredients:

1 cup rolled oats

2 cups whole wheat pastry flour

2 teaspoons baking soda

2 teaspoons cream of tartar

2 teaspoons cinnamon

½ teaspoon ground ginger

¼ teaspoon ground cloves

¼ teaspoon ground nutmeg

¼ teaspoon ground allspice

1 cup honey

1 cup unsweetened applesauce

1 can (16 ounces) pumpkin puree

2 egg whites, unbeaten

1 cup raisins

½ cup chopped dates

2 egg whites, lightly beaten

directions:

Preheat oven to 325°F. In large mixing bowl, combine oats, flour, baking soda, cream of tartar, cinnamon, ginger, cloves, nutmeg and allspice.

In medium bowl, mix honey, applesauce, pumpkin puree and 2 unbeaten egg whites. Gently stir into flour mixture and mix until just blended. Stir in raisins and dates. Gently stir in 2 lightly beaten egg whites. ***Do not overmix.***

Spoon batter into 10-inch nonstick fluted tube pan. Bake at 325°F. for 1 hour and 5 minutes, or until toothpick inserted in center comes out clean. Cool on wire rack for 30 minutes, and remove cake from pan.

Whaat we especially love about this recipe is the fact that it combines two nutritious foods that many people don't usually associate together: pumpkins and oats. And it is wheat-free so even people who are sensitive to wheat can enjoy it.

For simplicity, we use canned pumpkin, but you may want to make your own puree. If you do, pick a pumpkin that is between 6 and 7 inches in diameter, is firm and has a bright orange color. Remember that every raw pound of pumpkin will equal one cup of cooked.

The orange color of pumpkin is your clue that it is rich in beta carotene. Beta carotene is one of the antioxidant nutrients that is being called "the nutrient of the 1990's."

DAIRY FREE   WHEAT FREE   HEALTHY FIVE

Special Equipment

nonstick muffin pan

Temperature and Time

Bake at 350°F. for 25 minutes

Yield

16 muffins

Nutrition per Serving

Calories: 197
Carbohydrates: 47 grams
Protein: 3 grams
Fat: .5 gram
Calories from Fat: 2%
Cholesterol: 0 milligrams
Sodium: 170 milligrams
Dietary Fiber: 2 grams

pumpkin oat muffins

ingredients:

1½ cups rolled oats

2 cups oat flour (2½ cups rolled oats processed in blender about 2-3 minutes until finely ground)

1 teaspoon baking soda

1 teaspoon cream of tartar

1¼ teaspoons cinnamon

⅛ teaspoon ground nutmeg

¼ teaspoon ground cloves

¼ teaspoon ground ginger

½ cup honey

1 teaspoon vanilla

½ cup canned pumpkin puree

1 can (8 ounces) juice-packed crushed pineapple, undrained

¼ cup water

½ cup frozen pineapple juice concentrate (defrosted)

3 egg whites, lightly beaten

½ cup raisins

directions:

Preheat oven to 350°F. In large bowl, combine oats with oat flour, baking soda, cream of tartar, cinnamon, nutmeg, cloves and ginger; mix well. Set aside.

In medium bowl, mix together honey, vanilla, pumpkin, pineapple, water and juice concentrate; pour into flour mixture. Gently mix in egg whites. Stir in raisins. ***Do not overmix.*** Let batter set for 5 minutes to thicken. Using nonstick muffin pan, fill each muffin cup with batter.

Bake at 350°F. for 25 minutes, or until toothpick inserted near center comes out clean. Cool on wire rack for 5-10 minutes, and remove muffins from pan.

These bars make a tasty and simple alternative to traditional pumpkin pie. In fact, we especially like to make these bars for holiday dinners where there will be children present, because they seem to get a special pleasure in getting their very own dessert, rather than just a piece of a pie.

Since it can sometimes be difficult to get children to eat foods rich in beta carotene, such as broccoli and carrots, this recipe is a good tasting way to get them to eat it. Pumpkins are a rich source of this beneficial antioxidant.

Serving Suggestion:

Try serving these delicious bars covered with La Creme Whipped Topping (see page 175).

FAT-FREE DAIRY FREE HEALTHY FIVE

Special Equipment

8x11x2-inch nonstick baking dish

Temperature and Time

Bake at 350°F. for 45-50 minutes

Yield

24 bars

Nutrition per Serving

Calories: 116
Carbohydrates: 27 grams
Protein: 3 grams
Fat: Fat-Free*
Cholesterol: 0 milligrams
Sodium: 65 milligrams
Dietary Fiber: 3 grams

*All foods contain some fat. Less than .5 gram of fat per serving is nutritionally insignificant and considered to be "Fat-Free."

pumpkin pie bars

ingredients:

2½ cups whole wheat pastry flour

1 teaspoon cream of tartar

1 teaspoon baking soda

1¼ teaspoons cinnamon

¼ teaspoon ground cloves

½ teaspoon ground allspice

¼ teaspoon ground nutmeg

1 can (16 ounces) pumpkin puree

½ cup raisins

½ cup chopped dates

1 cup maple syrup

¼ cup honey

4 egg whites, lightly beaten

1 teaspoon vanilla

directions:

Preheat oven to 325°F. In large bowl, combine flour, cream of tartar, baking soda, cinnamon, cloves, allspice and nutmeg. Set aside.

In medium bowl, combine pumpkin, raisins, dates, syrup, honey, egg whites and vanilla. Gently stir into flour mixture and mix until just blended. *Do not overmix.* Pour mixture into 8x11x2-inch ovenproof glass baking dish.

Bake at 350°F. for 45-50 minutes, or until top is nicely browned. Cool on wire rack for 15 minutes. Cut into bars. Serve warm or cold.

O ne of our goals is not only to provide delicious recipes made without any added fat or high-fat ingredients, but also to incorporate really nutritious ingredients that are not normally found in baking cookbooks.

FAT-FREE   DAIRY FREE   HEALTHY FIVE

This is a recipe that fulfills that goal. The ingredient that gives this cake its lovely crimson color is beets! Many people do not like this vegetable because it has such a distinctively "earthy" flavor. But beets are a "super food." The greens are among the most nutrient-dense foods in all of nature.

One of our official tasters here at Health Valley absolutely despises the taste of beets. But when we served this recipe to him without telling him what was in it, he loved this cake and said it was one of his favorites in the whole book. When he was told about the beets, the cake wasn't the only thing that was blushing.

Serving Suggestion:

Enjoy this unique cake with Creamy Pineapple Topping (see page 165). If you wish to fill it, try the Pineapple Glaze (see page 177).

Special Equipment

2 9-inch nonstick baking pans

Temperature and Time

Bake at 325°F. for 35-40 minutes

Yield

16 servings

Nutrition per Serving

Calories: 198
Carbohydrates: 47 grams
Protein: 4 grams
Fat: Fat-Free*
Cholesterol: 0 milligrams
Sodium: 140 milligrams
Dietary Fiber: 3 grams

*All foods contain some fat. Less than .5 gram of fat per serving is nutritionally insignificant and considered to be "Fat-Free."

red blush cake

ingredients:

2½ cups whole wheat pastry flour

1½ teaspoons baking soda

1½ teaspoons cream of tartar

1 can (8 ounces) no salt whole beets, drained or 6 ounces steamed fresh beets, washed and peeled

1¼ cups honey

½ cup frozen orange juice concentrate (defrosted)

2 teaspoons vanilla

1 tablespoon finely grated orange peel

2 egg whites, unbeaten

1 can (8 ounces) juice-packed crushed pineapple, drained

¾ cup chopped dates

2 egg whites, lightly beaten

directions:

Preheat oven to 325°F. In large mixing bowl, combine flour, baking soda and cream of tartar. Set aside.

Puree drained beets in blender or food processor, approximately 2 minutes. Transfer beets to medium bowl; mix in honey, juice concentrate, vanilla, orange peel, 2 unbeaten egg whites, pineapple and dates. Stir into flour mixture until just blended. Gently stir in 2 lightly beaten egg whites. *Do not overmix.*

Spoon batter into 2 9x1½-inch nonstick round baking pans. Bake at 325°F. for 35-40 minutes, or until toothpick inserted in center comes out clean. Cool on wire rack for 20-30 minutes, and remove cakes from pans.

Thisis an exciting recipe–it's colorful and has an interesting texture because of the whole corn kernels it contains. It also features chile peppers, which are interesting nutritionally. The chile pepper is the most popular spice in the world. Capsaicin oil, which gives chiles their fire, has been shown to help increase metabolic rate. That means eating chiles can cause the body to burn more calories, which can be beneficial if you want to lose weight. The fact that this recipe is made without any added fat and it contains chiles makes it an ideal muffin to enjoy as part of a weight control program.

We prefer canned green chiles because their mild flavor blends well with the cornmeal taste, as well as its texture.

If you ever wish to use fresh chiles, look for the Anaheim variety, which are green before ripening, large and mild. To skin them, first spread the chiles on a baking sheet, and place them in the oven as close as possible to the broiler. Broil for about 10 minutes, until the skin is blistered, turning every few minutes until all sides of the chiles are blackened. Allow them to cool, then, with plastic gloves on, peel the skin from the flesh. Also, remove the seeds and the vein.

Be sure to wear gloves, otherwise the capsaicin oil–the element that gives chiles their fire–might burn your hands. Also, when working with chiles, never touch your face or, especially, your eyes.

**HEALTHY
FIVE**

Special Equipment

nonstick muffin pan

Temperature and Time

Bake at 425°F. for 15-20 minutes

Yield

16 servings

Nutrition per Serving

Calories: 140
Carbohydrates: 29 grams
Protein: 5 grams
Fat: 1 gram
Calories from Fat: 6%
Cholesterol: .8 milligram
Sodium: 120 milligrams
Dietary Fiber: 3 grams

southwestern corn muffins

ingredients:

1 cup corn meal

¾ cup whole wheat pastry flour

¾ teaspoon baking soda

1 teaspoon cream of tartar

3 egg whites, unbeaten

1⅛ cups lowfat buttermilk

⅓ cup honey

1 can (4 ounces) diced green chiles, drained

½ cup frozen corn kernels (defrosted)

¼ cup diced red peppers, steamed

directions:

Preheat oven to 425°F. In large mixing bowl, combine corn meal, flour, baking soda and cream of tartar. Set aside.

In medium bowl, stir together egg whites, buttermilk, honey, green chiles, corn and red peppers. Stir into corn meal mixture and mix until just blended. Pour into nonstick muffin pan, filling each cup half full.

Bake at 425°F. for 15-20 minutes, or until toothpick inserted in center comes out clean. Cool on wire rack for 10 minutes, and remove muffins from pan.

FAT-FREE   HEALTHY FIVE

Here's an alternative to the traditional pumpkin pie that appears to be almost decadently rich, yet actually qualifies as Fat-Free! Naturally, it is perfect at Thanksgiving or anytime during the fall and winter seasons, but it can be enjoyed all year long because you can use canned pumpkin, which is always available.

To prevent cracking the surface of the cheesecake after it comes out of the oven, use a knife to loosen the cake from the edges of the pan before removing it.

Here is another recipe that is a delicious way to get your beta carotene.

Advance Preparation

Day before drain 1 carton (32 ounces) plain, nonfat yogurt to make approximately 2 cups yogurt cheese (see page 129) Fat-Free Crust (see page 127)

Special Equipment

9-inch nonstick springform pan

Temperature and Time

Bake at 325°F. for 55-60 minutes

Yield

12 servings

Nutrition per Serving

Calories: 211
Carbohydrates: 46 grams
Protein: 7 grams
Fat: Fat-Free*
Cholesterol: 2 milligrams
Sodium: 100 milligrams
Dietary Fiber: 3 grams

We developed this recipe using Health Valley Fat-Free Granola with Date and Almond Flavor.

*All foods contain some fat. Less than .5 gram of fat per serving is nutritionally insignificant and considered to be "Fat-Free."

spicy pumpkin cheesecake

ingredients:

1 recipe Fat-Free Crust

2 cups nonfat yogurt cheese

1 cup pumpkin puree

1 cup pure maple syrup

1/3 cup evaporated skimmed milk

1 teaspoon vanilla

1/2 cup whole wheat pastry flour

2 1/2 tablespoons arrowroot

1 1/2 teaspoons cinnamon

1/8 teaspoon ground ginger

1/8 teaspoon ground cloves

1/8 teaspoon ground nutmeg

directions:

Prepare crust for 9-inch nonstick springform pan.

For filling, in large bowl, with electric mixer, beat together yogurt cheese, pumpkin puree, maple syrup, evaporated milk, vanilla, flour, arrowroot, cinnamon, ginger, cloves and nutmeg.

Pour filling into prepared nonstick springform pan. Smooth top with spatula. Bake at 325°F. for 55-60 minutes. Cheesecake is done when center is set but jiggles slightly when gently shaken. Remove cheesecake from oven. Loosen edges of cheesecake with knife to prevent cracking. Cool on wire rack for 1 hour.

Tomatoes are another vegetable that might not come readily to mind when you think about cake ingredients. But this is a simple cake to make, with a delicious flavor and a beautiful color. A slice of Spicy Tomato Cake will also help you to get your five servings of fruits and vegetables a day, since the recipe contains one can of tomato sauce, along with dates and raisins.

When the Harvard Medical School tracked the nutritional habits of 1,000 people for five years, one of the findings of the study was very interesting. People who included tomatoes or strawberries as a part of their weekly diets were the least likely to die from cancer. Tomatoes are rich in vitamins A and C, and also contain some fiber as well. What's more, they are low in both fat and sodium.

Serving Suggestion:

Another way to serve this cake is by glazing it with one-quarter cup of melted fruit-juice-sweetened apricot preserves.

FAT-FREE   DAIRY FREE   HEALTHY FIVE

Special Equipment

10-inch nonstick fluted tube pan

Temperature and Time

Bake at 325°F. for 55-60 minutes

Yield

16 servings

Nutrition per Serving

Calories: 206
Carbohydrates: 50 grams
Protein: 4 grams
Fat: Fat-Free*
Cholesterol: 0 milligrams
Sodium: 180 milligrams
Dietary Fiber: 4 grams

All foods contain some fat. Less than .5 gram of fat per serving is nutritionally insignificant and considered to be "Fat-Free."

spicy tomato cake

ingredients:

2⅓ cups whole wheat pastry flour

1 teaspoon + 1 teaspoon baking soda

1 teaspoon cream of tartar

1 teaspoon cinnamon

½ teaspoon ground cloves

½ teaspoon ground nutmeg

1 can (16 fluid ounces) tomato sauce (no-salt variety)

⅔ cup chopped dates

1¼ cups honey

1 teaspoon vanilla

3 egg whites, unbeaten

½ cup unsweetened applesauce

1 cup raisins

directions:

Preheat oven to 325°F. In large mixing bowl, combine flour, 1 teaspoon baking soda, cream of tartar, cinnamon, cloves and nutmeg. Set aside.

In blender, process on high speed, tomato sauce, dates and remaining 1 teaspoon baking soda until dates are pureed, about 2 minutes. Pour mixture into medium bowl. Add honey, vanilla, egg whites, applesauce and raisins. Stir into flour mixture and mix until just blended. ***Do not overmix.***

Spoon batter into 10-inch nonstick fluted tube pan. Bake at 325°F. for 55-60 minutes, or until toothpick inserted in center comes out clean. Cool on wire rack for 30 minutes, and remove cake from pan.

We've made things simple in this recipe by using sweet potato baby food puree. Remember, purees work as a fat substitution in our recipes, and they naturally allow you a substantial fat gram savings over butter, margarine or oil.

There is confusion, sometimes, about the differences between sweet potatoes and yams. Sweet potatoes have a pale colored skin, compared to the dark purplish skin on yams. Yams have darker-colored flesh and a sweeter flavor, but sweet potatoes are much higher in beta carotene, a potent antioxidant that current research suggests plays a role in cancer prevention. That's why we recommend sweet potatoes over yams. Beta carotene can also be converted by your body into vitamin A, which is an essential nutrient that helps keep your skin healthy, and protects your coronary system, as well.

When buying sweet potatoes in the store, choose firm, smooth, even-colored tubers with no soft spots. Scrub, but do not peel, before using.

FAT-FREE   **HEALTHY FIVE**

Special Equipment
nonstick muffin pan

Temperature and Time
Bake at 350°F. for 25 minutes

Yield
12 muffins

Nutrition per Serving
Calories: 177
Carbohydrates: 40 grams
Protein: 5 grams
Fat: Fat-Free*
Cholesterol: 0 milligrams
Sodium: 110 milligrams
Dietary Fiber: 4 gram

*All foods contain some fat. Less than .5 gram of fat per serving is nutritionally insignificant and considered to be "Fat-Free."

sweet potato muffins

ingredients:

2¼ cups whole wheat pastry flour

¾ teaspoon cream of tartar

¾ teaspoon baking soda

1¾ teaspoons cinnamon

½ teaspoon ground allspice

1 ripe medium banana, mashed

1 jar (6 ounces) sweet potato baby food puree

3 egg whites, lightly beaten

½ cup evaporated skimmed milk

½ cup pure maple syrup

1 teaspoon vanilla

¾ cup chopped dates

directions:

Preheat oven to 350°F. in medium bowl, combine flour, cream of tartar, baking soda, cinnamon and allspice; mix well. Set aside.

In separate bowl, combine banana, sweet potato puree, egg whites, evaporated milk, maple syrup and vanilla; stir into flour mixture. Stir in dates. Divide mixture evenly into nonstick muffin pan.

Bake at 350°F. for 25 minutes, or until toothpick inserted in center comes out clean. Cool on wire rack for 10 minutes, and remove muffins from pan.

These individual servings of pudding have a smooth, sweet flavor that keeps people here at Health Valley coming back to our test kitchen for more. You'll find that these pudding cups are easy to make, and are an excellent family dessert. The cookies make a "candied" crust.

A medium-sized sweet potato has five times the beta carotene you need each day, and beta carotene is a potent antioxidant that current research suggests plays a role in cancer prevention.

FAT-FREE   GREAT FOR KIDS   BETA-CAROTENE

HEALTHY FIVE

Special Equipment

8 4-inch custard cups

Temperature and Time

Bake at 425°F. for 35 minutes

Yield

8 servings

Nutrition per Serving

Calories: 220
Carbohydrates: 53 grams
Protein: 4 grams
Fat: Fat-Free**
Cholesterol: 0 milligrams
Sodium: 75 milligrams
Dietary Fiber: 3 grams

*We developed this recipe using Health Valley Fat-Free Date Delight Cookies.
**All foods contain some fat. Less than .5 gram of fat per serving is nutritionally insignificant and considered to be "Fat-Free."

sweet potato pudding cups

ingredients:

¾ cup Fat-Free finely ground cookie
crumbs (approximately 8 cookies)*

4 egg whites, lightly beaten

1½ cups cooked mashed sweet potato

1 cup and 3 tablespoons pure
maple syrup

¼ cup skimmed evaporated milk

1 teaspoon vanilla

½ teaspoon cinnamon

¼ teaspoon ground nutmeg

directions:

Preheat oven to 425°F. Divide cookie crumbs into 8 4-inch custard cups,
approximately 1½ tablespoons per cup, and gently press crumbs into
bottom of each cup. Set aside while preparing remaining ingredients.

In large bowl, combine egg whites, sweet potato, maple syrup, evaporated milk, vanilla and cinnamon. Pour mixture into 8 prepared custard
cups; sprinkle tops with nutmeg.

Place custard cups in baking pan and surround with hot water to depth
of 1 inch. Bake at 425°F. for 35 minutes, until nicely browned on top.

Serve warm or at room temperature.

If there ever were a treat that could get children to eat foods that are good for them but that they sometimes avoid, it is this one. Don't even tell them that one of the surprises of these delicious muffins is that it contains carrots. With all of the flavorful spices, maple syrup, honey and vanilla, they'll never even notice. But they'll still get the nutritional benefits.

Mothers have been telling their children to eat carrots for generations, and recent nutritional research is proving that moms really do know best. Carrots are rich in beta carotene, a nutrient that provides a variety of benefits. First of all, beta carotene is what is called a "precursor" to vitamin A. That means your body can use it to make vitamin A as it is needed. But in addition, beta carotene offers benefits not found in vitamin A. It is an antioxidant that appears to help protect the body against the effects of aging, and may help protect against certain forms of cancer.

DAIRY FREE   GREAT FOR KIDS   HEALTHY FIVE

Special Equipment

nonstick muffin pan

Temperature and Time

Bake at 350°F. for 30 minutes

Yield

16 muffins

Nutrition per Serving

Calories: 201
Carbohydrates: 47 grams
Protein: 4 grams
Fat: .5 gram
Calories from Fat: 2%
Cholesterol: 0 milligram
Sodium: 140 milligrams
Dietary Fiber: 3 grams

*We developed this recipe using Health Valley Fat-Free Granola with Date and Almond Flavor.

sweet carrot muffins

ingredients:

1½ cups whole wheat pastry flour

1 cup rolled oats

¾ teaspoon + ¾ teaspoon
baking soda

1½ teaspoons cream of tartar

2 teaspoons cinnamon

¼ teaspoon ground nutmeg

1 cup honey

⅓ cup pure maple syrup

2 teaspoons vanilla

3 egg whites, unbeaten

1 cup peeled and grated carrots

1 can (8 ounces) juice-packed
crushed pineapple, well drained

⅓ cup boiling water

¾ cup chopped dates

1 cup Fat-Free granola
(without fruit added)*

directions:

Preheat oven to 350°F. In large mixing bowl, combine flour, oats, three-quarter teaspoon baking soda, cream of tartar, cinnamon and nutmeg; mix well. Set aside.

In medium bowl, mix together honey, maple syrup, vanilla, egg whites, carrots and pineapple. Stir into flour mixture until just blended.

In blender, process on high speed water, dates and remaining three-quarter teaspoon baking soda until dates are pureed, approximately 2 minutes. Stir into flour mixture. ***Do not overmix.***

Spoon batter into nonstick muffin pan. In blender, pulse granola for 30 seconds, and sprinkle on top of batter.

Bake at 350°F. for 30 minutes, or until toothpick inserted in center comes out clean. Cool on wire rack for 10 minutes, and remove muffins from pan.

To create this recipe, we combined a variety of golden ingredients, including sweet potato puree, peaches and honey, together with a medley of spices to create a delicious and nutritious cake.

Sweet potatoes and peaches are both excellent sources of beta carotene, the antioxidant that is being called "the nutrient of the 1990's" because there is increasing evidence that a low-fat diet rich in beta carotene may help prevent heart disease and some forms of cancer.

Serving Suggestion:

As an alternative, we suggest glazing this lovely yet simple bundt cake with one-quarter cup of melted fruit-juice-sweetened peach preserves. Besides adding a classy touch, the glaze highlights the fruity taste of this cake that combines peaches with sweet potatoes.

FAT-FREE   DAIRY FREE   HEALTHY FIVE

Special Equipment

10-inch nonstick fluted pan

Temperature and Time

Bake at 325°F. for 55-60 minutes

Yield

16 servings

Nutrition per Serving

Calories: 218
Carbohydrates: 53 grams
Protein: 4 grams
Fat: Fat-Free*
Cholesterol: 0 milligrams
Sodium: 200 milligrams
Dietary Fiber: 4 grams

All foods contain some fat. Less than .5 gram of fat per serving is nutritionally insignificant and considered to be "Fat-Free."

sunshine cake

ingredients:

2⅓ cups whole wheat pastry flour

¾ teaspoon + 1½ teaspoons baking soda

1 teaspoon cream of tartar

2 teaspoons cinnamon

¼ teaspoon ground cloves

¼ teaspoon ground nutmeg

1 cup honey

⅓ cup pure maple syrup

2 teaspoons vanilla

1 can (16 ounces) juice-packed peaches, drained and chopped

2 egg whites, unbeaten

2 jars (4 ounces each) sweet potato baby food puree

¾ cup chopped dates

2 egg whites, lightly beaten

⅓ cup fruit-juice-sweetened peach preserves, melted

directions:

Preheat oven to 325°F. In large mixing bowl, combine flour, three-quarter teaspoon baking soda, cream of tartar, cinnamon, cloves and nutmeg. Set aside.

In medium bowl, mix honey, maple syrup, vanilla, peaches and 2 unbeaten egg whites. Stir into flour mixture until just blended.

In blender, process on high speed sweet potato puree, dates and 1½ teaspoons baking soda, until dates are pureed, approximately 2 minutes. Stir into flour mixture. Gently stir in 2 lightly beaten egg whites. *Do not overmix.*

Spoon batter into 10-inch nonstick fluted tube pan. Bake at 325°F. for 55-60 minutes, or until toothpick inserted in center comes out clean. Cool on wire rack for 30 minutes, and remove cake from pan. Drizzle melted preserves over top of cake. Allow preserves to drip over sides of cake.

I n this recipe, unsweetened applesauce is an important substitute for the fat that's used in traditional recipes. We were pleased by just how well the flavors of apple and zucchini blend together. Each serving of our zucchini bread fulfills 29 percent of the daily RDA of vitamin C.

Zucchini is a summer squash that can grow to an enormous size if left too long on the vine. So when purchasing it, look for young, tender and well-formed zucchini—the ones that are small and seem heavy for their size are best. The skin should be bright and free of blemishes. After washing, zucchini can be stored in the refrigerator for up to two weeks.

Serving Suggestion:

For an added treat, serve each slice with a dollop of plain, nonfat yogurt, or fruit-juice-sweetened preserves.

DAIRY FREE   HEALTHY FIVE

Special Equipment

10-inch nonstick fluted tube pan

Temperature and Time

Bake at 325°F. for 55-60 minutes

Yield

16 servings

Nutrition per Serving

Calories: 130
Carbohydrates: 29 grams
Protein: 4 grams
Fat: 1 gram
Calories from Fat: 7%
Cholesterol: 0 milligrams
Sodium: 170 milligrams
Dietary Fiber: 2 grams

zucchini bread ring

ingredients:

1½ cups grated zucchini

1½ cups rolled oats

1½ cups whole wheat pastry flour

2 teaspoons baking soda

2 teaspoons cream of tartar

2 teaspoons cinnamon

¼ teaspoon ground nutmeg

½ teaspoon ground allspice

½ cup honey

⅓ cup frozen pineapple juice concentrate (defrosted)

1 teaspoon vanilla

¾ cup unsweetened applesauce

1 can (8 ounces) juice-packed crushed pineapple, drained

2 egg whites, unbeaten

½ cup raisins

directions:

Preheat oven to 325°F. Set grated zucchini between paper towels and press to remove excess moisture.

In medium bowl, combine oats with flour, baking soda, cream of tartar, cinnamon, nutmeg and allspice; mix well. In separate bowl, combine honey, juice concentrate, vanilla, applesauce and crushed pineapple; stir into flour mixture. Gently mix in egg whites. Stir in raisins and well drained grated zucchini.

Pour batter into 10-inch nonstick fluted tube pan, and bake at 325°F. for 55-60 minutes. Cool 30 minutes, then remove from pan.

Cheesecakes Section

I f there is one dessert that is symbolic of dietary decadence it's cheesecake. After all, traditional recipes get their rich flavor and creamy texture from cream cheese, which is so high in fat that nearly two-thirds of the calories in a cheesecake are supplied by fat! That means a single serving of cheesecake can load you down with 33 grams of fat.

That's what makes the recipes in this section such a phenomenal achievement. They provide the rich flavor and creamy texture that you look for in cheesecake, but they are so low in fat that many of them actually qualify as Fat-Free!

You'll also find a wide variety of cheesecake recipes made without any added fat or high-fat ingredients. There are recipes to suit any taste, including those who love chocolate. Not only are these recipes low in calories and fat, they are also nutritional powerhouses. They provide a delicious way to get calcium, the essential mineral that prevents osteoporosis.

How to Make Ingredient Substitutions

Most of our cheesecake recipes use nonfat yogurt cheese and honey as main ingredients, but there are other healthy products that work well. We have experimented with them in the test kitchen and had good results. For example, you can replace honey with an equal amount of dry FruitSource.® If you want to experiment on your own, you can use this chart as a starting point:

Original Ingredient	Substitution
For 2 cups nonfat yogurt cheese*	**Use** 1 cup nonfat yogurt cheese and 1 package (8 ounces) Fat-Free cream cheese. Decrease arrowroot and whole wheat pastry flour by half.
	Or use 1 cup nonfat yogurt cheese and 1 cup Fat-Free (nonfat) sour cream. Decrease arrowroot and whole wheat pastry flour by half.
	Or use 1 package (8 ounces) Fat-Free cream cheese and 1 cup Fat-Free (nonfat) sour cream. Eliminate arrowroot and whole wheat pastry flour.

For 4 cups yogurt cheese, double the above.

A delicious crust is the foundation of many baked goods, including cheesecakes. Yet, it can be a real source of hidden fat. For example, the typical homemade 9-inch baked crust made with enriched flour will contain 900 calories, 60.1 grams of fat, and 60 percent of calories from fat.

That's why we've spent so much time carefully developing and refining this recipe. As you can see, it contains 629 calories and is Fat-Free, yet the flavor is still all there.

Use it for making all of the recipes in this chapter, except those that use chocolate or carob.

FAT-FREE DAIRY FREE

Special Equipment

9-inch nonstick springform pan

Temperature and Time

Bake for 12-15 minutes at 325°F.

Yield

1 9-inch crust

Nutrition per Serving

Calories: 629
Carbohydrates: 145 grams
Protein: 15 grams
Fat: Fat-Free**
Cholesterol: 0 milligrams
Sodium: 260 milligrams
Dietary Fiber: 17 grams

*We developed this recipe using Health Valley Fat-Free Granola with Date and Almond Flavor.
**All foods contain some fat. Less than .5 gram of fat per serving is nutritionally insignificant and considered to be "Fat-Free."

fat-free crust

ingredients:

1½ cups Fat-Free granola
(without fruit added)*

1 tablespoon frozen apple juice
concentrate (defrosted)

1 tablespoon honey

1 egg white, unbeaten

directions:

Preheat oven to 325°F. Grind granola in food processor for 2 minutes. Add juice concentrate, honey and egg white. Process minimally to blend ingredients, approximately 30 seconds.

Press granola mixture over bottom of 9-inch nonstick springform pan. Bake for 12-15 minutes at 325°F. Let cool while preparing filling.

Yogurt cheese is a basic ingredient if you want to cut down on fat. It is very versatile because you can use it as a nonfat substitute for cream cheese or sour cream. You can even use it as a topping by beating it and adding honey and vanilla, although it will not have the same texture as whipped cream. Yogurt cheese has the advantage of having only a third as many calories as cream cheese, yet it still is an excellent source of calcium.

FAT-FREE   **WHEAT FREE**

Per Tablespoon	Calories	Fat (grams)	Calories from Fat
Nonfat Yogurt Cheese	16	.05	3 percent
Cream Cheese	49	5.0	90 percent

Making nonfat yogurt cheese is easy, so don't be intimidated. All you have to do is drain off the liquid whey from plain nonfat yogurt. This process will take approximately 24 hours to achieve the consistency of cream cheese. It will keep in the refrigerator for approximately one week.

Important note: Some brands of yogurt contain gelatin or guar gum that prevent the whey from draining off as quickly. Read the label and avoid these brands. We've found that Dannon nonfat plain yogurt works really well.

Special Equipment

large strainer, drip coffee maker or yogurt cheese funnel

Temperature and Time

12-24 hours

Yield

approximately 2 cups or less

Nutrition per Serving

Calories: 502
Carbohydrates: 69 grams
Protein: 52 grams
Fat: Fat-Free*
Cholesterol: 17 milligrams
Sodium: 690 milligrams
Dietary Fiber: 0 grams

*All foods contain some fat. Less than .5 gram of fat per serving is nutritionally insignificant and considered to be "Fat-Free."

Coco Berry Cheesecake (See Cheesecakes Section)

Zucchini Bread Ring, *left*
(See Healthy Five Section)

Apricot Filled Banana Muffins,
(See Breads, Muffins & Cupcakes Section)

Citrus Golden Cake
(See Healthful Diet Section)

**Harvest Muffins
(See Healthy Five Section)**

**Honey Raisin
Cookies (See
Cookies & Bars
Section)**

**Date Granola Bars
(See Cookies &
Bars Section)**

**Crispy Rice Treats
(See Cookies & Bars Section**

Raspberry Cookie bars, *above* **and Black & White Brownies,** *left* **(See Cookies & Bars Section)**

Strawberry Angel Food Cake (See Cakes Section)

Peach Trifle
(See Fruit Desserts, Puddings & Pies Section)

nonfat yogurt cheese

ingredients:

1 (32 ounces) carton plain, nonfat yogurt

directions:

You may drain yogurt using any one of several different methods:

–use special yogurt cheese funnel designed for this specific purpose that is available in some health food and gourmet stores.

–use large strainer with either cheese cloth or coffee filters. Spoon in yogurt, refrigerate and let drain into large bowl or jar.

–use above method with drip coffee maker lined with double paper coffee filters.

Drain for desired time:

–12 hours or longer for whipped cream cheese consistency (use for our dessert topping recipes)

–24 hours or longer for cream cheese consistency (use for our cheese-cake recipes and dessert topping recipes)

This beautifully impressive summer dessert tastes best when eaten the day it is prepared. If you refrigerate it, remove the cheesecake from the refrigerator at least a half-hour before serving so it is at room temperature and all of the rich flavor comes through with every bite.

Beta carotene is found in apricots and other orange-colored fruits and vegetables. It is believed that the silicon in apricots will add shine back to your hair and help to rejuvenate your skin. Dried apricots also contain potassium, which is good for maintaining a healthy heart.

Advance Preparation

Day before drain 1 carton (32 ounces) plain, nonfat yogurt to make approximately 2 cups yogurt cheese (see page 129) Fat-Free Crust (see page 127)

Special Equipment

yogurt cheese funnel or similar device 9-inch non-stick springform pan

Temperature and Time

Bake at 325°F. for 50 minutes

Yield

12 servings

Nutrition per Serving

Calories: 220
Carbohydrates: 48 grams
Protein: 8 grams
Fat: Fat-Free*
Cholesterol: 2 milligrams
Sodium: 110 milligrams
Dietary Fiber: 2 grams

*All foods contain some fat. Less than .5 gram of fat per serving is nutritionally insignificant and considered to be "Fat-Free."

apricot cheesecake

ingredients:

1 recipe Fat-Free Crust

1 can (16 ounces) juice-packed apricots, drained

2 cups nonfat yogurt cheese

⅓ cup honey

¼ cup pure maple syrup

1 teaspoon vanilla

½ cup evaporated skimmed milk

2 tablespoons arrowroot

⅓ cup whole wheat pastry flour

3 egg whites, unbeaten

¼ cup + ¼ cup fruit-juice-sweetened apricot preserves, melted

directions:

Prepare crust for 9-inch nonstick springform pan.

Cut each apricot half into 5 slices and set aside.

For filling, in large bowl, with electric mixer, beat together yogurt cheese, honey, maple syrup, vanilla, evaporated milk, arrowroot and flour. Set aside.

In small bowl, with electric mixer on high, beat egg whites to soft peaks, about 2 minutes. Fold egg whites into cheese mixture and beat until well blended. Set aside.

Mix one-quarter cup preserves with half of apricots, reserving remainder.

Pour half of filling into prepared nonstick springform pan. Spread apricot mixture evenly over cheese mixture. Top with remaining cheese mixture. Smooth with spatula.

Bake at 325°F. for 50 minutes. Cheesecake is done when center appears set but jiggles slightly when gently shaken. Remove cheesecake from oven. Loosen edges with knife to prevent cracking. Cool on wire rack for 1 hour. Refrigerate for 6 hours, or until thoroughly chilled and set.

Just before serving, spread remaining one-quarter cup preserves over cheesecake and arrange remaining apricot slices on top.

The "secret" ingredient in this recipe is evaporated skimmed milk. It is Fat-Free yet contributes a creamy, rich flavor and a light texture.

This cheesecake gets its distinctive flavor from touches of lemon extract and orange marmalade that lend a pleasantly citrus flavor to the blueberries.

Although most of us are familiar with the cultivated form of blueberries, they also grow wild. In fact, they are second only to black-berries in being eaten mainly in the wild form.

Avoid buying blueberries in baskets with leaky bottoms, or purchasing blueberries that are discolored or have any fungus growing on them. Instead, look for small, plump, dusty-blue fruit.

Advance Preparation

Day before drain 1 carton (32 ounces) plain, nonfat yogurt to make approxi-mately 2 cups yogurt cheese (see page 129) Fat-Free Crust (see page 127)

Special Equipment

yogurt cheese funnel or similar device
9-inch nonstick springform pan

Temperature and Time

Bake at 325°F. for 60-70 minutes

Yield

12 servings

Nutrition per Serving

Calories: 216
Carbohydrates: 47 grams
Protein: 8 grams
Fat: Fat-Free*
Cholesterol: 2 milligrams
Sodium: 110 milligrams
Dietary Fiber: 3 grams

*All foods contain some fat. Less than .5 gram of fat per serving is nutritionally insignificant and considered to be "Fat-Free."

blueberry cheesecake

ingredients:

1 recipe Fat-Free Crust

2 cups nonfat yogurt cheese

⅓ cup honey

⅓ cup frozen apple juice concentrate (defrosted)

½ cup evaporated skimmed milk

1 teaspoon vanilla

½ teaspoon lemon extract

⅓ cup whole wheat pastry flour

2 tablespoons arrowroot

3 egg whites, unbeaten

2¼ cups blueberries (defrosted and drained if frozen)

4 tablespoons fruit-juice-sweetened blueberry preserves

4 tablespoons fruit-juice-sweetened orange marmalade

directions:

Prepare crust for 9-inch nonstick springform pan.

For filling, in large bowl, with electric mixer on high, beat together yogurt cheese, honey, juice concentrate, evaporated milk, vanilla and lemon extracts, flour and arrowroot. Set aside.

In small bowl, with electric mixer on high, beat egg whites to soft peaks, about 2 minutes. Fold egg whites into cheese mixture and beat until well blended. Pour half of filling into prepared nonstick springform pan.

In small bowl, mix blueberries, preserves and marmalade together. Spread three-quarter cup of fruit mixture evenly over cheese mixture. Top with remaining cheese mixture.

Bake at 325°F. for 60-70 minutes. Cheesecake is done when center is nearly set but jiggles slightly when shaken. Remove cake from oven. Loosen edges with knife to prevent cracking. Cool on wire rack for 1 hour. Refrigerate for 6 hours, or until thoroughly chilled and set. Just before serving, spread remaining fruit mixture over top of cheesecake.

FAT-FREE

This elegant dessert is one of our favorites. It combines the creamy richness of cheesecake with the distinctive flavor of chocolate. Yet it qualifies as Fat-Free, and contains no refined sugar and virtually no caffeine. Coco Berry Cheesecake looks as wonderful as it tastes, and it's sure to impress your guests and family as well.

To maintain its perfect appearance, we recommend that right after the cheesecake comes out of the oven, you run a knife around the inside edge of the nonstick springform pan to prevent the top of the cake from sticking to the pan and cracking as it cools.

This recipe gives you the choice of using either unsweetened cocoa powder, if you're a chocolate lover, or carob powder. Although unsweetened cocoa powder and carob powder aren't related, they can be substituted for each other with a one-to-one ratio.

Serving Suggestion:

To make this cheesecake even more elegant, decorate the border with fresh raspberries.

Advance Preparation

Day before drain 1 carton (32 ounces) plain, nonfat yogurt to make approximately 2 cups yogurt cheese (see page 129) Coco Frosting (see page 151)

Special Equipment

yogurt cheese funnel or similar device
9-inch nonstick springform pan

Temperature and Time

Bake at 325°F. for 50-60 minutes

Yield

14 servings

Nutrition per Serving

Calories: 185
Carbohydrates: 41 grams
Protein: 7 grams
Fat: Fat-Free*
Cholesterol: 1 milligram
Sodium: 95 milligrams
Dietary Fiber: 1 gram

All foods contain some fat. Less than .5 gram of fat per serving is nutritionally insignificant and considered to be "Fat-Free."

coco berry cheesecake

ingredients:

crust

¾ cup whole wheat pastry flour

2 tablespoons unsweetened cocoa powder or carob powder

½ teaspoon cinnamon

¼ teaspoon cream of tartar

¼ teaspoon baking soda

1 jar (2½ ounces) prune baby food puree

½ cup honey and 1 tablespoon honey

1 egg white, lightly beaten

½ teaspoon vanilla

filling

2 cups nonfat yogurt cheese

½ cup honey

1 teaspoon vanilla

2 tablespoon and 1 teaspoon arrowroot

3 egg whites, unbeaten

¼ cup fruit-juice-sweetened raspberry preserves

½ recipe Coco Frosting

Fresh raspberries

directions:

Preheat oven to 325°F. For crust, in medium bowl, sift together flour, cocoa or carob powder, cinnamon, cream of tartar and baking soda.

In small bowl, combine prune puree, honey, egg white and vanilla. Gently stir into flour mixture.

Pour mixture into bottom of 9-inch nonstick springform pan. Bake crust for 15 minutes. Let cool while preparing filling.

For filling, in medium bowl, with electric mixer on high, beat together yogurt cheese, honey, vanilla and arrowroot.

In small bowl, with electric mixer on high, beat egg whites to soft peaks, about 2 minutes. Fold egg whites into cheese mixture and beat until well blended.

Pour half of filling into prepared pan. Spread preserves evenly over cheese mixture and top with remaining cheese mixture. With knife, cut through cheesecake to form swirl. Smooth top with spatula.

Bake at 325°F. for 50-60 minutes. Cheesecake is done when center appears set but jiggles slightly when gently shaken. Remove cheesecake from oven. Loosen edges with knife to prevent cracking. Cool on wire rack for 1 hour. Refrigerate for 6 hours, or until thoroughly chilled and set.

To complete, frost with Coco Frosting, and top with fresh raspberries.

There are many different versions of cheesecake. Some are high and fluffy, while others are dense and rich. Many people refer to the rich and dense versions as "New York-style."

Since this recipe produces a thin, dense and rich dessert, we use the name "New York."

For a super-easy crust, we team up our Healthy Chip cookies with either chocolate or carob to produce a wonderfully rich chocolate flavor without the sugar or most of the caffeine.

This cheesecake makes an especially nice ending to a special dinner.

This recipe gives you the choice of using either unsweetened cocoa powder, if you're a chocolate lover, or carob powder. Although unsweetened cocoa powder and carob powder aren't related, they can be substituted for each other with a one-to-one ratio.

Serving Suggestion:

We suggest finishing this cheesecake with Creamy Berry Topping (see page 153).

Advance Preparation

Day before drain 1 carton (32 ounces) plain, nonfat yogurt to make approximately 2 cups yogurt cheese (see page 129)

Special Equipment

yogurt cheese funnel or similar device
9-inch nonstick springform pan

Temperature and Time

Bake at 300°F. for 60-70 minutes

Yield

10 servings

Nutrition per Serving

Calories: 160
Carbohydrates: 3 grams
Protein: 7 grams
Fat: Fat-Free*
Cholesterol: 0 milligrams
Sodium: 110 milligrams
Dietary Fiber: 1 gram

*All foods contain some fat. Less than .5 gram of fat per serving is nutritionally insignificant and considered to be "Fat-Free."
**We developed this recipe using Health Valley Healthy Chip Cookies.

new york coco cheesecake

ingredients:

crust

1⅛ cups finely ground
  Fat-Free cookie crumbs
  (approximately
  12 cookies)**

filling

2 cups nonfat yogurt cheese

½ cup and 2 tablespoons honey

1 teaspoon vanilla

⅛ teaspoon finely grated orange peel

2 tablespoons unsweetened
  cocoa powder or carob powder

2 tablespoons arrowroot

2 egg whites, unbeaten

directions:

Preheat oven to 300°F. For Crust, moisten fingers with water and press cookie crumbs over bottom and slightly up sides of 9-inch nonstick springform pan. Chill while preparing remaining ingredients.

For Filling, with electric mixer on high, beat yogurt cheese, honey, vanilla, orange peel, cocoa or carob powder, arrowroot and egg whites until thoroughly blended.

Pour filling into crust. Bake at 300°F. for 60-70 minutes. Cheesecake is done when center appears set but jiggles slightly when gently shaken. Remove cheesecake from oven. Loosen edges with knife to prevent cracking. Cool on wire rack for 1 hour. Refrigerate for 6 hours, or until thoroughly chilled and set.

FAT-FREE

If you like the rich and dense "New York-style" of cheesecake, but also want something that tastes refreshing at the end of the meal, you'll love this recipe. It is rich and creamy, yet the lemon adds light tangy flavor.

This recipe is so low in calories that it actually qualifies as Fat-Free. And like all of our cheesecake recipes, it is rich in calcium. This important mineral is essential for the formation and maintenance of strong bones and healthy teeth, and it's also necessary for a healthy heart. Since it is especially important for growing children and adolescence to get enough calcium, here is a delicious way to see that they get it.

Serving Suggestion:

When serving this dessert to guests, be sure to garnish it with fresh fruit to create an added accent.

Advance Preparation

Day before drain 2 carton (64 ounces) plain, nonfat yogurt to make approximately 4 cups yogurt cheese (see page 129) Fat-Free Crust (see page 127)

Special Equipment

yogurt cheese funnel or similar device
9-inch nonstick springform pan

Temperature and Time

Bake at 300°F. for 60-70 minutes

Yield

14 servings

Nutrition per Serving

Calories: 211
Carbohydrates: 43 grams
Protein: 10 grams
Fat: Fat-Free*
Cholesterol: 2 milligrams
Sodium: 140 milligrams
Dietary Fiber: 2 grams

All foods contain some fat. Less than .5 gram of fat per serving is nutritionally insignificant and considered to be "Fat-Free."

new york lemon cheesecake

ingredients:

1 recipe Fat-Free Crust

4 cups nonfat yogurt cheese

1 cup honey

2 teaspoons vanilla

¾ teaspoon lemon extract

¼ cup whole wheat pastry flour

3 tablespoons arrowroot

5 egg whites, unbeaten

directions:

Prepare crust for 9-inch nonstick springform pan.

For filling, in large bowl, with electric mixer on high, beat yogurt cheese, honey, vanilla and lemon extracts, flour, arrowroot and egg whites until thoroughly blended. Pour filling into prepared nonstick springform pan.

Bake at 300°F. for 60-70 minutes. Cheesecake is done when center appears set but jiggles slightly when shaken. Remove cheesecake from oven. Loosen edges with knife to prevent cracking. Cool on wire rack for 1 hour. Refrigerate for 6 hours, or until thoroughly chilled and set.

FAT-FREE

Wwanted to make a dessert as rich as the classic bavarian, but without all the cream, eggs and gelatin. We succeeded with this elegant recipe. It also makes a great presentation dessert, because of the sliced pears that are baked into the top.

Nutritionally, pears have a lot going for them. For example, a pear derives much of its sweetness from levulose, the fruit sugar that diabetics can tolerate more easily than other sugars. Also, pears contain more pectin than apples. Pectin is a beneficial form of soluble fiber that eases digestion.

Pears are also very heart healthy foods, because they contain high amounts of thiamin, niacin and folic acid, all B vitamins associated with cardiovascular health.

Advance Preparation

Day before drain 1 carton (32 ounces) plain, nonfat yogurt to make approximately 2 cups yogurt cheese (see page 129) Fat-Free Crust (see page 127)

Special Equipment

yogurt cheese funnel or similar device
9-inch nonstick springform pan

Temperature and Time

Bake at 325°F. for 55 minutes

Yield

12 servings

Nutrition per Serving

Calories: 201
Carbohydrates: 44 grams
Protein: 7 grams
Fat: Fat-Free*
Cholesterol: 1 milligram
Sodium: 100 milligrams
Dietary Fiber: 3 grams

*All foods contain some fat. Less than .5 gram of fat per serving is nutritionally insignificant and considered to be "Fat-Free."

pear bavarian cheesecake

ingredients:

1 recipe Fat-Free Crust

2 cans (16 ounces each) juice-packed pears, drained and sliced

2 cups nonfat yogurt cheese

½ cup pure maple syrup

1 teaspoon vanilla

2 tablespoons arrowroot

2 tablespoons whole wheat pastry flour

3 egg whites, unbeaten

½ cup raisins

¾ teaspoon cinnamon

¼ teaspoon ground nutmeg

directions:

Prepare crust for 9-inch nonstick springform pan.

Cut each pear half into 4 slices and set aside.

For filling, in large bowl, with electric mixer, beat together yogurt cheese, maple syrup, vanilla, arrowroot and flour. Set aside.

In small bowl, with electric mixer on high, beat egg whites to soft peaks, about 2 minutes. Fold egg whites into cheese mixture; mix until well blended. Pour half of filling into prepared nonstick springform pan.

Cover filling with half of pears. Sprinkle raisins and cinnamon over pears. Pour remaining filling on top and smooth with spatula. Arrange remaining pears on top of cheesecake and sprinkle with nutmeg.

Bake at 325°F. for 55 minutes. Cheesecake is done when center appears set but jiggles slightly when gently shaken. Remove cheesecake from oven. Loosen edges of cheesecake with knife to prevent cracking. Cool on wire rack for 1 hour. Refrigerate for 6 hours, or until thoroughly chilled and set.

Your taste buds will love how the tangy and sweet pineapple blends with the yogurt cheese in this recipe. From a nutritional standpoint, pineapple is a leader in one area– manganese. This trace mineral is essential in the metabolism of protein and carbohydrates. By eating just one slice of Pineapple Cheesecake, you are close to fulfilling the Safe and Adequate Range of between 2½ and 5 milligrams per day.

We recommend that right after the cheesecake comes out of the oven, you run a knife around the inside edge of the nonstick springform pan to prevent the top of the cake from sticking to the pan and cracking as it cools.

Advance Preparation

Day before drain 1 carton (32 ounces) plain, nonfat yogurt to make approximately 2 cups yogurt cheese (see page 129) Fat-Free Crust (see page 127)

Special Equipment

yogurt cheese funnel or similar device
9-inch nonstick springform pan

Temperature and Time

Bake at 325°F. for 60-70 minutes

Yield

12 servings

Nutrition per Serving

Calories: 189
Carbohydrates: 40 grams
Protein: 8 grams
Fat: Fat-Free*
Cholesterol: 2 milligrams
Sodium: 110 milligrams
Dietary Fiber: 2 grams

*All foods contain some fat. Less than .5 gram of fat per serving is nutritionally insignificant and considered to be "Fat-Free."

pineapple cheesecake

ingredients:

1 recipe Fat-Free Crust

filling

2 cups nonfat yogurt cheese

⅓ cup honey

½ cup frozen pineapple juice
concentrate (defrosted)

½ cup evaporated skimmed milk

1 teaspoon almond extract

⅓ cup whole wheat pastry flour

2 tablespoons arrowroot

3 egg whites, unbeaten

1 can (10 ounces) juice-packed
crushed pineapple, drained

glaze

1 can (10 ounces) juice-packed
crushed pineapple, undrained

1 teaspoon arrowroot

1 teaspoon water

directions:

Prepare crust for 9-inch nonstick springform pan.

For filling, in large bowl, with electric mixer, beat together yogurt cheese, honey, juice concentrate, evaporated milk, almond extract, flour and arrowroot. Set aside.

In small bowl, with electric mixer, beat egg whites to soft peak stage. Fold egg whites into cheese mixture and beat until well blended. Pour half of mixture into prepared nonstick springform pan. Spread pineapple evenly over cheese mixture. Top with remaining cheese mixture.

Bake at 325°F. for 60-70 minutes. Cheesecake is done when center appears set but jiggles slightly when shaken. Remove cheesecake from oven. Loosen edges of cake with knife to prevent cracking. Cool on wire rack for 1 hour. Refrigerate for 6 hours, or until thoroughly chilled and set.

For topping, drain pineapple reserving juice. Dissolve arrowroot in water. In small saucepan, whisk together pineapple juice and arrowroot mixture. Add crushed pineapple. Bring mixture to low boil over medium high heat, reduce heat to low and cook approximately 5 minutes until mixture thickens. Let cool. Just before serving top cheesecake with glaze.

FAT-
FREE

Ever since childhood, we've associated strawberries with warm weather and longer days. Perhaps that's why we have always looked forward to fresh strawberries and why we really prefer using fresh ones in this delicious cheesecake, although you can substitute frozen berries if fresh are not available.

Strawberries are favorites not only because of their distinctive juicy flavor, but also because they are an excellent source of vitamin C and other important nutrients.

Even though they are now available year round in most parts of the country, strawberries are most plentiful and flavorful from May through August. Select fruits that are solid with a good, even red color, and still have their caps attached. Remember when picking strawberries that no matter how appealing the big ones look, those of medium size are usually better tasting. Avoid baskets that are leaking through the bottom, and, of course, fruits that have anything fuzzy or foreign growing on them.

Advance Preparation

Day before drain 1 carton (32 ounces) plain, nonfat yogurt to make approximately 2 cups yogurt cheese (see page 129) Fat-Free Crust (see page 127)

Special Equipment

yogurt cheese funnel or similar device
9-inch nonstick springform pan

Temperature and Time

Bake at 325°F. for 60-70 minutes

Yield

12 servings

Nutrition per Serving

Calories: 193
Carbohydrates: 41 grams
Protein: 8 grams
Fat: Fat-Free*
Cholesterol: 2 milligrams
Sodium: 110 milligrams
Dietary Fiber: 3 grams

*All foods contain some fat. Less than .5 gram of fat per serving is nutritionally insignificant and considered to be "Fat-Free."

strawberry glazed cheesecake

ingredients:

1 recipe Fat-Free Crust

2 cups nonfat yogurt cheese

⅓ cup honey

⅓ cup frozen apple juice
concentrate (defrosted)

½ cup evaporated skimmed milk

1 teaspoon vanilla

¾ teaspoon orange extract

2 teaspoons finely grated orange peel

¼ cup whole wheat pastry flour

1½ tablespoons arrowroot

3 egg whites, lightly beaten

1½ cups sliced strawberries
(defrost and drain if frozen)

⅓ cup fruit-juice-sweetened
orange marmalade, melted

directions:

Prepare crust for 9-inch nonstick springform pan.

For filling, in large bowl, with electric mixer, beat together yogurt cheese, honey, juice concentrate, evaporated milk, vanilla, orange extract, orange peel, flour and arrowroot. Set aside.

In small bowl, with electric mixer on high, beat egg whites to soft peaks, about 2 minutes. Fold egg whites into cheese mixture and beat until well blended. Pour filling into prepared pan. Smooth top with spatula. Bake at 325°F. for 60-70 minutes. Cheesecake is done when center appears set but jiggles slightly when shaken. Remove cheesecake from oven. Loosen edges with knife to prevent cracking. Cool on wire rack for 1 hour. Refrigerate for 6 hours, or until thoroughly chilled and set.

Arrange strawberries on top of cheesecake. Dribble marmalade over strawberries.

Frostings, Sauces & Toppings Section

Frostings, sauces and toppings are the dessert categories that can be the main culprits when it comes to adding "hidden" fat. For example, traditional angel food cake is made with egg whites instead of whole eggs, so it is usually very low in fat. But it is often served with fruit, such as strawberries, and with whipped cream. The cake itself and the berries are low in fat and healthy, but the whipped cream is loaded with fat.

We know that frostings, sauces and toppings are important recipes because they so often provide the flourish, the color, and much of the flavor to cakes, puddings and other desserts. That's why we worked so hard to create delicious rich tasting frostings, sauces and toppings that are made without any added fat or high fat ingredients.

We even created a whipped topping that is a light and delicious substitute for whipped cream, and lets you cut both fat and calories.

Serving: (1 Tbsp)	Fat:	Calories:	% Calories from Fat
Whipped cream	6g	80	68
La Creme Whipped Topping from *Baking Without Fat*	Fat-Free	43	0

You may use Fat-Free cream cheese as a substitute for nonfat yogurt cheese in all of our Creamy Frostings. Avoid brands that contain artificial ingredients.

The rich flavor and creamy texture of this topping creates the illusion of it being high in fat. Actually, it qualifies as Fat-Free and contains no cholesterol. We use it in our Banana Cream Cake (see page 185), and it makes a wonderful topping for a variety of desserts, from puddings to cakes to plain nonfat yogurt.

This is not only a delicious and versatile recipe, but also a nutritionally beneficial one because bananas are a heart healthy food. They rank among the best natural sources of potassium, which studies have linked to controlling blood pressure. Also bananas contain a significant amount of soluble fiber that can help to lower blood cholesterol.

Serving Suggestion:

You may want to use this topping with our Banana Date Cake (see page 187).

FAT-FREE **DAIRY FREE** **WHEAT FREE**

GREAT FOR KIDS

Yield

1 cup (12 servings)

Nutrition per Serving

Calories: 41
Carbohydrates: 11 grams
Protein: 0 grams
Fat: Fat-Free*
Cholesterol: 0 milligrams
Sodium: 0 milligrams
Dietary Fiber: 0 grams

*All foods contain some fat. Less than .5 gram of fat per serving is nutritionally insignificant and considered to be "Fat-Free."

caramelized banana topping

ingredients:

½ cup pure maple syrup
1 large ripe banana, sliced

directions:

In medium saucepan over medium high heat, bring syrup to boil. Reduce heat to medium low and add banana slices. Cook for 5-7 minutes, or until bananas are golden brown and maple syrup has thickened.

For years, recipes that feature chocolate presented a real dilemma for the health-conscious. There is really nothing that can substitute for the distinctive, almost addictive, taste of chocolate, but along with the flavor came fat, sugar and caffeine.

One of the breakthroughs of this book is that we offer you a solution. We've created a frosting recipe using unsweetened cocoa powder to provide the great chocolate taste you love, with virtually no fat, sugar and caffeine.

This flavorful frosting completes the Coco Berry Cheesecake (see page 135) and Frosted Coco Cupcakes (see page 229) recipes. We also use it in our Boston Cream Cake (see page 191), Coco Silk Cake (see page 197) and Sachertorte (see page 213). But don't stop there. We're sure that you will find many other uses for this delicious nonfat treat.

This recipe gives you the choice of using either unsweetened cocoa powder, if you're a chocolate lover, or carob powder. Although unsweetened cocoa powder and carob powder aren't related, they can be substituted for each other with a one-to-one ratio.

Serving Suggestion:

You may want to use Coco Frosting with our Coco Garden Cake (see page 97).

FAT-FREE   WHEAT FREE   GREAT FOR KIDS

Yield

⅔ cup (12 servings)

Nutrition per Serving

Calories: 38
Carbohydrates: 9 grams
Protein: 1 gram
Fat: Fat-Free*
Cholesterol: 0 milligrams
Sodium: 110 milligrams
Dietary Fiber: 0 grams

*All foods contain some fat. Less than .5 gram of fat per serving is nutritionally insignificant and considered to be "Fat-Free."

coco frosting

ingredients:

¼ cup nonfat dry milk solids

¼ cup water

¼ cup sifted unsweetened cocoa
   powder or carob powder

¼ cup honey and 1 tablespoon honey

1½ teaspoon vanilla

directions:

In medium saucepan, mix nonfat dry milk solids in water until dissolved. Over medium heat, stir in sifted unsweetened cocoa powder or carob powder and honey. Cook and stir for 15-20 minutes until mixture is thickened. Remove from heat and stir in vanilla.

Let cool 10 minutes, and frosting is ready to use. Frosting will continue to harden as it cools. Recipe makes enough frosting for 12 cupcakes or 1 9-inch cake layer.

note: To use this recipe as a sauce or topping, decrease cooking time to 3 minutes and serve while still hot or warm.

O ne of the wonderful things about berries is the fact that there are so many different varieties, each with its own distinctive color and flavor. There's everything from the slightly tart and tangy varieties, such as raspberries, to the sweet and distinctively flavored varieties, such as strawberries and blueberries.

This topping gives you a chance to use any variety of berry you want, so you can tailor the taste, depending on what you plan on serving it with. If you prefer a sweeter flavor, try strawberries or blueberries. For something more complex and a bit tart, make this recipe with either raspberries or blackberries.

Besides being delicious, berries are very nutritious. Many varieties, such as strawberries and raspberries, are good sources of vitamin C.

Serving Suggestion:

Try this recipe with the Citrus Garden (see page 95), Orange (see page 209) or Lemon Cream (see page 201) cakes.

FAT-FREE   WHEAT FREE   GREAT FOR KIDS

Advance Preparation

Day before drain 1 carton (32 ounces) plain, nonfat yogurt to make approximately 2 cups yogurt cheese (see page 129)

Special Equipment

yogurt cheese funnel

Yield

1½ cups (24 servings)

Nutrition per Serving

Calories: 20
Carbohydrates: 4 grams
Protein: less than 1 gram
Fat: Fat-Free*
Cholesterol: 0 milligrams
Sodium: 10 milligrams
Dietary Fiber: 0 grams

*All foods contain some fat. Less than
.5 gram of fat per serving is nutritionally
insignificant and considered to be
"Fat-Free."

creamy berry topping

ingredients:

½ cup nonfat yogurt cheese

⅓ cup pure maple syrup

½ tablespoon nonfat milk dry solids

1 teaspoon vanilla

⅔ cup fresh or slightly defrosted frozen unsweetened berries (strawberries, blueberries, raspberries or blackberries)

directions:

In medium bowl, with electric mixer, beat together yogurt cheese, maple syrup, milk solids and vanilla until well blended.

If using strawberries, slice berries lengthwise, otherwise use whole; combine with yogurt mixture.

Serve 2 tablespoons over each slice of cake.

C innamon is a spice that has been used
since ancient times. Its warm, distinct
aroma and flavor make it an ideal complement
for a variety of foods. For example, apples
and cinnamon seem to have been made for
each other.

We are very fond of cinnamon, so we knew
we had to include a sauce that featured it in
this book. This tangy dessert sauce adds a delicious cinnamon complement to our cakes, but
it can be used on a variety of other recipes. It
features evaporated skimmed milk to provide
the creaminess and it's quick and easy to
prepare.

Serving Suggestion:

You may want to use Creamy Cinnamon
Sauce with our Chunky Apple Cake (see
page 193).

FAT-   GREAT
FREE   FOR KIDS

Yield

1 cup (16 servings)

Nutrition per Serving

Calories: 23
Carbohydrates: 5 grams
Protein: 1 gram
Fat: Fat-Free*
Cholesterol: 0 milligrams
Sodium: 15 milligrams
Dietary Fiber: 0 grams

*All foods contain some fat. Less than
.5 gram of fat per serving is nutritionally
insignificant and considered to be
"Fat-Free."

creamy cinnamon sauce

ingredients:

1 tablespoon whole wheat
  pastry flour

¾ cup evaporated skimmed milk

2 tablespoons honey

2 tablespoons frozen apple juice
  concentrate (defrosted)

½ teaspoon cinnamon

½ teaspoon vanilla

directions:

In small saucepan, over medium high heat, whisk together flour, evaporated milk, honey, juice concentrate and cinnamon. Bring mixture to low boil, reduce heat to low and cook approximately 5 minutes until mixture thickens. **Stir in vanilla.** Let cool slightly.

L emons are among the most versatile of fruit. Their juice can highlight the flavors of everything from fish to vegetables to desserts and sorbets. The clean, fresh aroma of lemons and the tart tangy taste are uniquely refreshing. We've taken advantage of both the refreshing flavor and the bright aroma of lemons to create a fabulous frosting recipe. This frosting lends a subtle tartness to cakes and other baked items. And, its light color can add just the right amount of brightness and festivity that makes a dessert "special."

Lemons are valuable not only for their taste and aroma, but also for their nutrients, including vitamin C. This recipe also calls for yogurt cheese, so it's a good source of calcium as well.

Serving Suggestion:

This frosting is a natural for Lemon Cream Cake (see page 201). You might also want to try it with Citrus Garden Cake (see page 95) and Pumpkin Delight Cake (see page 101).

FAT-
FREE

WHEAT
FREE

Advance Preparation

Day before drain 1 carton (16 ounces) plain, nonfat yogurt to make approximately 1 cup yogurt cheese (see page 129)

Special Equipment

yogurt cheese funnel

Yield

1½ cups (16 servings) enough to fill and frost 2 9-inch cakes

Nutrition per Serving

Calories: 49
Carbohydrates: 10 grams
Protein: 2 grams
Fat: Fat-Free*
Cholesterol: 0 milligrams
Sodium: 30 milligrams
Dietary Fiber: 0 grams

*All foods contain some fat. Less than .5 gram of fat per serving is nutritionally insignificant and considered to be "Fat-Free."

creamy lemon frosting

ingredients:

1 cup nonfat yogurt cheese

½ cup and 2 tablespoons
   pure maple syrup

3 tablespoon nonfat dry milk solids

½ teaspoon lemon extract

1 teaspoon finely grated lemon peel

directions:

In medium bowl, with electric mixer, beat together yogurt cheese, maple syrup, milk solids, lemon extract and lemon peel until well blended.

note: To frost 1 9-inch cake, reduce recipe by half, for a yield of three-quarter cup.

Maple syrup is a natural sweetener with a rich and distinct flavor that has always been a favorite in our kitchen. We wanted to take advantage of the special flavor maple syrup offers and create a creamy topping that you can use over a variety of desserts. This recipe combines maple flavor with a potent "secret" ingredient that gives it its rich creamy texture–evaporated skimmed milk. Even though this recipe qualifies as Fat-Free, it tastes like it's made with whole cream.

Serving Suggestion:

You may want to use Creamy Maple Sauce with our Carrot Pineapple Cake (See page 93).

Yield

1 cup (16 servings)

Nutrition per Serving

Calories: 13
Carbohydrates: 2 grams
Protein: 1 gram
Fat: Fat-Free*
Cholesterol: 0 milligrams
Sodium: 15 milligrams
Dietary Fiber: 0 grams

All foods contain some fat. Less than .5 gram of fat per serving is nutritionally insignificant and considered to be "Fat-Free."

creamy maple sauce

ingredients:

½ teaspoon arrowroot

½ teaspoon whole wheat pastry flour

2 teaspoons water

¾ cup evaporated skimmed milk

1 tablespoon pure maple syrup

½ teaspoon vanilla

directions:

In small saucepan, dissolve arrowroot and flour in water; whisk in evaporated milk and maple syrup. Bring mixture to low boil over medium high heat, reduce heat to low and cook approximately 5 minutes until mixture thickens. **Stir in vanilla.** Let cool slightly.

There are several coffee substitutes on the market now that can add a roasted coffee flavor to cooking without adding any caffeine. They are made from natural dark-roasted grain, and contain nothing artificial. By combining coffee substitute with unsweetened cocoa powder, we have created a rich mocha flavor without any fat, sugar or caffeine.

We use this frosting in the Coco-Mo Angel Cake (see page 195).

This recipe gives you the choice of using either unsweetened cocoa powder, if you're a chocolate lover, or carob powder. Although unsweetened cocoa powder and carob powder aren't related, they can be substituted for each other, with a one-to-one ratio.

Serving Suggestion:

For something different, try this frosting on the Brownies (see page 237).

FAT-FREE **WHEAT FREE**

Advance Preparation

Day before drain 1 carton (16 ounces) plain, nonfat yogurt to make approximately 1 cup yogurt cheese (see page 129)

Special Equipment

yogurt cheese funnel

Yield

1½ cups (24 servings), enough to fill and frost 2 9-inch cakes

Nutrition per Serving

Calories: 36
Carbohydrates: 8 grams
Protein: 1 gram
Fat: Fat-Free*
Cholesterol: 0 milligrams
Sodium: 20 milligrams
Dietary Fiber: 0 grams

All foods contain some fat. Less than .5 gram of fat per serving is nutritionally insignificant and considered to be "Fat-Free."

creamy mocha frosting

ingredients:

1 cup nonfat yogurt cheese

½ cup and 2 tablespoons
pure maple syrup

3 tablespoons nonfat dry
milk solids

3 tablespoons unsweetened cocoa
powder or carob powder

2 tablespoons powdered
coffee substitute

1 teaspoon vanilla

directions:

In medium bowl, with electric mixer, beat together yogurt cheese, maple syrup, milk solids, cocoa or carob powder, coffee substitute and vanilla extract until well blended.

note: To frost 1 9-inch cake, reduce recipe by half, for a yield of three-quarter cup. We use Pero as our coffee substitute.

The orange is a fruit that has been enjoyed since ancient times. It can lend its distinct sweet flavor and refreshing fragrance to everything from poultry to pancakes. We wanted to create an orange frosting that would complement a wide variety of cakes and other baked goods.

We use nonfat dry milk solids and yogurt cheese to add a richness to this frosting that seems as if it could only come from whole milk. They also provide beneficial calcium with so little fat that this recipe qualifies as Fat-Free.

Serving Suggestion:

This frosting will enhance either the Orange Cake (see page 209), or the Citrus Garden Cake (see page 95). And for something different, try it with Spicy Tomato Cake (see page 113).

Advance Preparation

Day before drain 1 carton (16 ounces) plain, nonfat yogurt to make approximately 1 cup yogurt cheese (see page 129)

Special Equipment

yogurt cheese funnel

Yield

1½ cups (24 servings) enough to fill and frost 2 9-inch cakes

Nutrition per Serving

Calories: 18
Carbohydrates: 4 grams
Protein: 1 gram
Fat: Fat-Free*
Cholesterol: 0 milligrams
Sodium: 10 milligrams
Dietary Fiber: 0 grams

All foods contain some fat. Less than .5 gram of fat per serving is nutritionally insignificant and considered to be "Fat-Free."

creamy orange frosting

ingredients:

1 cup nonfat yogurt cheese

½ cup and 2 tablespoons
   pure maple syrup

2 tablespoons frozen orange juice
   concentrate (defrosted)

3 tablespoons nonfat dry
   milk solids

½ teaspoon orange extract

1 teaspoon finely grated orange peel

directions:

In medium bowl, with electric mixer, beat together yogurt cheese, maple syrup, juice concentrate, milk solids, orange extract and orange peel until well blended.

note: To frost 1 9-inch cake, reduce recipe by half, for a yield of three-quarter cup.

The pineapple is a quintessential tropical fruit. It tastes almost decadently sweet, yet has the acidity to be refreshing in the hottest weather. That's why we were so anxious to create a topping that features pineapple. This topping can lend a tropical touch to cakes and other desserts. It's incredibly easy to make, once you have the yogurt cheese made. That's why we recommend keeping some yogurt cheese in the refrigerator. It really is one of the essential keys to creating your own creamy desserts without fat.

Serving Suggestion:

You may wish to substitute Creamy Pineapple Topping for the Pineapple Glaze used as part of our Aloha Cake (See page 91).

FAT-FREE   WHEAT FREE

Advance Preparation

Day before drain 1 carton (16 ounces) plain, nonfat yogurt to make approximately 1 cup yogurt cheese (see page 129)

Special Equipment

yogurt cheese funnel

Yield

1⅓ cups (16 servings) enough to fill and frost 2 9-inch cakes

Nutrition per Serving

Calories: 31
Carbohydrates: 7 grams
Protein: 1 gram
Fat: Fat-Free*
Cholesterol: 0 milligrams
Sodium: 15 milligrams
Dietary Fiber: 0 grams

All foods contain some fat. Less than .5 gram of fat per serving is nutritionally insignificant and considered to be "Fat-Free."

creamy pineapple topping

ingredients:

½ cup nonfat yogurt cheese

⅓ cup pure maple syrup

1½ tablespoons nonfat dry
milk solids

1 teaspoon vanilla

¼ teaspoon coconut extract

1 can (8 ounces) unsweetened
crushed pineapple, drained

directions:

In medium bowl, with electric mixer, beat together yogurt cheese, maple syrup, milk solids, vanilla and coconut extracts until blended. Stir in crushed pineapple.

note: To frost 1 9-inch cake, reduce recipe by half, for a yield of approximately three-quarter cup.

Vanilla is a staple spice whose rich, distinctive flavor and aroma make it one of the most versatile of flavorings. We've created a vanilla frosting with a creamy texture that does not depend on fat at all for its richness.

Instead of using cream cheese or some other high fat ingredient to make this frosting, we use nonfat yogurt cheese. The comparison between the two ingredients is eye opening.

One ounce of cream cheese contains 100 calories, almost 10 grams of fat and 89 percent of calories from fat. Compare that with the same amount of nonfat yogurt cheese that contains 25 calories and is so low in fat that it actually qualifies as Fat-Free. So you save almost 10 grams of fat per ounce. And cream cheese has four times the calories as yogurt cheese.

Serving Suggestion:

Use this frosting to bring out the taste in cakes, such as the Carrot Raisin Cake (see page 89).

FAT-FREE   WHEAT FREE   GREAT FOR KIDS

Advance Preparation

Day before drain 1 carton (16 ounces) plain, nonfat yogurt to make approximately 1 cup yogurt cheese (see page 129)

Special Equipment

yogurt cheese funnel

Yield

1½ cups (24 servings) enough to fill and frost 2 9-inch cakes

Nutrition per Serving

Calories: 34
Carbohydrates: 7 grams
Protein: 1 gram
Fat: Fat-Free*
Cholesterol: 0 milligrams
Sodium: 20 milligrams
Dietary Fiber: 0 grams

All foods contain some fat. Less than .5 gram of fat per serving is nutritionally insignificant and considered to be "Fat-Free."

creamy vanilla frosting

ingredients:

1 cup nonfat yogurt cheese

½ cup and 2 tablespoons
   pure maple syrup

3 tablespoon nonfat dry milk solids

2 teaspoons vanilla

directions:

In medium bowl, with electric mixer, beat together yogurt cheese, maple syrup, milk solids and vanilla until well blended.

note: To frost 1 9-inch cake, reduce recipe by half, for a yield of three-quarter cup.

Because there is nothing that tastes quite like chocolate and because so many people adore the taste, we wanted to offer a variety of recipes that feature the taste of chocolate without all the fat, sugar and caffeine usually associated with it.

By using cocoa powder, we created this smooth, airy frosting that is light in texture yet rich in flavor.

This recipe gives you the choice of using either unsweetened cocoa powder, if you're a chocolate lover, or carob powder. Although unsweetened cocoa powder and carob powder aren't related, they can be substituted for each other, with a one-to-one ratio.

Serving Suggestion:

You may want to use Fluffy Coco Frosting with our Brownies (see page 237).

Yield

2 cups (16 servings)

Nutrition per Serving

Calories: 28
Carbohydrates: 7 grams
Protein: 1 gram
Fat: Fat-Free*
Cholesterol: 0 milligrams
Sodium: 10 milligrams
Dietary Fiber: 0 grams

*All foods contain some fat. Less than
.5 gram of fat per serving is nutritionally
insignificant and considered to be
"Fat-Free."

fluffy coco frosting

ingredients:

⅔ cup pure maple syrup

2 egg whites

½ teaspoon cream of tartar

1 tablespoon unsweetened cocoa powder or carob powder

1 teaspoon vanilla

directions:

In medium saucepan over medium-high heat, bring maple syrup to boiling point, and boil for 3 minutes, stirring frequently.

In top of double boiler, with electric mixer, beat egg whites with cream of tartar until foamy, approximately 5 minutes.

Slowly drizzle hot maple syrup into egg whites, beating constantly on high speed for 4-6 minutes, or until frosting is thick enough to spread. Use rubber spatula to scrape down sides of pan frequently. Remove from heat; beat in cocoa or carob powder and vanilla.

The finished frosting should be smooth and fluffy, yet hold stiff peaks.

O ne of our goals in developing this book was to offer you an opportunity to be able to tailor the personality of the recipes to meet your own tastes and different occasions. The way that you frost a cake can change the way it looks and tastes. That's why we've created both creamy and fluffy versions of our most popular frostings, including the ones that feature lemon.

This light, lemony frosting features finely grated lemon peel to add extra flavor to this colorful frosting. We use it in the Strawberry Angel Food Cake (see page 217).

Serving Suggestion:

You may want to use Fluffy Lemon Frosting with our Honey Lemon Cake (see page 199).

Yield

2 cups (16 servings)

Nutrition per Serving

Calories: 38
Carbohydrates: 8 grams
Protein: 1 gram
Fat: Fat-Free*
Cholesterol: 0 milligrams
Sodium: 20 milligrams
Dietary Fiber: 0 grams

All foods contain some fat. Less than .5 gram of fat per serving is nutritionally insignificant and considered to be "Fat-Free."

fluffy lemon frosting

ingredients:

⅔ cup pure maple syrup

2 egg whites

½ teaspoon cream of tartar

¼ teaspoon lemon extract

1 teaspoon finely grated lemon peel

directions:

In medium saucepan over medium-high heat, bring maple syrup to boiling point, and boil for 3 minutes, stirring frequently.

In top of double boiler, with electric mixer, beat egg whites with cream of tartar until foamy, approximately 5 minutes.

Slowly drizzle hot maple syrup into egg whites, beating constantly on high speed for 4-6 minutes, or until frosting is thick enough to spread. Use rubber spatula to scrape down sides of pan frequently. Remove from heat; beat in lemon extract and lemon peel.

The finished frosting should be smooth and fluffy, yet hold stiff peaks.

note: For a flavor variation replace the lemon extract and peel with equal amounts of orange extract and finely grated orange peel.

This frosting will add a "party look" to baked goods, and works especially well with our layer cakes. We use it in our Black Forest Cake (see page 189), and Neapolitan Ice Cream Cake (see page 207).

We do not recommend using raw egg whites because of the danger of salmonella contamination. It's easy to kill this harmful bacteria, simply by cooking egg whites on top of a double boiler. For this recipe, heat the egg whites before using them.

Serving Suggestion:

You may want to use Fluffy Vanilla Frosting with our Carrot Raisin Cake (See page 89).

FAT-FREE   DAIRY FREE   WHEAT FREE

Yield

2 cups (16 servings)

Nutrition per Serving

Calories: 36
Carbohydrates: 8 grams
Protein: 0 grams
Fat: Fat-Free*
Cholesterol: 0 milligrams
Sodium: 10 milligrams
Dietary Fiber: 0 grams

All foods contain some fat. Less than .5 gram of fat per serving is nutritionally insignificant and considered to be "Fat-Free."

fluffy vanilla frosting

ingredients:

⅔ cup pure maple syrup

2 egg whites

½ teaspoon cream of tartar

1 teaspoon vanilla

directions:

In medium saucepan over medium-high heat, bring maple syrup to boiling point, and boil for 3 minutes, stirring frequently.

In top of double boiler over boiling water, with electric mixer, beat egg whites with cream of tartar until foamy, approximately 5 minutes.

Slowly drizzle hot maple syrup into egg whites, beating constantly on high speed for 4-6 minutes, or until frosting is thick enough to spread. Use rubber spatula to scrape down sides of pan frequently. Remove from heat; beat in vanilla extract.

The finished frosting should be smooth and fluffy, yet hold stiff peaks.

note: For a variation, add one-quarter teaspoon almond extract instead of the vanilla.

Whipped cream is one of those ingredients that adds a distinctive texture and appearance to desserts, but at the cost of an enormous amount of fat and calories. Our challenge was to create a substitute for whipped cream that has the wonderfully light texture and appearance of whipped cream, but without the fat and calories. Since we obviously could not use cream or even regular milk, we had to be inventive. The result of our efforts is a recipe we're quite proud of. We believe you'll find la creme whipped topping is similar to traditional whipped cream in flavor and texture, but without all of the fat. In fact, you save nearly 10 grams of fat in every tablespoon of this recipe compared to whipped cream. And there's four times as many calories in whipped cream.

Serving Suggestion:

Use as you would whipped cream on cakes, fruit cremes and pies.

Yield

4 cups (12 servings)

Nutrition per Serving

Calories: 43
Carbohydrates: 8 grams
Protein: 2 grams
Fat: Fat-Free*
Cholesterol: 0 milligrams
Sodium: 40 milligrams
Dietary Fiber: 0 grams

All foods contain some fat. Less than .5 gram of fat per serving is nutritionally insignificant and considered to be "Fat-Free."

la creme whipped topping

ingredients:

½ can (6 fluid ounces)
   evaporated skimmed milk

2 tablespoons pure maple syrup
1 teaspoon vanilla

directions:

Pour evaporated milk into large metal bowl and place in freezer until ice crystals form along edge of bowl, minimum of 30 minutes. Chill electric mixer beaters at same time.

Remove bowl and beaters from freezer. Add maple syrup and vanilla to evaporated milk. Using electric mixer, beat on high until mixture is creamy and stiff, about 5 minutes. For best results, use immediately.

We developed the glazes in this book to provide you with even more versatility when it comes to personalizing the recipes. You can use our glazes on top of cake recipes in place of frosting, or as a filling between cake layers and then put a frosting on top of the cake. You can also use the glazes as a topping for nonfat frozen yogurt or pudding.

This pineapple glaze can add a tropical flavor to cakes or puddings because it combines the flavors of pineapples and coconut, but without any fat.

We use Pineapple Glaze as part of our Aloha Cake (See page 91).

Yield

1½ cups (16 servings)

Nutrition per Serving

Calories: 33
Carbohydrates: 9 grams
Protein: 0 grams
Fat: Fat-Free*
Cholesterol: 0 milligrams
Sodium: 0 milligrams
Dietary Fiber: 0 grams

*All foods contain some fat. Less than .5 gram of fat per serving is nutritionally insignificant and considered to be "Fat-Free."

pineapple glaze

ingredients:

1 can (16 ounces) juice-packed
  crushed pineapple

1 tablespoon arrowroot

⅓ cup pure maple syrup

½ teaspoon coconut extract
  (optional)

directions:

Drain crushed pineapple, reserving one-quarter cup juice.

In medium saucepan over medium heat, dissolve arrowroot in reserved juice. Stir in maple syrup and cook until thickened, approximately 5 minutes. Remove from heat and add crushed pineapple and coconut extract.

This is a tasty, easy-to-prepare topping that you can serve warm over any number of recipes, from cakes to pancakes to puddings.

Apples are a good source of fiber, especially soluble fiber. That's good news, since eating a low fat diet rich in soluble fiber has been shown to lower blood cholesterol for a healthier heart. It also helps to regulate the body's blood sugar level.

Serving Suggestion:

You may want to use Spicy Apple Topping with our Frozen Fruit Cremes (see page 285).

FAT-FREE DAIRY FREE WHEAT FREE

GREAT FOR KIDS

Yield

2 cups (16 servings)

Nutrition per Serving

Calories: 36
Carbohydrates: 9 grams
Protein: 0 grams
Fat: Fat-Free*
Cholesterol: 0 milligrams
Sodium: 0 milligrams
Dietary Fiber: 0 grams

*All foods contain some fat. Less than .5 gram of fat per serving is nutritionally insignificant and considered to be "Fat-Free."

spicy apple topping

ingredients:

2 large cooking apples,
  peeled and thinly sliced

¾ cup apple juice

⅓ cup raisins

½ teaspoon cinnamon

2 tablespoons honey

2 tablespoons arrowroot

2 tablespoons water

½ teaspoon vanilla

directions:

In saucepan over medium heat, combine sliced apples, apple juice, raisins, cinnamon and honey. Simmer uncovered until apples are just tender, about 8-10 minutes.

Dissolve arrowroot in water. Add to apple mixture. Cook and stir until thickened and bubbly, about 4 minutes. Stir in vanilla. Let cool slightly.

G lazing a cake is a simple way to dress it up, and enhance its appearance. You can also set pieces of dried fruit into the glaze to give it an even more fancy appearance, as well as enhanced nutrition. If you're planning to decorate the glaze with pieces of fruit, mix 1 teaspoon of arrowroot for each half cup of glaze. The arrowroot will thicken the glaze and allow you to set in dried fruits. It will also change the glaze's appearance slightly, giving it more of a transparent sheen.

Serving Suggestion:

You may wish to substitute Strawberry Glaze for the Fluffy Lemon Frosting used as part of our Strawberry Angel Food Cake (see page 217).

FAT-FREE   DAIRY FREE   WHEAT FREE

GREAT FOR KIDS

Yield

¾ cups (16 servings)

Nutrition per Serving

Calories: 36
Carbohydrates: 9 grams
Protein: 0 grams
Fat: Fat-Free*
Cholesterol: 0 milligrams
Sodium: 0 milligrams
Dietary Fiber: 0 grams

*All foods contain some fat. Less than .5 gram of fat per serving is nutritionally insignificant and considered to be "Fat-Free."

strawberry glaze

ingredients:

2 cups + ½ cup fresh or frozen
   sliced unsweetened strawberries

¼ cup pure maple syrup

directions:

In saucepan, mix 2 cups strawberries and maple syrup. Cook over medium heat until thickened, stirring frequently, approximately 20 minutes.

Remove from heat and stir in remaining half cup strawberries.

Cakes Section

There is something inherently festive about a cake. It can turn even a simple dinner at home into an occasion. Perhaps that's because cakes are associated with so many special celebrations. After all, what would a birthday party or a wedding be without a cake?

When we were developing the recipes for this section, we were aware that you want to serve cakes that look as special as they taste. We're especially proud of these recipes because they go beyond what other cookbooks offer you. In this section, you'll find cakes that look spectacular, and that taste as good as they look. But they're not just sweet treats filled with empty calories. They get their sweetness and flavor from fruits, fruit puree and fruit juice, so they provide many important natural nutrients and fiber. And the flour used is whole grain pastry flour to provide you with the natural B vitamins and fiber that are missing from white flour. We're most proud of the fact that there is no added fat of any kind and no high fat ingredients used in any of these recipes. In fact, many are so low in fat that they qualify as Fat-Free.

To give you an idea of just how much fat and calories you can save with these recipes, here is a comparison between the Banana Date Cake in this section and a traditional Banana Cake recipe made with fat:

One Serving	Fat (grams)	Calories
Traditional Banana Cake	11g	288
Banana Date Cake from *Baking Without Fat*	**Fat-Free**	**220**

So now you can serve cakes that no one has to feel guilty about enjoying, because they're low in fat and nutritious, yet still festive and fun.

The very name "cream cake" usually warns you that the recipe is going to be loaded with fat. But in this case, we've been able to create a cake with a creamy texture that qualifies as Fat-Free. The secret is the bananas. They have a naturally creamy texture without the fat normally associated with creaminess.

To create this tasty cake, we began with a smaller version of our banana date cake recipe, added vanilla pudding/filling in the middle and topped it all off with caramelized banana topping. The result is a banana-lover's dream that is richly satisfying yet totally healthy.

Eating bananas is a good way to keep your heart healthy. They rank among the best natural sources of potassium, which studies have linked to controlling blood pressure. Also bananas contain a significant amount of soluble fiber that can help to lower blood cholesterol.

FAT-FREE

Advance Preparation

Vanilla Pudding/Filling (see page 305)
Caramelized Banana Topping (see page 149)

Special Equipment

2 9x1½-inch nonstick round baking pans

Temperature and Time

Bake at 325°F. for 30 minutes

Yield

16 servings

Nutrition per Serving

Calories: 151
Carbohydrates: 37 grams
Protein: 2 grams
Fat: Fat-Free*
Cholesterol: 0 milligrams
Sodium: 110 milligrams
Dietary Fiber: 2 grams

*All foods contain some fat. Less than .5 gram of fat per serving is nutritionally insignificant and considered to be "Fat-Free."

banana cream cake

ingredients:

1 cup and 2½ tablespoons whole wheat pastry flour

½ teaspoon + ¾ teaspoon baking soda

¼ teaspoon cream of tartar

½ teaspoon cinnamon

⅛ teaspoon ground nutmeg

¾ cups honey

2½ tablespoons pure maple syrup

¾ teaspoon vanilla

2 egg whites, lightly beaten

1 ripe medium banana, pureed

1 ripe medium banana, sliced

½ cup boiling water

½ cup chopped dates

½ recipe Vanilla Pudding/Filling

1 recipe Caramelized Banana Topping

directions:

Preheat oven to 325°F. In large mixing bowl, combine flour, half teaspoon baking soda, cream of tartar, cinnamon and nutmeg. Set aside.

In medium bowl, mix honey, maple syrup, vanilla, egg whites, pureed banana and sliced banana. Stir into flour mixture and mix until **just** blended.

In blender, process on high speed, boiling water, dates and three-quarter teaspoon baking soda until dates are pureed, about 2 minutes. Stir into flour mixture. ***Do not overmix.***

Spoon batter into 2 9x1½-inch nonstick round baking pans. Bake at 325°F. for 30 minutes, or until toothpick inserted in center comes out clean. Cool on wire racks for 10 minutes, and remove cakes from pans.

While baking, prepare Vanilla Pudding/Filling and Caramelized Banana Topping.

Fill cake layers by spreading Vanilla Pudding/Filling between cake layers, and top with Caramelized Banana Topping.

This is one of our favorite recipes for getting children to eat foods that are good for them in a form they really enjoy. A touch of frosting turns this recipe into a child's healthy birthday cake.

Bananas are an excellent source of energy for active children, as well as a rich source of the mineral potassium, which is one of the electrolytes the body needs to maintain the proper fluid balance.

To make your own puree for this recipe, be sure that the bananas you choose are ripe and soft to the touch. The color should be bright solid yellow, or preferably, flecked with brown. In fact, very brown bananas that have gotten too ripe for eating are perfect for making puree. When you're planning on making puree, simply buy extra bananas ahead of time, eat some of them, and let a few of them turn nice and ripe.

Serving Suggestion:

You may want to fill and glaze this cake, using one-quarter cup of melted fruit-juice-sweetened berry or apricot preserves per layer. Or try our Creamy Maple Sauce (see page 159), or Caramelized Banana Topping (see page 149).

FAT-FREE   DAIRY FREE   GREAT FOR KIDS

Special Equipment

2 9x1½-inch nonstick round baking pans

Temperature and Time

Bake at 325°F. for 35-40 minutes

Yield

16 servings

Nutrition per Serving

Calories: 220
Carbohydrates: 55 grams
Protein: 4 grams
Fat: Fat-Free*
Cholesterol: 0 milligrams
Sodium: 210 milligrams
Dietary Fiber: 3 grams

*All foods contain some fat. Less than .5 gram of fat per serving is nutritionally insignificant and considered to be "Fat-Free."

banana date cake

ingredients:

2⅓ cups whole wheat pastry flour

¾ teaspoon + 1½ teaspoons
 baking soda

1 teaspoon cream of tartar

½ teaspoon cinnamon

¼ teaspoon ground nutmeg

1½ cups honey

¼ cup pure maple syrup

2 teaspoons vanilla

2 egg whites, unbeaten

2 very ripe medium bananas,
 pureed (about 1½ cups)

1 ripe medium banana, diced

½ cup boiling water

¾ cup chopped dates

2 egg whites, lightly beaten

directions:

Preheat oven to 325°F. In large mixing bowl, combine flour, three-quarter teaspoon baking soda, cream of tartar, cinnamon and nutmeg. Set aside.

In medium bowl, mix honey, maple syrup, vanilla, 2 unbeaten egg whites, pureed banana and diced banana. Stir into flour mixture and mix until **just** blended.

In blender, process on high speed boiling water, dates and 1½ teaspoons baking soda until dates are pureed, about 2 minutes. Stir into flour mixture. Gently stir in 2 lightly beaten egg whites. *Do not overmix.*

Spoon batter into 2 9x1½-inch nonstick round baking pans. Bake at 325°F. for 35-40 minutes, or until toothpick inserted in center comes out clean. Cool on wire racks for 10 minutes, and remove cakes from pans.

As delicious as traditional Black Forest Cake is, it certainly rates a black mark when it comes to fat and calories. By the time you add up the chocolate butter frosting, the whipped cream and the chocolate shavings, a slice of this traditional German dessert will contain 20 grams of fat and 532 calories. Contrast that to our healthy version, which qualifies as Fat-Free, with just 188 calories. So you save 20 grams of fat and nearly 344 calories in every slice!

In this recipe, we still use the classic flavor combination of chocolate and cherries, but cut the fat and eliminate the refined sugar by using unsweetened cocoa powder and fruit-juice-sweetened cherry preserves.

If you don't want to use cocoa powder in this recipe, you can substitute carob powder. Although the two ingredients aren't related, they can be substituted for each other, with a one-to-one ratio.

Advance Preparation

Fluffy Vanilla Frosting (see page 173)

Special Equipment

2 9x1½-inch nonstick round baking pans

Temperature and Time

Bake at 325°F. for 15-20 minutes

Yield

16 servings

Nutrition per Serving

Calories: 188
Carbohydrates: 45 grams
Protein: 3 grams
Fat: Fat-Free*
Cholesterol: 0 milligrams
Sodium: 80 milligrams
Dietary Fiber: 2 grams

*All foods contain some fat. Less than .5 gram of fat per serving is nutritionally insignificant and considered to be "Fat-Free."

black forest cake

ingredients:

1¾ cups whole wheat pastry flour

¾ teaspoon cream of tartar

¾ teaspoon baking soda

1 teaspoon cinnamon

⅓ cup unsweetened cocoa powder
  or carob powder

¾ cup unsweetened applesauce

1¼ cups honey

3 egg whites, lightly beaten

1 teaspoon vanilla

¾ cup fruit-juice-sweetened
  cherry preserves

1 recipe Fluffy Vanilla Frosting

directions:

Preheat oven to 325°F. In large bowl, sift together flour, cream of tartar, baking soda, cinnamon and cocoa or carob powder. Set aside.

In medium bowl, combine applesauce, honey, egg whites and vanilla. Gently stir into flour mixture and mix until **just** blended. ***Do not overmix.***

Spoon batter into 2 9x1½-inch nonstick round baking pans. Bake at 325°F. for 15-20 minutes, or until toothpick inserted in center comes out clean. Cool on wire rack for 15 minutes, and remove from pan.

Let cake cool additional 20 minutes and prepare Fluffy Vanilla Frosting.

Fill cake layers by spreading preserves between cake layers, and top with Fluffy Vanilla Frosting.

The very name "Boston Cream Cake" conjures up images of a rich treat that is high in fat. But we've managed to create a version of this cake with the rich flavor you expect that actually qualifies as Fat-Free. It contains no white flour, no butter, margarine or vegetable shortening, no refined sugar, no whole milk and no whole eggs, which are all found in the traditional recipe.

Instead, we have substituted whole wheat pastry flour that is milled from the whole grain, so that the minerals and vitamins are preserved, along with pure honey, fruit puree and natural flavoring.

We think you'll be pleasantly surprised by how delicious a "cream" cake can be without any cream whatsoever.

FAT-FREE

Advance Preparation

Vanilla Pudding/Filling (see page 305)
Coco Frosting (see page 151)

Special Equipment

2 9x1½-inch nonstick round baking pans

Temperature and Time

Bake at 325°F. for 30 minutes

Yield

16 servings

Nutrition per Serving

Calories: 135
Carbohydrates: 32 grams
Protein: 3 grams
Fat: Fat-Free*
Cholesterol: 0 milligrams
Sodium: 100 milligrams
Dietary Fiber: 2 grams

*All foods contain some fat. Less than .5 gram of fat per serving is nutritionally insignificant and considered to be "Fat-Free."

boston cream cake

ingredients:

1½ cups whole wheat pastry flour

1 teaspoon baking soda

¾ teaspoon cream of tartar

¾ cup honey

¼ cup frozen orange juice concentrate (defrosted)

1-2 tablespoons water (as needed)

1 teaspoon vanilla

⅛ teaspoon orange extract

¾ tablespoon finely grated orange peel

1 egg white, unbeaten

1 jar (4 ounces) apricot baby food puree

1 egg white, lightly beaten

½ recipe Vanilla Pudding/Filling

1 recipe Coco Frosting

directions:

Preheat oven to 325°F. In large bowl, combine flour, baking soda and cream of tartar. Set aside.

In medium bowl, mix honey, juice concentrate, water, vanilla, orange extract, orange peel, 1 unbeaten egg white and apricot puree. Stir into flour mixture until **just** blended. Gently stir in 1 lightly beaten egg white. *Do not overmix.*

Spoon batter into 2 9x1½-inch nonstick round baking pans. Bake at 325°F. for 30 minutes, or until toothpick inserted in center comes out clean. Cool on wire racks for 10 minutes, and remove cakes from pans. Let cake cool an additional 20 minutes and prepare Vanilla Pudding/ Filling and Coco Frosting.

Fill cake layers by spreading Vanilla Pudding/Filling between cake layers, and top with Coco Frosting.

Applesauce cake has long been a favorite family dessert, but the traditional recipe can be higher in fat than it is in applesauce. If concern for fat has caused you to remove this recipe from your repertoire, we have good news for you. We've created a Fat-Free version that uses a trio of spices–cinnamon, nutmeg and cloves–to compliment the flavor of baking apples.

Apples are not only one of the most popular fruits, they are also rich in fiber, including pectin, which is a form of soluble fiber that can help lower blood cholesterol.

When baking, we suggest you use organically grown whole wheat pastry flour. It differs from whole wheat flour in that it has less gluten, which means a lighter finished product.

Serving Suggestion:

For a flavorful way to fill and top this cake, try our Creamy Cinnamon Sauce (see page 155).

DAIRY FREE   GREAT FOR KIDS

Special Equipment

2 9x1½-inch nonstick round baking pans

Temperature and Time

Bake at 325°F. for 40-45 minutes

Yield

16 servings

Nutrition per Serving

Calories: 125
Carbohydrates: 26 grams
Protein: 4 grams
Fat: 1 gram
Calories from Fat: 7%
Cholesterol: 0 milligrams
Sodium: 170 milligrams
Dietary Fiber: 3 grams

chunky apple cake

ingredients:

2½ cups whole wheat pastry flour

1½ teaspoons baking soda

1½ teaspoons cream of tartar

2 teaspoons cinnamon

¼ teaspoon ground cloves

¼ teaspoon ground nutmeg

1½ cups honey

2 teaspoons vanilla

⅓ cup unsweetened applesauce

2 jars (2½ ounces each) prune baby food puree

⅓ cup frozen apple juice concentrate (defrosted)

2 egg whites, unbeaten

2½ cups peeled and chopped baking apples

½ cups dark raisins

2 egg whites, lightly beaten

directions:

Preheat oven to 325°F. In large bowl, combine flour, baking soda, cream of tartar, cinnamon, cloves and nutmeg. Set aside.

In medium bowl, mix honey, vanilla, applesauce, prune puree, juice concentrate and 2 unbeaten egg whites. Fold in chopped apples and raisins. Stir into flour mixture and mix until **just** blended. Gently stir in 2 lightly beaten egg whites. ***Do not overmix.***

Spoon batter into 2 9x1½-inch nonstick round baking pans.
Bake at 325°F. for 40-45 minutes, or until toothpick inserted in center comes out clean. Cool on wire racks for 10 minutes, and remove cakes from pans.

The key ingredient in making angel food cake is whipped egg whites, which give the cake its light texture. The reason for whipping egg whites is to trap air, and use it as a natural leavening. The more air, the better.

Some home cooks are intimidated when it comes to whipping egg whites. They have visions of French chefs using balloon whisks and copper bowls to give the whites maximum volume. Wire whisks are still the best tools for whipping egg whites, but they are tiring to the wrist and arm. You can achieve excellent results with a lot less effort by using an electric mixer. The secret is to start at a slower speed so you don't break down the whites, then gradually increasing the speed of the mixer. Usually, the biggest problem that home cooks encounter is overbeating the whites. Once this has happened, the ability of the egg white to hold air is lost, and the whites will have a dry appearance. With practice, you will quickly be able to tell when the whites are stiff, yet not dry.

In this recipe, we also use cream of tartar to help increase the volume of the egg whites.

Advance Preparation
Creamy Mocha Frosting (see page 161)

Special Equipment
10-inch nonstick fluted tube pan

Temperature and Time
Bake at 325°F. for 40-45 minutes

Yield
14 servings

Nutrition per Serving
Calories: 146
Carbohydrates: 32 grams
Protein: 5 grams
Fat: Fat-Free*
Cholesterol: 0 milligrams
Sodium: 60 milligrams
Dietary Fiber: 0 grams

*All foods contain some fat. Less than .5 gram of fat per serving is nutritionally insignificant and considered to be "Fat-Free."

coco-mo angel cake

ingredients:

10 egg whites

1 teaspoon cream of tartar

1⅓ cups pure maple syrup

¾ cup and 2 tablespoons
   whole wheat pastry flour

¼ cup unsweetened cocoa powder
   or carob powder

1 teaspoon vanilla

¼ teaspoon finely grated orange peel

1 recipe Creamy Mocha Frosting

directions:

Preheat oven to 325°F. In large bowl, with electric mixer, beat egg whites at moderate speed until frothy. Add cream of tartar and beat whites until they hold soft peaks. Gradually beat in maple syrup at high speed and beat whites until stiff.

Gently fold in flour, cocoa or carob powder, vanilla and orange peel. Spoon batter into ungreased 10-inch nonstick fluted tube pan. Bake at 325°F. for 40-45 minutes, or until toothpick inserted in center comes out clean. Remove from oven, and invert cake pan on cooling rack until completely cooled. To remove cake from pan, loosen edges with spatula.

Prepare Creamy Mocha Frosting.

When cake is completely cool, spread Creamy Mocha Frosting over top of cake.

This elegant cake takes its name from the silky appearance of the Coco Frosting that is part of the recipe. The finished cake has an elegant shiny appearance that is "dressed up" enough even for a formal dinner.

This recipe proves once again that you can create special occasion desserts without refined flour, sugar, butter or unhealthy ingredients.

You have the option of using cocoa powder if you're a chocolate lover, or carob powder. Although the two ingredients aren't related, they can be substituted for each other, with a one-to-one ratio.

FAT-
FREE

Advance Preparation

Vanilla Pudding/Filling
(see page 305)
Coco Frosting (see
page 151)

Special Equipment

2 9x 1½-inch nonstick
round baking pans

Temperature and Time

Bake at 325°F. for 15-20
minutes

Yield

16 servings

Nutrition per Serving

Calories: 172
Carbohydrates: 41 grams
Protein: 4 grams
Fat: Fat-Free*
Cholesterol: 0 milligrams
Sodium: 80 milligrams
Dietary Fiber: 2 grams

*All foods contain some fat. Less than
.5 gram of fat per serving is nutritionally
insignificant and considered to be
"Fat-Free."

coco silk cake

ingredients:

1¾ cups whole wheat pastry flour

⅓ cup unsweetened cocoa powder
or carob powder

¾ teaspoon cream of tartar

¾ teaspoon baking soda

1 teaspoon cinnamon

¾ cup unsweetened applesauce

1¼ cups honey

3 egg whites, lightly beaten

1 teaspoon vanilla

½ recipe Vanilla Pudding/Filling

1 recipe Coco Frosting

directions:

Preheat oven to 325°F. In large bowl, sift together flour, cocoa or carob powder, cream of tartar, baking soda and cinnamon. Set aside.

In medium bowl, combine applesauce, honey, egg whites and vanilla. Gently stir into flour mixture and mix until **just** blended. ***Do not overmix.***

Spoon batter into 2 9x1½-inch nonstick round baking pans. Bake at 325°F. for 15-20 minutes, or until toothpick inserted in center comes out clean. Cool on wire rack for 15 minutes, and remove from pan.

Let cake cool additional 20 minutes and make Vanilla Pudding/Filling and Coco Frosting.

Fill cake layers by spreading Vanilla Pudding/Filling between cake layers, and top with Coco Frosting.

This versatile cake can be dressed up or down, depending upon the occasion. Serve it plain or with some fresh fruit for a sensational everyday dessert. Or fill it and top it with Fluffy Lemon Frosting and garnish with fresh fruit for a dessert worthy of a fancy dinner party. Or glaze it with our Creamy Berry Topping, for a delicious combination of fruity flavors for a festive garden luncheon.

This cake is so low in fat that it qualifies as Fat-Free. You can feel good about serving it often.

Serving Suggestion:

Fill and top with Fluffy Lemon Frosting (see page 171) or Creamy Lemon Frosting (see page 157). Or glaze with Creamy Berry Topping (see page 153).

Special Equipment

2 9x1½-inch nonstick round baking pans

Temperature and Time

Bake at 325°F. for 35-40 minutes

Yield

14 servings

Nutrition per Serving

Calories: 164
Carbohydrates: 38 grams
Protein: 3 grams
Fat: Fat-Free*
Cholesterol: 0 milligrams
Sodium: 135 milligrams
Dietary Fiber: 3 grams

*All foods contain some fat. Less than .5 gram of fat per serving is nutritionally insignificant and considered to be "Fat-Free."

honey lemon cake

ingredients:

2½ cups whole wheat pastry flour

1½ teaspoons baking soda

1½ teaspoons cream of tartar

1 cup honey

¾ cup frozen apple juice
concentrate (defrosted)

2 teaspoons vanilla

¼ teaspoon lemon extract

2 teaspoons finely grated lemon peel

2 egg whites, unbeaten

1 cup unsweetened applesauce

2 egg whites, lightly beaten

directions:

Preheat oven to 325°F. In large bowl, combine flour, baking soda and cream of tartar. Set aside.

In medium bowl, mix honey, juice concentrate, vanilla, lemon extract, lemon peel, 2 unbeaten egg whites and applesauce. Stir into flour mixture until **just** blended. Gently stir in 2 lightly beaten egg whites. *Do not overmix.*

Spoon batter into 2 9x1½-inch nonstick round baking pans. Bake at 325°F. for 35-40 minutes, or until toothpick inserted in center comes out clean. Cool on wire racks for 10 minutes, and remove cakes from pans.

The traditional Lemon Chiffon Cake recipe calls for seven whole eggs and a half cup of oil. As a result, a single serving without frosting has 13 grams of fat.

FAT-FREE

We wanted to offer you a lemon cake with all the refreshing flavor of chiffon cake, but without all the fat. So we developed this recipe that calls for just one egg white and no oil whatsoever. The word "cream" in the recipe title refers to the filling, not to the use of cream or fat. It also refers to the fact that this recipe tastes so decadently delicious that any guests you serve it to won't even realize that it's a "healthy" dessert.

A topping of sliced strawberries and blueberries make this cake festive and colorful, as well as adding flavor. Frozen strawberries and blueberries are available all year long, but when fresh berries are available in season, we recommend you use them to make this cake even more delicious.

Advance Preparation
Lemon Pudding/Filling (see page 289)

Special Equipment
2 9x1½-inch nonstick round baking pans

Temperature and Time
Bake at 325°F. for 25-30 minutes

Yield
16 servings

Nutrition per Serving
Calories: 169
Carbohydrates: 39 grams
Protein: 4 grams
Fat: Fat-Free*
Cholesterol: 0 milligrams
Sodium: 120 milligrams
Dietary Fiber: 2 grams

*All foods contain some fat. Less than
.5 gram of fat per serving is nutritionally
insignificant and considered to be
"Fat-Free."

lemon cream cake

ingredients:

1½ cups whole wheat pastry flour

1 teaspoon baking soda

¾ teaspoon cream of tartar

¾ cup honey

6 tablespoons frozen apple juice concentrate (defrosted)

1 teaspoon vanilla

⅛ teaspoon lemon extract

1 teaspoon finely grated lemon peel

1 egg white, unbeaten

½ cup unsweetened applesauce

1 egg white, lightly beaten

1 recipe Lemon Pudding/Filling

¼ cup + ¼ cup fruit-juice-sweetened strawberry and/or blueberry preserves, melted

½ cup sliced strawberries

½ cup blueberries (defrosted if frozen)

directions:

Preheat oven to 325°F. In large bowl, combine flour, baking soda and cream of tartar. Set aside.

In medium bowl, mix honey, juice concentrate, vanilla, lemon extract, lemon peel, 1 unbeaten egg white and applesauce. Stir into flour mixtureuntil **just** blended. Gently stir in 1 lightly beaten egg white. *Do not overmix.*

Spoon batter into 2 9x1½-inch nonstick round baking pans. Bake at 325°F. for 25-30 minutes, or until toothpick inserted in center comes out clean. Cool on wire racks for 10 minutes, and remove cakes from pans. Let cakes cool additional 20 minutes.

Prepare Lemon Pudding/Filling.

Fill cake with three-quarter cup Pudding between layers; drizzle one-quarter melted preserves over pudding. Place second layer over preserves; spread remaining Pudding over top.

Next place sliced strawberries and blueberries over top; drizzle remaining melted preserves over berries. Chill for a minimum of 30 minutes and serve.

This light airy cake gets its distinctive citrus flavor from a combination of fruit-juice-sweetened orange marmalade and mandarin oranges.

Mandarin oranges are much closer cousins to the tangerine and the tangelo than they are to the navel orange. All three peel and section easily.

Like all citrus fruits, mandarin oranges are high in vitamin C and are an excellent source of vitamin B1.

FAT-FREE   DAIRY FREE

Special Equipment

10-inch nonstick tube pan

Temperature and Time

Bake at 325°F. for 55-60 minutes

Yield

14 servings

Nutrition per Serving

Calories: 134
Carbohydrates: 30 grams
Protein: 4 grams
Fat: Fat-Free*
Cholesterol: 0 milligrams
Sodium: 45 milligrams
Dietary Fiber: 2 grams

*All foods contain some fat. Less than .5 gram of fat per serving is nutritionally insignificant and considered to be "Fat-Free."

mandarin chiffon cake

ingredients:

10 egg whites

1 teaspoon cream of tartar

1 cup pure maple syrup

1 cup whole wheat pastry flour

1 teaspoon vanilla

1 teaspoon finely grated orange peel

1 teaspoon orange extract

⅓ cup fruit-juice-sweetened orange marmalade, melted

2 cans (10½ ounces each) juice-packed mandarin oranges, drained

directions:

Preheat oven to 325°F. In large bowl, with electric mixer, beat egg whites at moderate speed until frothy. Add cream of tartar and beat whites until they hold soft peaks. Gradually beat in maple syrup at high speed and beat whites until stiff.

In medium bowl, mix together flour, vanilla, orange peel and orange extract and gently fold into egg whites. Spoon batter into ungreased 10-inch nonstick fluted tube pan. Cut through batter with serrated knife to remove air bubbles.

Bake at 325°F. for 55-60 minutes, or until toothpick inserted in center comes out clean. Remove from oven, and invert cake pan on wire rack until completely cooled, approximately 30 minutes. To remove cake from pan, loosen edges with metal spatula.

When cake is completely cooled, slice in half horizontally using serrated knife; set aside.

Mix melted preserves and mandarin oranges. Fill cake layer with half orange mixture. Place halves together and spread remaining orange mixture evenly on top.

M ocha is the very popular flavor combination of coffee and chocolate. Until
recently, we have been like many health-
conscious people and avoided mocha because
both coffee and chocolate contain caffeine,
and chocolate usually contains both sugar and
fat as well.

This recipe shares our secret with you for
enjoying the distinctive mocha flavor in a
healthy form by using unsweetened cocoa
powder and dry coffee substitute in place of
chocolate and coffee. So you can get all the
enjoyment of mocha, while avoiding the caffeine, sugar and fat.

To add even greater flavor excitement, we
combine the mocha flavor with mandarin
oranges. The combination of mocha with
mandarin oranges not only tastes wonderful,
but the colors even complement each other so
this cake looks as exciting as it tastes.

If you don't want to use cocoa powder in this
recipe, you can substitute carob powder.
Although the two ingredients aren't related,
they can be substituted for each other, with a
one-to-one ratio.

FAT-
FREE

Advance Preparation

Creamy Mocha Frosting
(see page 161)

Special Equipment

2 9x1½-inch nonstick
round baking pans

Temperature and Time

Bake at 325°F. for 15-20
minutes

Yield

16 servings

Nutrition per Serving

Calories: 204
Carbohydrates: 48 grams
Protein: 5 grams
Fat: Fat-Free*
Cholesterol: 0 milligrams
Sodium: 100 milligrams
Dietary Fiber: 2 grams

*All foods contain some fat. Less than
.5 gram of fat per serving is nutritionally
insignificant and considered to be
"Fat-Free."

mocha mandarin torte

ingredients:

1¾ cups whole wheat pastry flour

¾ teaspoon cream of tartar

¾ teaspoon baking soda

1 teaspoon cinnamon

⅓ cup unsweetened cocoa powder
  or carob powder

1 tablespoon dry coffee
  substitute beverage

¾ cup unsweetened applesauce

1 jar (2½ ounces) prune
  baby food puree

1¼ cups honey

3 egg whites, lightly beaten

1 teaspoon vanilla

¼ teaspoon orange extract

1 can (10½ ounces) juice-packed
  mandarin oranges, drained

1 recipe Creamy Mocha Frosting

directions:

Preheat oven to 325°F. In large bowl, sift together flour, cream of tartar, baking soda, cinnamon, cocoa or carob powder and coffee substitute. Set aside.

In medium bowl, combine applesauce, prune puree, honey, egg whites, vanilla and orange extracts. Gently stir into flour mixture and mix until **just** blended. *Do not overmix.*

Spoon batter into 2 9x1½-inch nonstick round baking pans. Bake at 325°F for 15-20 minutes, or until toothpick inserted in center comes out clean. Cool on wire rack for 15 minutes, and remove from pan.

Let cake cool additional 20 minutes. Reserve 12 mandarin orange sections; coarsely chop remaining oranges.

Prepare Mocha Frosting.

To assemble torte, spread half cup frosting over bottom layer, followed by chopped mandarin oranges and another layer of half cup frosting on top and arrange remaining mandarin oranges around edge of cake. Serve cake chilled.

Neapolitan ice cream, with its colorful layers of different flavored ice cream is a childhood favorite that many health-conscious adults have long since given up. We've updated this old favorite in the form of a Fat-Free cake.

Frozen Fruit Creme (see page 285), and Creamy Vanilla Frosting (see page 167) are used to create a fancy-style party cake.

To get the most flavor from this cake, allow it to soften in the refrigerator for 15 minutes before you serve it, so that it will reach the correct consistency.

If you don't want to use cocoa powder in this recipe, you can substitute carob powder. Although the two ingredients aren't related, they can be substituted for each other, with a one-to-one ratio.

Serving Suggestion:

For a topping, try the Strawberry Glaze (see page 181).

Advance Preparation

Frozen Fruit Creme (see page 285)
Creamy Vanilla Frosting (see page 167)

Special Equipment

9-inch nonstick springform pan

Temperature and Time

Bake crust at 325°F. for 15 minutes

Yield

12 servings

Nutrition per Serving

Calories: 189
Carbohydrates: 42 grams
Protein: 6 grams
Fat: Fat-Free*
Cholesterol: 0 milligrams
Sodium: 95 milligrams
Dietary Fiber: 2 grams

*All foods contain some fat. Less than .5 gram of fat per serving is nutritionally insignificant and considered to be "Fat-Free."

neapolitan ice cream cake

ingredients:

¾ cup whole wheat pastry flour

2 tablespoons unsweetened cocoa powder or carob powder

¼ teaspoon cream of tartar

¼ teaspoon baking soda

½ teaspoon cinnamon

1 jar (2½ ounces) prune baby food puree

½ cup honey and 1 tablespoon honey

1 egg white, lightly beaten

½ teaspoon vanilla

1 recipe Frozen Fruit Creme

1 recipe Creamy Vanilla Frosting

directions:

Preheat oven to 325°F. For crust, in medium bowl, sift together flour, cocoa or carob powder, cream of tartar, baking soda and cinnamon. In small bowl, combine prune puree, honey, egg white and vanilla. Gently stir into flour mixture.

Pour mixture into bottom of 9-inch nonstick springform pan. Bake crust for 15 minutes. Let cool while preparing filling.

For filling, prepare Frozen Fruit Creme using fresh or frozen strawberries and fruit-juice-sweetened strawberry preserves. Spoon into prepared crust, and place in freezer for 1 hour.

Prepare Creamy Vanilla Frosting and spread on top of filling. Place in freezer until entire ice cream cake is firm, approximately 1 additional hour. If made well in advance, remove from freezer about 15 minutes before serving for best texture.

I f you like the clean, refreshing taste of oranges, this is the recipe for you.

Many orange cakes are really just a sponge cake with orange-flavored filling holding the layers together. This one provides plenty of real zesty orange flavor from a combination of orange juice concentrate, orange extract and grated orange peel mixed right into the batter.

What makes this cake more remarkable is the fact that it is Fat-Free, so you can enjoy it anytime without the slightest bit of guilt.

Serving Suggestion:

For even more flavor, fill and glaze this cake with one-quarter cup of melted fruit-juice-sweetened orange marmalade per layer.

FAT-FREE   DAIRY FREE

Special Equipment

2 9x1½-inch nonstick round baking pans

Temperature and Time

Bake at 325°F. for 35-40 minutes

Yield

16 servings

Nutrition per Serving

Calories: 193
Carbohydrates: 46 grams
Protein: 4 grams
Fat: Fat-Free*
Cholesterol: 0 milligrams
Sodium: 135 milligrams
Dietary Fiber: 3 grams

*All foods contain some fat. Less than .5 gram of fat per serving is nutritionally insignificant and considered to be "Fat-Free."

orange cake

ingredients:

2½ cups whole wheat pastry flour

1½ teaspoons baking soda

1½ teaspoons cream of tartar

1½ cups honey

½ cup frozen orange juice concentrate (defrosted)

2 teaspoons vanilla

¼ teaspoon orange extract

1½ tablespoons finely grated orange peel

2 egg whites, unbeaten

2 jars (4 ounces each) apricot baby food puree

2 egg whites, lightly beaten

directions:

Preheat oven to 325°F. In large mixing bowl, combine flour, baking soda and cream of tartar. Set aside.

In medium bowl, mix honey, juice concentrate, vanilla, orange extract, orange peel, 2 unbeaten egg whites and apricot puree. Stir into flour mixture until **just** blended. Gently stir in 2 lightly beaten egg whites. *Do not overmix.*

Spoon batter into 2 9x1½-inch nonstick round baking pans. Bake at 325°F. for 35-40 minutes, or until toothpick inserted in center comes out clean. Cool on wire racks for 10 minutes, and remove cakes from pans.

Although we normally prefer fresh fruit to canned, pineapple recipes are the exception, because canned pineapple actually works better in baking than the fresh version. Fortunately, canned pineapple retains most of the nutrients of fresh, making this recipe as healthy as it is delicious. We recommend using pineapple packed in its own juice, without any added sugar.

Serving Suggestion:

The way we like to serve this cake is with a glaze of fruit-juice-sweetened apricot preserves. It highlights the flavors of the cake perfectly and looks beautiful.

FAT-FREE   **DAIRY FREE**

Special Equipment

2 9x1½-inch nonstick round baking pans

Temperature and Time

Bake at 325°F. for 40-45 minutes

Yield

16 servings

Nutrition per Serving

Calories: 173
Carbohydrates: 41 grams
Protein: 4 grams
Fat: Fat-Free*
Cholesterol: 0 milligrams
Sodium: 135 milligrams
Dietary Fiber: 3 grams

*All foods contain some fat. Less than .5 gram of fat per serving is nutritionally insignificant and considered to be "Fat-Free."

pineapple cake

ingredients:

2½ cups whole wheat pastry flour

1½ teaspoons baking soda

1½ teaspoons cream of tartar

1 teaspoon cinnamon

1 cup and 3 tablespoons honey

⅓ cup frozen pineapple juice concentrate (defrosted)

2 teaspoons vanilla

2 egg whites, unbeaten

1 can (8 ounces) juice-packed crushed pineapple, well drained

2 jars (4 ounces each) apricot with tapioca baby food puree

2 egg whites, lightly beaten

directions:

Preheat oven to 325°F. In large mixing bowl, mix together flour, baking soda, cream of tartar and cinnamon. Set aside.

In medium bowl, mix honey, juice concentrate, vanilla, 2 unbeaten egg whites, drained pineapple and apricot puree. Stir into flour mixture until **just** blended. Gently stir in 2 lightly beaten egg whites. *Do not overmix.*

Spoon batter into 2 9x1½-inch nonstick round baking pans. Bake at 325°F. for 40-45 minutes, or until toothpick inserted in the center comes out clean. Cool on wire racks for 10 minutes, and remove cakes from pans.

T his famous Viennese cake was created over 150 years ago by Franz Sacher for Prince Metternich of Austria. It is renowned for its dense chocolate fudge flavor.

Of course, the original version is far from low in calories and fat, with 6 ounces of chocolate, ¾ cup butter, 1 cup of sugar and 6 egg yolks.

So it was a challenge to create a healthy version of this classic without any added fat or high fat ingredients.

The result? We believe you will find this to be so deliciously dense and full of fudge flavor that it's hard to believe it's Fat-Free. Even Franz, himself, would approve. The cake is completed with Coco Frosting (see page 151).

If you don't want to use cocoa powder in this recipe, you can substitute carob powder. Although the two ingredients aren't related, they can be substituted for each other, with a one-to-one ratio.

Serving Suggestion:

If desired, serve with La Creme Whipped Topping (see page 175).

Advance Preparation

Coco Frosting (see page 151)

Special Equipment

9-inch nonstick springform pan

Temperature and Time

Bake at 325°F. for 45-50 minutes

Yield

16 servings

Nutrition per Serving

Calories: 197
Carbohydrates: 48 grams
Protein: 3 grams
Fat: Fat-Free*
Cholesterol: 0 milligrams
Sodium: 60 milligrams
Dietary Fiber: 2 grams

All foods contain some fat. Less than .5 gram of fat per serving is nutritionally insignificant and considered to be "Fat-Free."

sachertorte

ingredients:

1¾ cups whole wheat pastry flour

¼ cup unsweetened cocoa powder
or carob powder

½ teaspoon cream of tartar

½ teaspoon baking soda

1 teaspoon cinnamon

½ cup unsweetened applesauce

1 cup and 3 tablespoons honey

3 egg whites, lightly beaten

1 teaspoon vanilla

⅓ cup + ⅓ cup fruit-juice-sweetened
apricot preserves, melted

1 recipe Coco Frosting

directions:

Preheat oven to 325°F. In large bowl, sift together flour, cocoa or carob powder, cream of tartar, baking soda and cinnamon. Set aside.

In medium bowl, combine applesauce, honey, egg whites and vanilla. Gently stir into flour mixture and mix until **just** blended. ***Do not over-mix.*** Swirl in one-third cup apricot preserves.

Spread mixture into 9-inch nonstick springform pan. Bake at 325°F. for 45-50 minutes, or until toothpick inserted in center comes out clean. Cool on wire rack for 20 minutes, and remove from pan. While cake is still warm, spread remaining one-third cup preserves over top of cake.

Let cake cool additional 20 minutes and prepare Coco Frosting.

Drizzle Frosting over top of cake.

There's an old joke that says there's really only one fruit cake, and it gets passed around from person to person during the holiday season without ever being eaten.

Many people do not like the heavy taste of traditional fruit cake, and even those who do often avoid it because of all the fat and calories it contains.

This is a lighter, healthy alternative to fruit cake that everyone will enjoy. Like fruit cake, it features dried fruit, but that's where the resemblance ends. This spice cake is Fat-Free and much lower in calories.

We feature dried fruit in this recipe both for its wonderful flavor and for its nutritional value. Because the water has been removed from dried fruit, ounce for ounce, it contains as many as seven times the nutrients of fresh fruit. So it's a wonderful source of quick energy when you need a pick-me-up.

Serving Suggestion:

You may want to fill and glaze this cake with one-quarter cup of melted fruit-juice-sweetened orange marmalade per layer. Or try our Creamy Cinnamon Sauce (see page 155), or Creamy Maple Sauce (see page 159).

FAT-FREE   DAIRY FREE

Special Equipment

2 9x1½-inch nonstick round baking pans

Temperature and Time

Bake at 325°F. for 40-45 minutes

Yield

16 servings

Nutrition per Serving

Calories: 220
Carbohydrates: 54 grams
Protein: 4 grams
Fat: Fat-Free*
Cholesterol: 0 milligrams
Sodium: 140 milligrams
Dietary Fiber: 3 grams

All foods contain some fat. Less than .5 gram of fat per serving is nutritionally insignificant and considered to be "Fat-Free."

spice cake

ingredients:

2½ cups whole wheat pastry flour

1½ teaspoons baking soda

1½ teaspoons cream of tartar

1 teaspoon cinnamon

½ teaspoon ground cloves

1 teaspoon ground nutmeg

½ teaspoon ground allspice

1½ cups honey

⅓ cup frozen orange juice concentrate (defrosted)

1 teaspoon vanilla

2 egg whites, unbeaten

½ cup unsweetened applesauce

1 jar (2½ ounces) prune baby food puree

½ cup raisins

½ cup chopped dates

¾ cup chopped dried apples

2 egg whites, lightly beaten

directions:

Preheat oven to 325°F. In large mixing bowl, combine flour, baking soda, cream of tartar, cinnamon, cloves, nutmeg and allspice. Set aside.

In medium bowl, mix honey, juice concentrate, vanilla, 2 unbeaten egg whites, applesauce, prune puree, raisins, dates and dried apples. Stir into flour mixture and mix until **just** blended. Gently stir in 2 lightly beaten egg whites. ***Do not overmix.***

Spoon batter into 2 9x1½-inch nonstick round baking pans. Bake at 325°F. for 40-45 minutes, or until toothpick inserted in center comes out clean. Cool on wire racks for 10 minutes, and remove cakes from pans.

Traditional angel food cake has always been low in fat because it is primarily made from egg whites. But the whipped cream it is often served with turns it into a high-fat dessert.

In this recipe, we keep the egg whites, and show you how to add plenty of flavor without fat by finishing the angel food cake with our Fluffy Lemon Frosting (see page 171) and strawberries.

Besides being everyone's favorite berry, strawberries may help to diminish the effects of second-hand smoke.

Researchers at Case Western Reserve University studied the effects of a naturally occurring chemical called ellagitannin contained in strawberries. They found that ellagic acid may block harmful chemicals from the environment from converting into damaging substances once they are inside the body.

Serving Suggestion:

Because of its light and airy nature, we suggest that you garnish this cake right before serving. If you garnish it ahead of time, the cake will fall. Also, if you have a cake divider, make your slices with it instead of a knife.

FAT-FREE   GREAT FOR KIDS

Advance Preparation

Fluffy Lemon Frosting (see page 171)

Special Equipment

10-inch nonstick tube pan

Temperature and Time

Bake at 325°F. for 45-50 minutes

Yield

14 servings

Nutrition per Serving

Calories: 114
Carbohydrates: 25 grams
Protein: 3 grams
Fat: Fat-Free*
Cholesterol: 0 milligrams
Sodium: 45 milligrams
Dietary Fiber: 0 grams

*All foods contain some fat. Less than .5 gram of fat per serving is nutritionally insignificant and considered to be "Fat-Free."

strawberry angel food cake

ingredients:

10 egg whites

1 teaspoon cream of tartar

1 cup pure maple syrup

1¼ cups whole wheat pastry flour

1 teaspoon vanilla

¼ teaspoon lemon extract

1 recipe Fluffy Lemon Frosting

1 cup fresh strawberries, sliced

directions:

Preheat oven to 325°F. In large bowl, with electric mixer, beat egg whites at moderate speed until frothy. Add cream of tartar and beat egg whites until they hold soft peaks. Gradually beat in maple syrup at high speed and beat whites until stiff.

In medium bowl, mix together flour, vanilla and lemon extracts, and gently fold into egg whites. Spoon batter into ungreased 10-inch non-stick fluted tube pan. Cut through batter with serrated knife to remove air bubbles.

Bake at 325°F. for 45-50 minutes, or until toothpick inserted in center comes out clean. Remove from oven, and invert cake pan on cooling rack until completely cooled, approximately 30 minutes. To remove cake from pan, loosen edges with metal spatula.

Prepare Fluffy Lemon Frosting.

When cake is completely cooled, slice in half horizontally using serrated knife. Fill cake layer with half Frosting and strawberries, reserving some for garnish. Place halves together and spread remaining Frosting on top; garnish with reserved strawberries.

Breads, Muffins & Cupcakes Section

W e were motivated to write this book because of our anger and indignation over the amount of fat "hidden" in foods that are normally considered to be "healthy." A good example of this can be found in muffins. Most people think of a muffin as a healthy food to start the day, filled with beneficial fiber and the nutrition of fruit. But the traditional banana muffin recipe is made with oil, milk and a whole egg, so a single muffin can contain 7 grams of fat. Compare that to the version we've developed that is fat-free.

Serving (1 muffin)	Fat (grams)	Calories
Traditional Blueberry Muffin recipe	7g	184
Baking Without Fat **Blueberry Muffin recipe**	**Fat-Free**	**99**

You'll save similar amounts of fat and calories with the other recipes in this section. For example, the traditional corn bread recipe contains 8 grams of fat per serving, or 10 times more fat than the version in this book that has one gram of fat.

C orn bread is a traditional southern favorite with a slightly sweet taste. The only problem with corn bread is the amount of fat used to make it. In fact, one popular variation calls for frying 5 slices of bacon and using the fat drippings as the oil to make corn bread. This recipe we developed combines apples, raisins and honey for a sweeter version of corn bread that you can enjoy as a dessert. Since it contains no added fat and no cholesterol, you can enjoy it without feeling guilty about the delicious taste.

Serving Suggestion:

Try serving this corn bread with a dab of honey on the side.

**GREAT
FOR KIDS**

Temperature and Time

Bake at 400°F. for 30 minutes

Yield

8 servings

Nutrition per Serving

Calories: 200
Carbohydrates: 44 grams
Protein: 5 grams
Fat: 1 gram
Calories from Fat: 4%
Cholesterol: 0 milligrams
Sodium: 220 milligrams
Dietary Fiber: 3 grams

apple raisin corn bread

ingredients:

1 cup corn meal

½ cup whole wheat pastry flour

1 teaspoon baking soda

1 teaspoon cream of tartar

3 egg whites, unbeaten

1¼ cups lowfat buttermilk

⅓ cup honey

1 cup chopped baking apples, peeled
(approximately 2 apples)

½ cup raisins

directions:

Preheat oven to 400°F. In large mixing bowl, combine corn meal, flour, baking soda and cream of tartar. Set aside.

In medium bowl, combine egg whites, buttermilk, honey, apples and raisins; mix until blended. Stir into corn meal mixture until just blended. Pour into an 8-inch square ovenproof glass baking dish.

Bake at 400°F. for 30 minutes, or until nicely browned.

Bananas are an excellent source of potassium, which is important for the maintenance of body fluid, acid-base balance and the transmission of nerve impulses.

A delicious way to enjoy the benefits of bananas is in muffins. Here is a healthy version made without any added fat, so you save 6 grams of fat in every muffin, compared with the traditional recipe.

Remember that the riper the banana, the sweeter the muffin.

WHEAT   GREAT
FREE   FOR KIDS

Special Equipment

nonstick muffin pan

Temperature and Time

Bake at 350°F. for 25 minutes

Yield

12 servings

Nutrition per Serving

Calories: 144
Carbohydrates: 31 grams
Protein: 3 grams
Fat: 1 gram
Calories from Fat: 6%
Cholesterol: 0 milligrams
Sodium: 130 milligrams
Dietary Fiber: 3 grams

apricot filled banana muffins

ingredients:

1¾ cups rolled oats

½ cup oat bran

1 teaspoon baking soda

1 teaspoon cream of tartar

¾ teaspoon cinnamon

⅛ teaspoon ground nutmeg

¾ cup pureed banana (approximately 1½ ripe medium bananas)

⅓ cup honey

2 tablespoons pure maple syrup

1 teaspoon vanilla

½ cup nonfat milk

3 egg whites, lightly beaten

¼ cup fruit-juice-sweetened apricot preserves

directions:

Preheat oven to 350°F. Pulse rolled oats and oat bran in food processor for 10 seconds. In medium bowl, combine oat mixture, baking soda, cream of tartar, cinnamon and nutmeg; mix well. Set aside.

In small bowl, combine pureed banana, honey, maple syrup, vanilla and milk; pour into cereal mixture. Stir until **just** blended. Gently mix in egg whites. *Do not overmix.*

Using nonstick muffin pan, fill each muffin cup with batter, top each with 1 teaspoon preserves. Bake at 350°F. for 20-25 minutes. Cool on wire rack for 10 minutes, and remove muffins from pan.

This version of the popular blueberry muffin is made with oats and oat bran rather than wheat flour, so it can be enjoyed even by people with a wheat sensitivity or allergy.

Even if you are not sensitive to wheat, we recommend that you also include oat bran in your diet because it is rich in a different kind of fiber than wheat bran. The predominant fiber in oat bran is water soluble. Studies have shown that a low fat diet rich in soluble fiber can help lower blood cholesterol levels to help you maintain a healthier heart and circulatory system.

FAT-FREE   WHEAT FREE   GREAT FOR KIDS

Special Equipment

nonstick muffin pan

Temperature and Time

Bake at 350°F. for 25 minutes

Yield

12 servings

Nutrition per Serving

Calories: 99
Carbohydrates: 22 grams
Protein: 2 grams
Fat: Fat-Free*
Cholesterol: 0 milligrams
Sodium: 100 milligrams
Dietary Fiber: 2 grams

*All foods contain some fat. Less than .5 gram of fat per serving is nutritionally insignificant and considered to be "Fat-Free."

blueberry muffins

ingredients:

1¾ cups rolled oats

½ cup oat bran

¾ teaspoon baking soda

½ teaspoon cinnamon

¾ cup unsweetened applesauce

½ cup honey

1 teaspoon vanilla

½ cup nonfat milk

3 egg whites, lightly beaten

1 cup frozen blueberries (defrosted and well drained)

directions:

Preheat oven to 350°F. Pulse rolled oats and oat bran in food processor for 10 seconds. Reserve 2 tablespoons oat mixture; in medium bowl, combine remaining oat mixture with baking soda and cinnamon; mix well. Set aside.

In small bowl, combine applesauce, honey, vanilla and milk; pour into oat mixture. Stir until **just** blended. Gently mix in egg whites. *Do not overmix.*

Dust well drained and dried blueberries with 2 tablespoons reserved oat mixture; gently fold blueberries into batter. Divide mixture evenly into nonstick muffin pan and bake at 350°F. for 20-25 minutes, or until toothpick inserted in center comes out clean. Cool on wire rack for 10 minutes, and remove muffins from pan.

When you bake without fat, you should be aware that the ingredients may not look or act the same way they do when you use fat in the form of shortening.

For example, the batter for this corn bread will appear watery at first, but it will firm up as it cooks in the oven.

We recommend using stoneground corn meal in this recipe because it provides the toothsome texture of classic cornbread. And if you have a choice between yellow corn and white corn, you should be aware that yellow corn is a better source of magnesium and beta carotene.

As you probably know, beta carotene is being recognized as a very important nutrient for the 1990's. Studies have shown that a low fat diet which contains foods rich in beta carotene may reduce the risk of heart disease and some forms of cancer.

Serving Suggestion:

Try serving this corn bread with a dab of honey on the side.

GREAT FOR KIDS

Temperature and Time

Bake at 400°F. for 30 minutes

Yield

8 servings

Nutrition per Serving

Calories: 155
Carbohydrates: 32 grams
Protein: 5 grams
Fat: 1 gram
Calories from Fat: 6%
Cholesterol: 0 milligrams
Sodium: 220 milligrams
Dietary Fiber: 2 grams

corn bread

ingredients:

1 cup corn meal
½ cup whole wheat pastry flour
1 teaspoon baking soda
1 teaspoon cream of tartar

1¼ cups lowfat buttermilk
3 egg whites, unbeaten
⅓ cup honey

directions:

Preheat oven to 400°F. In large mixing bowl, combine corn meal, flour, baking soda and cream of tartar. Set aside.

In small bowl, combine buttermilk, egg whites and honey. Stir into corn meal mixture until just blended. Pour into an 8-inch square ovenproof glass baking dish.

Bake at 400°F. for 30 minutes, or until toothpick inserted in center comes out clean. Cool on wire rack for 10 minutes, and remove corn bread from pan.

The "secret" to this recipe is using a ripe banana to lend a creamy texture and natural sweetness in place of fat and refined sugar. The banana also complements the chocolate flavor of the cocoa powder to produce a rich flavored cupcake that is fat-free.

This recipe gives you the option of using cocoa powder if you're a chocolate lover, or substituting carob powder. Although the two ingredients aren't related, they can be substituted one-for-one for each other.

FAT-FREE   **GREAT FOR KIDS**

Advance Preparation

Coco Frosting
(see page 151)

Special Equipment

nonstick muffin pan

Temperature and Time

Bake at 325°F. for 35-40 minutes

Yield

12 servings

Nutrition per Serving

Calories: 164
Carbohydrates: 39 grams
Protein: 3 grams
Fat: Fat-Free*
Cholesterol: 0 milligrams
Sodium: 65 milligrams
Dietary Fiber: 2 grams

*All foods contain some fat. Less than .5 gram of fat per serving is nutritionally insignificant and considered to be "Fat-Free."

frosted coco cupcakes

ingredients:

1½ cups whole wheat pastry flour

¼ cup unsweetened cocoa powder
or carob powder

½ teaspoon cinnamon

½ teaspoon cream of tartar

½ teaspoon baking soda

1 ripe medium banana, mashed
(½ cup)

¾ cup unsweetened applesauce

1 cup honey

2 egg whites, lightly beaten

1 teaspoon vanilla

¾ cup Coco Frosting

directions:

Preheat oven to 325°F. In medium bowl, sift together flour, cocoa or carob powder, cinnamon, cream of tartar and baking soda. Set aside.

In separate medium bowl, beat together banana, applesauce, honey, egg whites and vanilla. Stir into flour mixture, and mix until **just** blended. ***Do not overmix.*** Divide mixture evenly into nonstick muffin pan (fill each cup almost to top).

Bake at 325°F. for 35-40 minutes. Cupcakes are done when toothpick inserted in the center comes out clean. Cool on wire rack for 10 minutes, and remove muffins from pan.

Top with Coco Frosting.

When you grate fresh ginger it isn't necessary to remove the skin, unless it is shriveled.

In our gingerbread recipe, we use both fresh and dried ginger. This may seem odd at first, but remember that dried and fresh ginger have such different tastes that one can't be used as a substitute for the other.

When you buy fresh ginger, look for younger roots, since the older ones can be quite fibrous and difficult to use. Buy a finger-long section from the larger main root. When you break off the piece you need, there should be the pungent odor of ginger, as well as moisture where the break occurred. If it isn't this fresh, don't buy it.

Fresh ginger will keep in the refrigerator for a number of weeks. Ginger is a bit like cheese in that it can develop a blue mold and still be safe to use. Simply cut the moldy section off and use the rest.

Serving Suggestion:

For a real treat, top this gingerbread with either La Creme Whipped Topping (see page 175) or Creamy Maple Sauce (see page 159).

FAT-FREE   **DAIRY FREE**   **GREAT FOR KIDS**

Special Equipment

8-inch square ovenproof glass baking dish

Temperature and Time

Bake at 325°F. for 35-40 minutes

Yield

16 servings

Nutrition per Serving

Calories: 98
Carbohydrates: 23 grams
Protein: 2 grams
Fat: Fat-Free*
Cholesterol: 0 milligrams
Sodium: 55 milligrams
Dietary Fiber: 2 grams

All foods contain some fat. Less than .5 gram of fat per serving is nutritionally insignificant and considered to be "Fat-Free."

gingerbread

ingredients:

1¾ cups whole wheat pastry flour

½ teaspoon baking soda

½ teaspoon cream of tartar

1 teaspoon ground ginger

1 teaspoon cinnamon

⅛ teaspoon ground cloves

1 jar (4 ounces) pear
baby food puree

1 jar (2½ ounces) prune
baby food puree

1 teaspoon grated fresh ginger

1 teaspoon finely grated orange peel

½ cup honey

¼ cup molasses

2 egg whites, lightly beaten

½ cup boiling water

directions:

Preheat oven to 325°F. In large bowl, combine flour, baking soda, cream of tartar, ginger, cinnamon and cloves. Set aside.

In medium bowl, mix together pear puree, prune puree, ginger, orange peel, honey, molasses, egg whites and boiling water. Gently stir into flour mixture. With electric mixer, beat at medium high speed for 1 minute, or until well blended.

Pour into 8-inch square ovenproof glass baking dish. Bake at 325°F. for 35-40 minutes, or until nicely browned. Cool on wire rack for 15 minutes. Cut into squares.

Cookies & Bars Section

We created this book to meet the needs of health-conscious individuals in today's busy world. We recognize that there are times when you need good tasting, nutritious and satisfying foods that you can take along with you as a light meal, or to provide a between meals, quick energy "pick-me-up."

These fruit bars and cookies can meet your needs. Unlike most cookies that simply supply "empty" calories from fat and refined sugar, the recipes in this section are nutritious foods that you can feel good about enjoying.

Of course, we've kept in mind the fact that you eat cookies and fruit bars for enjoyment. So in addition to being nutritious, these recipes are also good tasting.

By cutting out all the added fat, refined sugar and white flour, and by replacing them with fruit purees, fruit juices and whole grain pastry flour, we have created delicious, healthy recipes that you can use for dessert, as high energy snacks, or even as a light meal that you can take with you.

By cutting the fat, we also cut calories. For example, the traditional recipe for Oatmeal Raisin Cookies has 51% more calories than the version you'll find in this section. Here is a comparison of the fat and calories in the two recipes:

Serving (1 cookie)	Fat (grams)	Calories
Traditional Oatmeal Raisin Cookie	6g	145
Baking Without Fat **Oatmeal Raisin Cookie**	1g	**96**

H ere is a recipe that looks much more difficult to make than it really is. It's actually
easy to achieve the lovely "black and white"
effect by using a dull-edged knife to swirl
together the ingredients.

One of the "secrets" of this recipe is the way
we use prune puree as a substitute for butter.
The rich prune flavor accents the chocolate
flavor of the cocoa.

You have the option of substituting carob
powder for the unsweetened cocoa powder if
you have an aversion to cocoa. Although the
two ingredients aren't related, they can be substituted one-for-one for each other.

FAT-
FREE

GREAT
FOR KIDS

Advance Preparation

Day before drain 1 carton
(32 ounces) plain, nonfat
yogurt to make approx-
imately 1 cup yogurt
cheese (see page 129)

Special Equipment

9x13-inch nonstick baking
dish

Temperature and Time

Bake at 325°F. for
45 minutes

Yield

36 servings

Nutrition per Serving

Calories: 82
Carbohydrates: 19 grams
Protein: 2 grams
Fat: Fat-Free*
Cholesterol: 0 milligrams
Sodium: 30 milligrams
Dietary Fiber: 1 gram

*All foods contain some fat. Less than
.5 gram of fat per serving is nutritionally
insignificant and considered to be
"Fat-Free."

black & white brownies

ingredients:

Brownie Batter

1½ cups whole wheat pastry flour

¼ cup unsweetened cocoa powder or carob powder

1 teaspoon cinnamon

½ teaspoon cream of tartar

½ teaspoon baking soda

2 jars (2½ ounces each) prune baby food puree

1 cup honey and 3 tablespoons honey

2 egg whites, lightly beaten

1¼ teaspoons vanilla

Yogurt Batter

1 cup nonfat yogurt cheese

¾ cup maple syrup

1 tablespoon whole wheat pastry flour

2 teaspoons vanilla

directions:

Preheat oven to 325°F. For brownie batter, in large bowl, sift together flour, cocoa or carob powder, cinnamon, cream of tartar and baking soda. Set aside.

In medium bowl, combine prune puree, honey, egg whites and vanilla. Stir into brownie mixture and mix until **just** blended. *Do not overmix.*

For yogurt batter, in separate medium bowl, with electric mixer, beat together yogurt cheese, maple syrup, flour and vanilla until well blended.

Pour brownie batter on bottom of 9x13-inch nonstick baking dish. Add yogurt batter. Swirl both batters together with knife to marbleize.

Bake at 325°F. for 45 minutes. Cool on wire rack for 15 minutes, and remove from pan.

The he secret to the incredible texture of these brownies is the prune puree. Prunes are a fruit that people sometimes ridicule, but they are both nutritious and an ideal match for the taste of chocolate. The flavors of the two seem to complement each other beautifully. The prune puree also provides a rich, creamy texture. You'll swear it tastes like there's butter in this recipe, but there isn't.

As in all our recipes that feature a chocolate taste, you have the option of substituting carob powder for unsweetened cocoa powder. Although the two ingredients aren't related, they can be substituted one-for-one for each other.

FAT-FREE   **DAIRY FREE**   **GREAT FOR KIDS**

Special Equipment

8x11x2-inch nonstick baking pan

Temperature and Time

Bake at 325°F. for 35-40 minutes

Yield

24 servings

Nutrition per Serving

Calories: 87
Carbohydrates: 21 grams
Protein: 2 grams
Fat: Fat-Free*
Cholesterol: 0 milligrams
Sodium: 35 milligrams
Dietary Fiber: 1 gram

*All foods contain some fat. Less than .5 gram of fat per serving is nutritionally insignificant and considered to be "Fat-Free."

brownies

ingredients:

1½ cups whole wheat pastry flour

⅓ cup unsweetened cocoa powder
   or carob powder

1 teaspoon cinnamon

½ teaspoon cream of tartar

½ teaspoon baking soda

2 jars (2½ ounces each) prune
   baby food puree

¼ cup unsweetened applesauce

1 cup and 3 tablespoons honey

2 egg whites, lightly beaten

1½ teaspoons vanilla

directions:

Preheat oven to 325°F. In large bowl, sift together flour, cocoa or carob powder, cinnamon, cream of tartar and baking soda. Set aside.

In medium bowl, combine prune puree, applesauce, honey, egg whites and vanilla. Gently stir into flour mixture and mix until **just** blended. *Do not overmix.*

Spread mixture in 8x11x2-inch ovenproof glass baking dish. Bake at 325°F for 35-40 minutes, or until toothpick inserted in center comes out clean. Cool on wire rack for 15 minutes, and remove from pan.

FAT-FREE **DAIRY FREE** **GREAT FOR KIDS**

Please be aware that when you bake without fat, the ingredients don't react the way you may be accustomed to when you bake with fat. These cookies are a good example of that. The first time you bake them, you will probably think that they are not done after the 12 minutes indicated in the directions because they will still be very soft. So you will be tempted to bake them an extra few minutes, but don't! This will cause the bottoms of the cookies to burn. Remember that as these cookies cool, they will become firmer in texture.

If you enjoy a chewier cookie, try this recipe. The secret is in the crispy brown rice cereal we use. Brown rice provides better nutrition than white rice because it is unpolished, which means the bran layer – along with its vitamins and fiber – is not removed as it is with white rice.

Special Equipment

nonstick cookie sheet

Temperature and Time

Bake at 350°F. for
12 minutes

Yield

30 servings

Nutrition per Serving**

Calories: 197
Carbohydrates: 46 grams
Protein: 4 grams
Fat: Fat-Free***
Cholesterol: 0 milligrams
Sodium: 25 milligrams
Dietary Fiber: 2 grams

*We developed this recipe using Health Valley Brown Rice Fruit Lites Cereal.
**A serving is three cookies.
***All foods contain some fat. Less than .5 gram of fat per serving is nutritionally insignificant and considered to be "Fat-Free."

chewy spice cookies

ingredients:

1 cup whole wheat pastry flour

1¼ cups crisp brown rice cereal*

1 cup rolled oats

½ teaspoon baking soda

½ teaspoon cream of tartar

1 teaspoon cinnamon

½ teaspoon ground allspice

¼ teaspoon ground cloves

¼ teaspoon ground nutmeg

½ cup honey

½ cup frozen apple juice concentrate (defrosted)

1 jar (2½ ounces) prune baby food puree

1 teaspoon vanilla

½ cup raisins

directions:

Preheat oven to 350°F. In large bowl, combine flour, cereal, oats, baking soda, cream of tartar, cinnamon, allspice, cloves and nutmeg; mix well. Set aside.

In medium saucepan, combine honey, juice concentrate and prune puree. Bring to boil over medium high heat, stirring constantly; reduce heat and simmer 1 minute. Remove from heat and add vanilla and raisins. Gently stir into cereal mixture.

Drop batter by rounded teaspoons onto nonstick cookie sheet.

Bake at 350°F. for 12 minutes. Cookies may appear undercooked, they get crisper as they cool. Cool for 5 minutes, and remove cookies from sheet.

This cookie is a particular favorite with children. And parents can feel good about coco crispy treats because instead of being filled with saturated fat and refined sugar, they're full of healthy ingredients.

We use brown rice cereal in this recipe because brown rice is an intact grain. Everything that nature put into it is still there, including the fiber and two grams of protein per cup.

This recipe offers you the option of using either unsweetened cocoa powder if you're a chocolate lover, or carob powder. Although the two ingredients aren't related, they can be substituted for each other, with a one-to-one ratio.

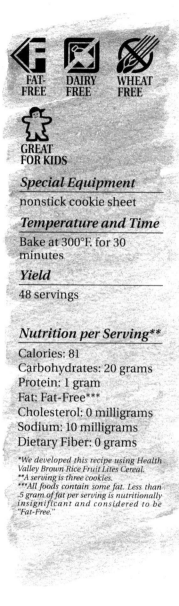

FAT-FREE DAIRY FREE WHEAT FREE

GREAT FOR KIDS

Special Equipment

nonstick cookie sheet

Temperature and Time

Bake at 300°F. for 30 minutes

Yield

48 servings

Nutrition per Serving**

Calories: 81
Carbohydrates: 20 grams
Protein: 1 gram
Fat: Fat-Free***
Cholesterol: 0 milligrams
Sodium: 10 milligrams
Dietary Fiber: 0 grams

*We developed this recipe using Health Valley Brown Rice Fruit Lites Cereal.
**A serving is three cookies.
***All foods contain some fat. Less than .5 gram of fat per serving is nutritionally insignificant and considered to be "Fat-Free."

coco crispy treats

ingredients:

2 egg whites, unbeaten

¾ cup pure maple syrup

1½ tablespoons unsweetened
   cocoa powder or carob powder

4 cups crisp brown rice cereal*

1 teaspoon almond extract

directions:

Preheat oven to 300°F. In large bowl, beat egg whites until soft peaks form. Gradually add maple syrup, and beat until egg whites are stiff. Gently stir in cocoa or carob powder, cereal and almond extract.

Drop batter by teaspoons onto nonstick cookie sheet.

Bake at 300°F. for 30 minutes, or until cookies are lightly browned. Cool on wire rack for about 5 minutes, or until cookies become firm. Remove immediately to prevent from sticking to sheet.

Judging by how quickly these cookies disappeared whenever we made them in our test kitchen, they are one of the most popular recipes in this book.

Keep in mind the first time you make them that the meringue will still appear very soft and not quite done even after it has turned brown. These cookies will get a crisper texture as they cool, so don't overbake them.

We recommend that you let these cookies cool before you attempt to remove them from the pan, otherwise they will tear. They are best enjoyed as soon as you remove them from the pan because they have a tendency to absorb the moisture from the air and get soggy if you let them sit for too long. Of course, everyone at Health Valley ate them so quickly that we never had a problem with them sitting around for too long.

One of the secrets to the taste of these cookies is using almond extract to get the unique flavor of almonds, without any of the fat.

FAT-FREE DAIRY FREE WHEAT FREE

GREAT FOR KIDS

Special Equipment
nonstick cookie sheet

Temperature and Time
Bake at 300°F. for 30 minutes

Yield
48 servings

Nutrition per Serving**
Calories: 79
Carbohydrates: 19 grams
Protein: 1 gram
Fat: Fat-Free***
Cholesterol: 0 milligrams
Sodium: 10 milligrams
Dietary Fiber: 0 grams

*We developed this recipe using Health Valley Brown Rice Fruit Lites Cereal.
**A serving is three cookies.
***All foods contain some fat. Less than .5 gram of fat per serving is nutritionally insignificant and considered to be "Fat-Free."

crispy rice treats

ingredients:

2 egg whites, unbeaten

¾ cup pure maple syrup

4 cups crisp brown rice cereal*

1 teaspoon almond extract

directions:

Preheat oven to 300°F. In large bowl, beat egg whites until soft peaks form. Gradually add maple syrup, and beat until egg whites are stiff. Gently fold in cereal and almond extract.

Drop batter by teaspoons onto nonstick cookie sheet (do not use non-stick cooking spray).

Bake at 300°F. for 30 minutes, or until cookies are lightly browned. Cool on wire rack for about 5 minutes, or until cookies become firm. Remove immediately to prevent from sticking to sheet.

If you have been looking for a treat to go into school lunches, this is it. These snack bars are not only popular with children, but moms love them too, because they're filled with real nutrition instead of refined sugar and fat. They're also extremely convenient because they can be baked in advance and stored in air-tight containers in the freezer. Then these bars can go right from the freezer into your child's lunch sack, and they will have thawed by the time your child is ready to enjoy them.

FAT-FREE **DAIRY FREE** **GREAT FOR KIDS**

Special Equipment

8x11x2-inch nonstick baking pan

Temperature and Time

Bake at 350°F. for 30-35 minutes

Yield

24 servings

Nutrition per Serving

Calories: 120
Carbohydrates: 28 grams
Protein: 2 grams
Fat: Fat-Free**
Cholesterol: 0 milligrams
Sodium: 30 milligrams
Dietary Fiber: 1 gram

*We developed this recipe using Health Valley Brown Rice Fruit Lites Cereal.
**All foods contain some fat. Less than .5 gram of fat per serving is nutritionally insignificant and considered to be "Fat-Free."

date filled cookie bars

ingredients:

1¾ cups rolled oats

2 cups crisp brown rice cereal*

1½ cups whole wheat pastry flour

½ teaspoon baking soda

½ teaspoon cream of tartar

1 cup honey

¾ cup frozen apple juice
concentrate (defrosted)

1 teaspoon vanilla

1 teaspoon almond extract

filling

¾ cup boiling water

¾ cup chopped dates

¼ cup raisins

directions:

Preheat oven at 350°F. In large bowl, combine rolled oats, cereal, flour, baking soda and cream of tartar. Set aside.

In small saucepan, bring honey and juice concentrate to boil over medium high heat, stirring constantly. Remove from heat; cool for 5 minutes. Add vanilla and almond extracts. Gently stir into cereal mixture.

For filling, in blender or food processor, process on high speed boiling water, dates and raisins until pureed, approximately 2 minutes.

In 8x11x2-inch ovenproof glass baking dish, press 2 cups of the cereal mixture in bottom of pan. Using back of wooden spoon, spread filling on top of cereal mixture, and top with remaining cereal mixture.

Bake at 350°F. for 30-35 minutes, or until nicely browned. Cool on wire rack for 20 minutes. Cut into 24 bars.

T hese bars are made from a grain combination of rolled oats and crisp brown rice, so they can be enjoyed even by people who are sensitive to wheat.

We recommend that whenever possible, you buy organically grown grains. Selecting organic grains not only assures you of food safety, but it also helps create a market for organic foods, so that more farmers will feel that it pays to raise food without fertilizers, pesticides, fungicides or herbicides. Organic farming helps protect our pure water supplies and our precious topsoil.

DAIRY FREE   **WHEAT FREE**   **GREAT FOR KIDS**

Special Equipment
10½x15½x1-inch nonstick cookie sheet

Temperature and Time
Bake at 325°F. for 20-25 minutes

Yield
24 servings

Nutrition per Serving
Calories: 135
Carbohydrates: 31 grams
Protein: 2 grams
Fat: .5 grams
Calories from Fat: 3%
Cholesterol: 0 milligrams
Sodium: 0 milligrams
Dietary Fiber: 2 grams

*We developed this recipe using Health Valley Brown Rice Fruit Lites Cereal.

date granola bars

ingredients:

3 cups rolled oats

3 cups crisp brown rice cereal*

1½ cups + ¾ cup chopped dates

½ cup boiling water

½ cup honey

⅓ cup frozen apple juice
  concentrate (defrosted)

1½ teaspoons cinnamon

⅛ teaspoon ground nutmeg

2 teaspoons vanilla

1 teaspoon orange extract

directions:

Preheat oven to 325°F. Spread oats on cookie sheet and toast at 325°F. for 10-15 minutes, or until nicely browned.

In large bowl, combine toasted oats, cereal and 1½ cups dates. Set aside.

In blender or food processor, process remaining ¾ cup dates with boiling water, approximately 2 minutes. In medium saucepan, combine date mixture with honey, juice concentrate, cinnamon and nutmeg. Bring mixture to boil over medium high heat, stirring constantly; reduce heat and simmer 1 minute. Remove from heat and add vanilla and orange extracts. Gently stir into cereal mixture.

Press mixture, compressing with back of wooden spoon, onto 10½x15½x1-inch nonstick cookie sheet.

Bake at 325°F. for 20-25 minutes, or until bars are lightly browned. Cool on wire rack for 10 minutes. Cut into 24 bars, and place on rack to air dry.

The energy boost you'll feel from eating these delicious bars comes from all of the dried fruits and whole grains that they contain. Dried fruit is an especially good source of energy because it contains the nutrients of whole fruit, but with most of the water removed. As a result, dried fruit has as much as seven times the amount of nutrients, ounce for ounce, as the same fruit in fresh form.

These energy bars are made from a combination of oats and rice, so they can even be enjoyed by people who are sensitive to wheat.

FAT-FREE DAIRY FREE WHEAT FREE

GREAT FOR KIDS

Temperature and Time

Bake at 350°F. for 25 minutes

Yield

24 servings

Nutrition per Serving

Calories: 88
Carbohydrates: 21 grams
Protein: 2 grams
Fat: Fat-Free**
Cholesterol: 0 milligrams
Sodium: 35 milligrams
Dietary Fiber: 1 gram

*We developed this recipe using Health Valley Brown Rice Fruit Lites Cereal.
**All foods contain some fat. Less than .5 gram of fat per serving is nutritionally insignificant and considered to be "Fat-Free."

energy bars

ingredients:

⅓ cup honey

⅓ cup frozen apple juice
   concentrate (defrosted)

⅔ cup chopped dates

⅔ cup raisins

⅔ cup finely chopped
   dried apricots

1 tablespoon lemon juice

½ cup rolled oats

½ cup crisp brown rice cereal*

¾ cup oat flour (1⅓ cups rolled oats
   processed in blender about
   2-3 minutes until finely ground)

½ teaspoon baking soda

½ teaspoon cream of tartar

½ teaspoon cinnamon

¼ teaspoon ground nutmeg

¼ teaspoon ground cloves

1 teaspoon vanilla

1 teaspoon finely grated orange peel

3 egg whites, lightly beaten

directions:

Preheat oven to 350°F. In medium saucepan over medium-high heat, bring honey and juice concentrate to boil, stirring constantly. Add dates, raisins, apricots and lemon juice; reduce heat to low and simmer for 10 minutes. Remove from heat and cool for 5 minutes.

In large bowl, combine rolled oats, cereal, flour, baking soda, cream of tartar, cinnamon, nutmeg and cloves. Stir in fruit mixture, vanilla, orange peel and egg whites; mix until well blended.

Spread batter into 8-inch square ovenproof glass baking dish and bake at 350°F. for 25 minutes or until nicely browned. Cool on wire rack for 20 minutes. Cut into 24 bars.

It upsets us when food companies sell products under the guise of being healthy that are actually loaded with fat. A prime example is granola. Even though manufacturers have bowed to public pressure and removed the coconut oil from their products, many have simply replaced it with other unhealthy forms of fat. For example, the most popular commercial brand of granola cereal contains over 41 percent of calories from fat and is made with partially hydrogenated cottonseed oil. Hydrogenation is the process that artificially makes unsaturated fat more saturated, and results in trans fatty acids. There is now concern that trans fatty acids may contribute to heart disease as much or more than saturated fats do.

FAT-FREE   DAIRY FREE   GREAT FOR KIDS

Special Equipment
nonstick cookie sheet

Temperature and Time
Bake at 350°F. for
10 minutes

Yield
36 servings

Nutrition per Serving**
Calories: 137
Carbohydrates: 33 grams
Protein: 3 grams
Fat: Fat-Free***
Cholesterol: 0 milligrams
Sodium: 75 milligrams
Dietary Fiber: 3 grams

*We developed this recipe using Health Valley Fat-Free Granola with Date and Almond Flavor.
**A serving is two cookies.
***All foods contain some fat. Less than .5 gram of fat per serving is nutritionally insignificant and considered to be "Fat-Free."

granola cookies

ingredients:

1½ cups fat-free granola
(without fruit added)*

1½ cups whole wheat pastry flour

¾ teaspoon baking soda

¾ teaspoon cream of tartar

1 teaspoon cinnamon

¼ teaspoon ground cloves

¼ teaspoon ground nutmeg

¾ cup honey

1 jar (4 ounces) sweet potato
baby food puree

2 egg whites, lightly beaten

1 teaspoon vanilla

1 cup raisins

directions:

Preheat oven to 350°F. Grind granola in food processor for 2 minutes. In large bowl, mix together ground granola, flour, baking soda, cream of tartar, cinnamon, cloves and nutmeg. Set aside.

In medium bowl, combine honey, sweet potato puree, egg whites, vanilla and raisins. Gently stir into flour mixture and mix until **just** blended. *Do not overmix.*

Drop by rounded teaspoons onto nonstick cookie sheet; allow room for cookies to spread. Bake at 350°F. for 10 minutes, or until lightly browned. Be careful not to over-brown cookie bottoms. Cool on wire rack for 5 minutes, and remove cookies from sheet.

H oney is a natural sweetener that has been revered since ancient times. In fact, the Bible refers to a particularly idyllic location as "the land of milk and honey."

This recipe takes full advantage of the unique flavor of honey to produce a cookie that is especially sweet and delicious. It is a version of the traditional oatmeal cookie, made from a combination of oat flour, rice and rolled oats for a crisp texture and slightly nutty flavor.

It is wheat free, so it can be enjoyed even by people who are sensitive to wheat.

DAIRY FREE   WHEAT FREE

Special Equipment
nonstick cookie sheet

Temperature and Time
Bake at 350°F. for 10-12 minutes

Yield
36 servings

Nutrition per Serving**

Calories: 187
Carbohydrates: 43 grams
Protein: 3 grams
Fat: 1 gram
Calories from Fat: 5%
Cholesterol: 0 milligrams
Sodium: 55 milligrams
Dietary Fiber: 1 gram

*We developed this recipe using Health Valley Brown Rice Fruit Lites Cereal.
**A serving is three cookies.

honey raisin cookies

ingredients:

1 cup oat flour (1¼ cups rolled oats processed in blender about 2-3 minutes until finely ground)

2 cups crisp brown rice cereal*

1 cup rolled oats

½ teaspoon baking soda

½ teaspoon cream of tartar

1½ teaspoons cinnamon

¼ teaspoon ground nutmeg

¾ cup honey

¾ cup unsweetened applesauce

1 teaspoon vanilla

¾ cup dark raisins

directions:

Preheat oven to 350°F. In large bowl, combine oat flour, cereal, oats, baking soda, cream of tartar, cinnamon and nutmeg; mix well and set aside.

Heat honey in small saucepan over medium heat for 2-3 minutes or until melted. Remove from heat, and add applesauce, vanilla and raisins. Gently stir into cereal mixture.

Drop by rounded teaspoon onto nonstick cookie sheets. Bake at 350°F. for 10-12 minutes. Cookies may appear undercooked; they get crisper as they cool. Allow cookies to cool 5 minutes before removing from sheet.

These cookies taste sweet and spicy with just a hint of orange. To make them, we combine three different grains, each for a different purpose. Wheat gives the cookie its bulk; oats, its slightly nutty flavor, and rice its wonderfully crisp texture.

**DAIRY
FREE**

Special Equipment

nonstick cookie sheet

Temperature and Time

Bake at 350°F. for 10-12 minutes

Yield

30 servings

Nutrition per Serving**

Calories: 158
Carbohydrates: 37 grams
Protein: 3 grams
Fat: .5 grams
Calories from Fat: 3%
Cholesterol: 0 milligrams
Sodium: 50 milligrams
Dietary Fiber: 2 grams

**We developed this recipe using Health Valley Brown Rice Fruit Lites Cereal.
**A serving is two cookies.*

oatmeal date cookies

ingredients:

1 cup whole wheat pastry flour

1½ cups rolled oats

1½ cups crisp brown rice cereal*

½ teaspoon baking soda

½ teaspoon cream of tartar

1½ teaspoons cinnamon

¼ teaspoon ground nutmeg

¼ teaspoon ground allspice

¾ cup honey

½ cup unsweetened applesauce

1 teaspoon grated orange peel

¾ cup chopped dates

2 egg whites, lightly beaten

directions:

Preheat oven to 350°F. In large mixing bowl, mix together flour, oats, cereal, baking soda, cream of tartar, cinnamon, nutmeg and allspice. Set aside.

In medium bowl, combine honey, applesauce, orange peel, dates and egg whites. Gently stir into flour mixture, and mix until **just** blended. *Do not overmix.*

Drop by rounded teaspoon onto nonstick cookie sheets. Lightly pat down each mound. Bake at 350°F. for 10-12 minutes, or until cookies are nicely browned. Allow cookies to cool 5 minutes before removing from sheet.

O atmeal raisin cookies are a traditional favorite that people never seem to get tired of. The distinctive flavor and chewy texture make this cookie a form of "comfort" food that is reassuring and that just makes you feel good.

This recipe offers all the solid enjoyment of the traditional recipe, but without the fat and refined sugar. Instead, it uses unsweetened applesauce as a fat substitute, and to lend a naturally sweet flavor.

The oats provide the chewy texture and mild, slightly nutty flavor that is so comforting. Rolling the oats is a process in which the grain is first hulled, then steamed and finally flattened into flakes. It is easy to turn rolled oats into oat flour simply by putting a cup or so into a blender or food processor, and grinding on medium high for about 10 seconds. Then sift the flour before you use it to remove any larger pieces.

DAIRY FREE   **GREAT FOR KIDS**

Special Equipment
nonstick cookie sheet

Temperature and Time
Bake at 350°F. for 12 minutes

Yield
30 servings

Nutrition per Serving*
Calories: 193
Carbohydrates: 43 grams
Protein: 5 grams
Fat: 1 gram
Calories from Fat: 5%
Cholesterol: 0 milligrams
Sodium: 180 milligrams
Dietary Fiber: 2 grams

*A serving is two cookies.

oatmeal raisin cookies

ingredients:

2 cups whole wheat pastry flour

2 cups rolled oats

2 teaspoons baking soda

1¾ teaspoons cinnamon

¼ teaspoon ground nutmeg

¼ teaspoon ground allspice

¾ cup honey

½ cup apple juice concentrate (defrosted)

¼ cup applesauce

2 teaspoons vanilla

¾ cup raisins

3 egg whites, lightly beaten

directions:

Preheat oven to 350°F. In large bowl, combine flour, oats, baking soda, cinnamon, nutmeg and allspice; mix well.

In medium bowl, combine honey, juice concentrate, applesauce, vanilla, raisins and egg whites. Gently stir into flour mixture, and mix until **just** blended. ***Do not overmix.***

Drop by heaping teaspoon onto nonstick cookie sheet. Lightly pat down each mound. Bake at 350°F. for 12 minutes. Allow cookies to cool slightly before removing from sheet.

DAIRY FREE **WHEAT FREE** **GREAT FOR KIDS**

H ere is another example of the fact that when you bake without fat the ingredients react very differently than when you use fat. These bars do <u>not</u> look like other bars do when they are done baking. So it is important to follow the directions carefully and bake for 35-40 minutes or just until the bars turn a nice golden brown color, even though the texture may still seem too soft and gooey. That's because the bars will harden as they cool, and overbaking will cause them to burn or be too hard.

An even bigger difference between this granola bar recipe and others is the amount of fat they contain. Traditional recipes call for oils and other forms of fat, including nuts and even coconut. So they can contain 6 grams of fat per 1-ounce serving. Ounce for ounce, that's more fat than you find in hamburger! With this recipe, you can enjoy the same delicious flavor without a lot of fat.

Special Equipment
nonstick cookie sheet

Temperature and Time
Bake at 325°F. for 35-40 minutes

Yield
24 servings

Nutrition per Serving
Calories: 126
Carbohydrates: 29 grams
Protein: 3 grams
Fat: 1 gram
Calories from Fat: 7%
Cholesterol: 0 milligrams
Sodium: 0 milligrams
Dietary Fiber: 1 gram

We developed this recipe using Health Valley Brown Rice Fruit Lites Cereal.

raisin granola bars

ingredients:

3 cups rolled oats

3 cups crisp brown rice cereal*

1½ cups currants or other
  finely chopped dried fruit

¾ cup chopped dates

½ cup hot water

½ cup honey

⅓ cup frozen apple juice
  concentrate (defrosted)

1½ teaspoons cinnamon

⅛ teaspoon ground nutmeg

2 teaspoons vanilla

1 teaspoon almond extract

directions:

Preheat oven to 325°F. Spread oats on cookie sheet and toast at 325°F. for 10-15 minutes, or until nicely browned.

In large bowl, combine toasted oats, rice cereal and currants; set aside.

Process dates and hot water in blender, about 2 minutes. Combine date mixture with honey, juice concentrate, cinnamon and nutmeg in medium saucepan. Bring mixture to boil over medium-high heat, stirring constantly; reduce heat and simmer for 1 minute. Remove from heat and add vanilla and almond extracts. Gently stir into cereal fruit mixture.

Press mixture, compressing with back of moistened wooden spoon onto nonstick cookie sheet. Bake at 325°F. for 35-40 minutes, or until bars are light brown. Remove from oven; cool 10 minutes and cut into 24 bars. Place on rack to air dry.

Commercially prepared jams contain as much refined sugar as they do fruit. In fact, government labeling laws say that in order to use the name "preserves" or "jelly," companies have to add as much sugar as they do fruit. That's why fruit-juice-sweetened preserves with no added sugar have to be called "fruit spreads" and names other than "preserves."

In spite of this marketing handicap, juice-sweetened preserves have grown in popularity. To our taste, they are superior to preserves with all the sugar because you get a purer fruit flavor. You can taste for yourself in this recipe.

In making it, you'll see instructions that tell you to make a batter that consists of the cereal grains and the sweeteners, and to pat this batter down in the bottom of a nonstick baking pan. Because the batter is too sticky to work comfortably with your hands, we suggest that you use the bottom of a glass jar that has been moistened.

In the next step, you apply preserves to the mixture, before adding another layer of batter. Since the preserves come out of the jar in sticky clumps that are hard to work with, we suggest that you stir it in a small bowl before applying it.

By using these two tips, you'll find this recipe simple and easy to follow.

DAIRY FREE   GREAT FOR KIDS

Special Equipment

8x11x2-inch nonstick baking pan

Temperature and Time

Bake at 350°F. for 30 minutes

Yield

24 servings

Nutrition per Serving

Calories: 149
Carbohydrates: 35 grams
Protein: 2 grams
Fat: .5 gram
Calories from Fat: 3%
Cholesterol: 0 milligrams
Sodium: 30 milligrams
Dietary Fiber: 1 gram

We developed this recipe using Health Valley Brown Rice Fruit Lites Cereal.

raspberry cookie bars

ingredients:

1¾ cups rolled oats

2 cups crisp brown rice cereal*

1½ cups whole wheat pastry flour

½ teaspoon baking soda

½ teaspoon cream of tartar

1 cup honey

¾ cup frozen apple juice
   concentrate (defrosted)

1 teaspoon vanilla

1 teaspoon almond extract

1 jar (10 ounces) fruit-juice-
   sweetened raspberry preserves

directions:

Preheat oven to 350°F. In large bowl, combine oats, cereal, flour, baking soda and cream of tartar. Set aside.

In small saucepan, bring honey and juice concentrate to boil over medium-high heat, stirring constantly. Reduce heat and simmer for 1 minute. Remove from heat; cool for 5 minutes. Add vanilla and almond extracts. Gently stir into cereal mixture.

In 8x11x2-inch ovenproof glass baking dish, press 2 cups of cereal mixture in bottom of pan; reserve remaining cereal mixture. Melt preserves, pour over mixture and spread evenly; top with reserved cereal mixture.

Bake at 350°F. for 30 minutes, or until nicely browned. Cool on wire rack for 20 minutes. Cut into 24 bars.

This is a great recipe for introducing children to the joys of baking wholesome, fat-free food. It gives children a chance to get involved in a "hands on" way ... literally. That's because these cookies get their name from the technique of making a thumbprint in the wet dough of each one, into which you drop a teaspoon of preserves. The resulting cookies are not only colorful and sweetly delicious, but something that children can take pride in having made "with their own hands." For variety, use several different fruit flavors to fill in the thumbprints.

FAT-FREE **DAIRY FREE** **GREAT FOR KIDS**

Special Equipment

nonstick cookie sheets

Temperature and Time

Bake at 350°F. for
15 minutes

Yield

36 servings

Nutrition per Serving**

Calories: 149
Carbohydrates: 36 grams
Protein: 3 grams
Fat: Fat-Free***
Cholesterol: 0 milligrams
Sodium: 190 milligrams
Dietary Fiber: 4 grams

*We developed this recipe using Health Valley Fat-Free Granola with Date and Almond Flavor.
**A serving is two cookies.
***All foods contain some fat. Less than .5 gram of fat per serving is nutritionally insignificant and considered to be "Fat-Free."

thumbprint cookies

ingredients:

1½ cups fat-free granola
(without fruit added)*

1½ cups whole wheat pastry flour

¾ teaspoon baking soda

¾ teaspoon cream of tartar

1 teaspoon cinnamon

⅛ teaspoon ground cloves

⅛ teaspoon ground nutmeg

¾ cup honey

1 jar (4 ounces) sweet potato
baby food puree

2 egg whites, lightly beaten

1 teaspoon vanilla

1 cup raisins

1 jar (10 ounces) fruit-juice-
sweetened strawberry preserves

directions:

Preheat oven to 350°F. Grind granola in food processor for 2 minutes. In large bowl, mix together ground granola, flour, baking soda, cream of tartar, cinnamon, cloves and nutmeg. Set aside.

In medium bowl, combine honey, sweet potato puree, egg whites, vanilla and raisins. Gently stir into flour mixture and mix until **just** blended. *Do not overmix.*

Drop by rounded teaspoons onto nonstick cookie sheets. Wet thumb with water, and make thumbprint in cookie. Using teaspoon drop 1 teaspoon of preserves in center of cookie. Bake at 350°F. about 15 minutes, or until lightly browned. Be careful not to overbrown cookie bottoms. Cool on wire rack for 5 minutes, and remove cookies from sheet.

H ere is an interesting variation on the traditional oatmeal cookie recipe. Instead of
adding raisins, we've substituted chunks of
dried pineapple and papaya, and finely grated
orange peel to create a refreshing flavor twist.
We also season this recipe with cinnamon,
vanilla, coconut extract and pureed apricots
for a delightful melange of flavors.

The apricot puree we use substitutes for the
fat in traditional recipes, and adds beta
carotene – all at once. And apricots contain silicon, a mineral associated with adding shine to
your hair and helping to rejuvenate your skin.

Special Equipment

nonstick cookie sheet

Temperature and Time

Bake at 350°F. for 12-15
minutes

Yield

48 servings

Nutrition per Serving*

Calories: 195
Carbohydrates: 44 grams
Protein: 4 grams
Fat: 1 gram
Calories from Fat: 5%
Cholesterol: 0 milligrams
Sodium: 170 milligrams
Dietary Fiber: 1 gram

*A serving is three cookies.

tropical oatmeal cookies

ingredients:

2 cups whole wheat pastry flour

2 cups rolled oats

2 teaspoons baking soda

¼ teaspoon ground nutmeg

1 teaspoon cinnamon

1 teaspoon finely grated orange peel

¾ cup honey

⅓ cup frozen tropical fruit juice concentrate (defrosted)

2 jars (4 ounces each) apricot baby food puree

3 egg whites, unbeaten

2 teaspoons vanilla

½ teaspoon coconut extract

1 cup chopped dried pineapple and/or dried papaya

directions:

Preheat oven to 350°F. In large bowl, combine flour, oats, baking soda, nutmeg, cinnamon and orange peel. Set aside.

In medium bowl, combine honey, juice concentrate, apricot puree, egg whites, vanilla and coconut extracts, and dried fruit. Gently stir into flour mixture, and mix until **just** blended. ***Do not overmix.***

Drop by teaspoons onto nonstick cookie sheet. Bake at 350°F. for 12-15 minutes, or until lightly browned. Cool on wire rack for 10 minutes, and remove cookies from sheet.

Fruit Desserts, Puddings & Pies Section

O ne of the things that makes food so important in all our lives is the fact that it nourishes more than just our bodies. It can also enhance our feelings of well being and just plain make us feel better. In fact, there is now an increasing recognition of the value of "comfort foods"–foods that we naturally associate with home and nurturing. Certainly no list of "comfort foods" would be complete without puddings and pies. Baked goods like apple pie and bread pudding are foods that we automatically associate with home cooking and with family meals.

Because we recognize the importance of puddings and pies, we have devoted this section to versions of some old favorites with all the comfort and flavor intact, but with the fat, refined sugar and white flour removed. The versions you will find in this book will nourish your spirit every bit as well as the traditional recipes, but they will nourish your body even better.

You might not think of pies and puddings as being very high in fat, but that's just because so much of the fat in traditional recipes is "hidden." Take peach pie, for example. What could sound healthier than plump peaches with all their beneficial beta carotene, baked into a pie. The problem comes from the shortening in the crust, and often in the topping as well. One slice of peach pie made from a traditional recipe can contain 24 grams of fat! Compare the fat and calories in a traditional peach pie recipe with the one in this section:

Serving (1 slice)	Fat (grams)	Calories
Traditional Peach Pie	24g	442
Baking Without Fat Peach Tart	Fat-Free	159

B read pudding certainly qualifies as "comfort food." And although the recipe sounds like it should be high in complex carbohydrates and low in fat, the traditional recipe actually contains 6 or more grams of fat in a serving from milk and eggs. Although this is not an unreasonable amount of fat, we offer you our version of this classic recipe that offers all the comfort and enjoyment with less than a gram of fat.

Our recipe makes a perfect family dessert that can be enjoyed even during a busy week because it is simple to make and can be served at the table right out of the baking dish.

This is also a healthy recipe because it is not only low in fat but a good source of fiber from the abundance of bread and apples used to make it.

**GREAT
FOR KIDS**

Temperature and Time

Bake at 325°F. for 60-65 minutes

Yield

8 servings

Nutrition per Serving

Calories: 163
Carbohydrates: 35 grams
Protein: 6 grams
Fat: 1 gram
Calories from Fat: 6%
Cholesterol: 0 milligrams
Sodium: 150 milligrams
Dietary Fiber: 2 grams

apple bread pudding

ingredients:

6 slices fat-free whole wheat bread,
    cut into 1-inch cubes
    (approximately 3 cups)

1 cup evaporated skimmed milk

3 egg whites, lightly beaten

½ cup frozen apple juice
    concentrate (defrosted)

3 cups peeled and chopped baking
    apples (approximately 3 apples)

⅓ cup raisins

½ teaspoon finely grated lemon peel

1½ teaspoons cinnamon

½ teaspoon ground nutmeg

2 tablespoons pure maple syrup

1 teaspoon vanilla

directions:

Preheat oven to 325°F. In large bowl, add bread cubes, evaporated milk, egg whites, juice concentrate, apples, raisins, lemon peel, cinnamon, nutmeg, maple syrup and vanilla; mix well.

Pour mixture into 8-inch square ovenproof glass baking dish. Bake at 325°F. for 60-65 minutes, or until knife inserted near center comes out clean. Cool slightly. Serve warm or cold.

If there were such a thing as an all-American fruit, the apple would certainly qualify. Apples have been enjoyed throughout our history, and there are varieties that are appropriate for everything from eating out of hand to baking to making into pies and cobblers. For cooking, we suggest you use Rome Beauty, which is the most popular baking apple, or the all-purpose Granny Smith or Mackintosh.

We created this simple recipe to remind you of the crisps of yesteryear. By teaming apples with fat-free granola, each serving of this recipe provides 57 percent of the U.S. RDA for vitamin C.

As you enjoy it, you might keep in mind this quote from almost 150 years ago that we find amusing:

> "If every boy in America planted an apple tree in some useless corner, and tended it carefully, the net savings would in time extinguish the public debt."
>
> Amelia Simmons
> American Cookery
> 1845

How many apples would it take today, we wonder?

Serving Suggestion:

This tasty apple crisp can either be eaten alone, or served to guests over nonfat vanilla yogurt. Serve either hot or cold.

FAT-FREE   DAIRY FREE

Temperature and Time

Bake at 350°F. for 40 minutes

Yield

8 servings

Nutrition per Serving

Calories: 215
Carbohydrates: 54 grams
Protein: 2 grams
Fat: Fat-Free**
Cholesterol: 0 milligrams
Sodium: 35 milligrams
Dietary Fiber: 4 grams

*We developed this recipe using Health Valley Fat-Free Granola with Date and Almond Flavor.
**All foods contain some fat. Less than .5 gram of fat per serving is nutritionally insignificant and considered to be "Fat-Free."

apple crisp

ingredients:

filling

6 medium cooking apples, peeled and coarsely chopped

1 tablespoon lemon juice

¾ cup frozen apple juice concentrate (defrosted)

¾ teaspoon cinnamon

¼ teaspoon ground nutmeg

½ cup raisins

¼ cup chopped dates

topping

1½ cups fat-free granola (without fruit added)*

2 tablespoons frozen apple juice concentrate (defrosted)

directions:

Preheat oven to 350°F. In 8x11x2-inch ovenproof glass baking dish, stir together chopped apples, lemon juice, juice concentrate, cinnamon, nutmeg, raisins and dates.

For topping, grind granola with juice concentrate in food processor for 2 minutes.

Top apples with granola mixture. Bake covered at 350°F. for 30 minutes; remove cover and continue to bake additional 10 minutes until topping is lightly browned and fruit is tender.Cool on wire rack for 15 minutes. Serve warm or cold.

R ice pudding is another classic "comfort food" that is not only soothing but that also makes you feel nurtured and cared for.

We made this version without the milk and eggs of the traditional recipe to save you about 5 grams of fat a serving and to allow even those who have an allergy or sensitivity to milk products to be able to enjoy it. The combination of apples and brown rice provide beneficial fiber that is an important part of a healthy diet.

FAT-FREE   DAIRY FREE   WHEAT FREE

GREAT FOR KIDS

Special Equipment

8 custard cups

Temperature and Time

Bake at 325°F. for 50-60 minutes

Yield

8 servings

Nutrition per Serving

Calories: 195
Carbohydrates: 45 grams
Protein: 4 grams
Fat: Fat-Free***
Cholesterol: 0 milligrams
Sodium: 55 milligrams
Dietary Fiber: 2 grams

*We developed this recipe using Health Valley Fat-Free Soy Moo® Drink.
***All foods contain some fat. Less than .5 gram of fat per serving is nutritionally insignificant and considered to be "Fat-Free."

apple rice pudding

ingredients:

1⅓ cups fat-free soy beverage*

½ cup honey

3 egg whites

2 teaspoons vanilla

½ teaspoon finely grated
   orange peel

¼ teaspoon cinnamon

2 cups cooked brown rice
   (short grain preferred)**

2 cups cooking apples, peeled
   and chopped (approximately
   2-3 medium apples)

⅓ cup chopped dates

⅛ teaspoon ground nutmeg

directions:

Preheat oven to 325°F. In medium mixing bowl, combine soy beverage, honey, egg whites, vanilla, orange peel and cinnamon. With electric mixer, beat until smooth. Stir in rice, apples and dates. Spoon mixture into 8 custard cups. Sprinkle lightly with nutmeg.

Place custard cups in baking pan and surround with hot water to depth of 1 inch. Bake at 325°F. for 50-60 minutes, until nicely browned on top. Pudding will solidify as it cools. Remove from water bath to cool. Serve warm or cold.

**note: to make 2 cups cooked brown rice, use two-thirds cup raw brown rice and 1⅓ cups water.

This is a recipe you can enjoy all year long by using frozen peaches and blueberries, but it is especially delicious during the spring and summer when you can get fresh fruit in season.

We love recipes made with fresh peaches because they have such a distinctive and delicious flavor and they are also very nutritious. Among other beneficial nutrients, peaches are a good source of the antioxidant, beta carotene.

When choosing fresh peaches, look for fruit that is firm yet tender, without bruises. Most fresh peaches sold in supermarkets have been picked before they are fully ripe to allow time for shipping and handling, and many times they are still not ripe when you buy them. You can speed the ripening process by storing peaches unrefrigerated in a closed brown paper bag. Be sure to check them daily because they can get overripe very quickly. You can tell when peaches are ripe by their fragrant aroma and the fact that the flesh softens.

Serving Suggestion:

It's easy to reheat this crisp in single servings. Just use the HIGH (100% power) setting on your microwave and heat for 30 seconds.

FAT-FREE **DAIRY FREE**

Temperature and Time

Bake at 350°F. for
40 minutes

Yield

8 servings

Nutrition per Serving

Calories: 190
Carbohydrates: 46 grams
Protein: 2 grams
Fat: Fat-Free**
Cholesterol: 0 milligrams
Sodium: 35 milligrams
Dietary Fiber: 4 grams

*We developed this recipe using Health Valley Fat-Free Granola with Date and Almond Flavor.
**All foods contain some fat. Less than .5 gram of fat per serving is nutritionally insignificant and considered to be "Fat-Free."

blueberry peach fruit crisp

ingredients:

filling

1 bag (16 ounces) frozen
peach slices (defrosted)

1 box (10 ounces) frozen
blueberries (defrosted)

1 cup frozen apple juice
concentrate (defrosted)

¼ cup instant tapioca

¾ teaspoon cinnamon

topping

1¾ cups fat-free granola
(without fruit added)*

2 tablespoons frozen apple juice
concentrate (defrosted)

directions:

Preheat oven to 350°F. In 8-inch square ovenproof glass baking dish, stir together peaches, blueberries, juice concentrate, tapioca and cinnamon.

For topping, grind granola with juice concentrate in food processor, approximately 2 minutes.

Top fruit mixture with granola topping. Bake covered at 350°F. for 30 minutes; remove cover and continue to bake additional 10 minutes until topping is lightly browned and fruit is tender. Cool on wire rack for 15 minutes. Serve warm or cold.

This layered dessert provides a delicious contrast of tastes and textures. The bottom layer has a rich chocolate taste, while the center is a creamy custard that is covered by an airy meringue topping.

The center also contains sliced bananas. Since the bananas are barely heated in the finished dessert, it is important to use fresh, firm fruit. Look for bananas that have a nice yellow color without any brown spots.

Bananas are an excellent source of the mineral potassium, which is one of the electrolytes the body needs to maintain the proper fluid balance.

You have the option of using unsweetened cocoa powder if you're a chocolate lover, or carob powder. Although these two ingredients aren't related, they can be substituted for each other, with a one-to-one ratio.

FAT-
FREE

Special Equipment

10 2½-inch glass oven-proof dessert cups

Temperature and Time

Bake at 325°F. for 20-25 minutes
Bake at 375°F. for 5-10 minutes

Yield

10 servings

Nutrition per Serving

Calories: 196
Carbohydrates: 44 grams
Protein: 6 grams
Fat: Fat-Free*
Cholesterol: 0 milligrams
Sodium: 90 milligrams
Dietary Fiber: 2 grams

*All foods contain some fat. Less than .5 gram of fat per serving is nutritionally insignificant and considered to be "Fat-Free."

coco banana meringue

ingredients:

crust

¾ cup whole wheat pastry flour

2 tablespoons unsweetened
cocoa powder or carob powder

½ teaspoon cinnamon

¼ teaspoon cream of tartar

¼ teaspoon baking soda

1 jar (2½ ounces) prune
baby food puree

½ cup honey and
1 tablespoon honey

1 egg white, lightly beaten

½ teaspoon vanilla

custard

1 tablespoon arrowroot

3 tablespoons whole wheat
pastry flour

1 can (12 fluid ounces) evaporated
skimmed milk

3 tablespoons pure maple syrup

1 teaspoon vanilla

½ teaspoon almond extract

2 large bananas, thinly sliced

meringue

2 egg whites

¼ cup maple syrup

ground nutmeg (optional)

directions:

Preheat oven to 325°F. For crust, in medium bowl, sift together flour, cocoa or carob powder, cinnamon, cream of tartar and baking soda. In separate bowl, combine prune puree, honey, egg white and vanilla. Pour into flour mixture; stir until blended.Divide mixture into 10 2½-inch glass ovenproof dessert cups. Bake at 325°F. for 20-25 minutes, or until toothpick inserted in center comes out clean. Let cool while preparing custard.

For custard, in medium saucepan, over medium-high heat, whisk together arrowroot, flour, evaporated milk and maple syrup. Bring mixture to low boil. Reduce heat to low, and cook approximately 5 minutes until mixture thickens. Stir in vanilla and almond extracts; set aside. Let cool for 10 minutes. Add sliced bananas and pour cooled custard on top of each brownie cup.

For meringue, preheat oven to 375°F. In small bowl, with electric mixer on high, beat egg whites until foamy, slowly drizzle in maple syrup, and beat until stiff peaks form, about 2 minutes. Swirl meringue on top of each custard cup. If desired, lightly sprinkle ground nutmeg on top. Bake at 375°F. for 5-10 minutes until meringue is lightly browned.

This recipe is an excellent example of the way we have been able to take a traditional recipe and maintain the rich taste and texture, while eliminating the fat and cholesterol.

Traditional chocolate pudding calls for four egg yolks, which add 33 grams of fat and 1,090 milligrams of cholesterol to the recipe. Our version contains no eggs at all. Instead, we use whole wheat flour to give this pudding its thickness, and evaporated skim milk to supply the rich taste.

You have the option of using unsweetened cocoa powder if you're a chocolate lover, or carob powder. Although these two ingredients aren't related, they can be substituted for each other, with a one-to-one ratio.

FAT- GREAT
FREE FOR KIDS

Special Equipment

6 custard cups

Yield

6 servings

Nutrition per Serving

Calories:138
Carbohydrates: 30 grams
Protein: 5 grams
Fat: Fat-Free*
Cholesterol: 0 milligrams
Sodium: 70 milligrams
Dietary Fiber: 1 gram

*All foods contain some fat. Less than
.5 gram of fat per serving is nutritionally
insignificant and considered to be
"Fat-Free."

coco pudding/filling

ingredients:

¼ cup whole wheat pastry flour

2 tablespoons unsweetened cocoa powder or carob powder

1 can (12 fluid ounces) evaporated skimmed milk

½ cup and 1 tablespoon pure maple syrup

½ teaspoon vanilla

¼ teaspoon almond extract

directions:

In medium bowl, whisk together flour, cocoa or carob powder, evaporated milk and maple syrup. In medium saucepan over medium-high heat, bring mixture to low boil; reduce heat to low and cook until mixture thickens, approximately 5 minutes. Stir in vanilla and almond extracts. Let cool slightly.

Spoon into 6 custard cups. Serve warm or chill for 1 hour.

There are some flavors that just seem to be made for each other. Chocolate and raspberries make one of these ideal flavor combinations. Together they create a symphony of contrasting but harmonious flavors. Even the colors are lovely together.

This trifle blends cocoa and raspberry to create a dessert that is so pretty and so delicious that you can serve it at the most elegant dinner party and the taste will linger in the memory of your guests long after dinner has ended. This recipe is also ideal for a dinner party because you can make it the day before and it actually tastes better the next day. If time is of the essence, at least allow it to rest in the refrigerator for two hours before serving.

When they are available, use fresh raspberries to highlight the flavor of this dish.

You have the option of using unsweetened cocoa powder for a true chocolate taste, or carob powder. Although the two ingredients aren't related, they can be substituted for each other, with a one-to-one ratio.

FAT-FREE

Special Equipment

1-quart trifle dish

Yield

10 servings

Nutrition per Serving

Calories: 209
Carbohydrates: 48 grams
Protein: 6 grams
Fat: Fat-Free**
Cholesterol: 0 milligrams
Sodium: 85 milligrams
Dietary Fiber: 3 grams

*We developed this recipe using Health Valley Fat-Free Granola with Date and Almond Flavor.
**All foods contain some fat. Less than .5 gram of fat per serving is nutritionally insignificant and considered to be "Fat-Free."

coco raspberry trifle

ingredients:

¼ cup whole wheat pastry flour

2 tablespoons unsweetened cocoa powder or carob powder

1 can (12 fluid ounces) evaporated skimmed milk

½ cup and 1 tablespoon maple syrup

½ teaspoon vanilla

¼ teaspoon almond extract

2 cups fat-free granola (without added fruit)*

6 tablespoons fruit-juice-sweetened raspberry preserves, melted

1 bag (16 ounces) frozen raspberries, defrosted and drained, or 2 cups fresh raspberries

directions:

In medium saucepan, over medium-high heat, whisk together flour, cocoa or carob powder, evaporated milk and maple syrup. Bring mixture to low boil; reduce heat to low and cook approximately 5 minutes until mixture thickens. Stir in vanilla and almond extracts. Let cool slightly, approximately 5 minutes.

Pulse granola in food processor into coarse crumbs, approximately 1 minute. Arrange 1 cup of crumbs in bottom of 1-quart trifle dish.

Drizzle 3 tablespoons of melted preserves over crumbs. Spoon two-thirds cup of pudding over preserves. Arrange half of raspberries over pudding. Repeat layering procedure with remaining crumbs, preserves, pudding and raspberries.

note: Our trifle dish has straight sides, 8-inch diameter, 3 inches high. Recipe must be doubled if a larger trifle dish is used.

A pple pie is the All-American dessert in more ways than one. It is not only symbolic of this country, it is also a prime example of why we eat too much fat. Hidden in each serving of the traditional apple pie recipe is 25 grams of fat!

One of our main goals in creating this book was to expose the amount of fat "hidden" in the foods we love so much, and to offer alternative versions that offer the enjoyment without all the fat. Apple pie was one of our biggest challenges. Our solution was to create a unique variation with the crust on the top, instead of the bottom of the pie. The advantage is that we not only eliminate all the fat found in the traditional pie crust, but we also end up with a recipe that's simpler to make because there's none of the mixing and rolling associated with pie crusts. So you can enjoy this All-American dessert any time.

Serving Suggestion:

If desired, serve with Creamy Cinnamon Sauce (see page 155).

Temperature and Time

Bake at 325°F. for
30 minutes

Yield

8 servings

Nutrition per Serving

Calories: 133
Carbohydrates: 32 grams
Protein: 3 grams
Fat: Fat-Free**
Cholesterol: 0 milligrams
Sodium: 110 milligrams
Dietary Fiber: 2 grams

*We developed this recipe using Health Valley Fat-Free Granola with Date and Almond Flavor.
**All foods contain some fat. Less than .5 gram of fat per serving is nutritionally insignificant and considered to be "Fat-Free."

crustless apple pie

ingredients:

¼ cup + ¼ cup fat-free granola
   (without fruit added)*

1½ cups finely chopped, peeled
   and cored green cooking apples
   (about 2 medium apples)

1 tablespoon lemon juice

½ cup honey

¾ teaspoon cinnamon

¼ teaspoon ground allspice

2 egg whites, unbeaten

⅓ cup whole wheat pastry flour

½ teaspoon baking soda

½ teaspoon cream of tartar

⅓ cup plain nonfat yogurt

⅛ teaspoon ground nutmeg

directions:

Preheat oven to 325°F. Grind granola in food processor for 2 minutes; set aside.

In medium saucepan over low heat, simmer apples, lemon juice, honey, cinnamon and allspice for 10 minutes. Remove from stove and put mixture in medium bowl. Let cool for 10 minutes.

Add egg whites, flour, one-quarter cup ground granola, baking soda, and cream of tartar to apple mixture and mix well. Stir in yogurt and pour mixture into 9-inch ovenproof glass pie dish. Sprinkle top with one-quarter cup ground granola and nutmeg. Bake at 325°F for 30 minutes, or until top is set and lightly browned.

Cool on wire rack for 15 minutes. Serve warm or cold.

H ere's a wonderful, easy dessert that is especially refreshing to enjoy during the long hot days of summer. It can also be served as a complement to many of our other desserts, or as part of a more elaborate recipe, such as our Neapolitan Ice Cream Cake (see page 207).

This recipe gets its distinctive flavor from the fruit that is used. A nice selection of unsweetened frozen fruit is available in most stores. Of these, strawberries, raspberries, blackberries and peaches are best suited for this recipe if you want a smooth texture and uniform color. Because of their skins, blueberries and cherries do not puree as smoothly, however if you enjoy the flecks of peel and a slightly chunky texture, you may actually prefer these fruits.

You can also use fresh fruit, such as bananas for this dessert. Peel the fruit and cut it into slices and place them in a plastic bag or freezer container, and put them in the freezer. They will be frozen in a few hours and will keep for several months.

Canned pineapple also can be drained and spread in a single layer on a cooking sheet, then placed in the freezer for several hours until hard. This, too, can be used at once, or transferred to a freezer container for the future. If you enjoy berry picking during the summer, you can preserve your harvest in the same way and have some on hand out of season for making frozen desserts.

FAT-FREE   WHEAT FREE   GREAT FOR KIDS

Advance Preparation

Day before drain 1 carton (16 ounces) plain, nonfat yogurt to make approximately 1 cup yogurt cheese (see page 129)

Special Equipment

yogurt cheese funnel or similar device

Yield

6 servings

Nutrition per Serving

Calories: 80
Carbohydrates: 17 grams
Protein: 4 grams
Fat: Fat-Free*
Cholesterol: 0 milligrams
Sodium: 50 milligrams
Dietary Fiber: 1 gram

*All foods contain some fat. Less than .5 gram of fat per serving is nutritionally insignificant and considered to be "Fat-Free."

frozen fruit creme

ingredients:

2 cups unsweetened frozen fruit

2 tablespoons + 1 tablespoon
  fruit-juice-sweetened preserves

1 cup nonfat yogurt cheese

⅓ cup nonfat dry milk solids

½ teaspoon vanilla

directions:

In food processor, combine frozen fruit, 2 tablespoons preserves, yogurt cheese, nonfat dry milk solids and vanilla, and puree until smooth, approximately 2 minutes. Stir in 1 tablespoon preserves.

Spoon into bowls and serve at once, or transfer to freezing container and place in freezer for 30 minutes for soft ice cream consistency.

The refreshingly fruity taste of this recipe will satisfy anyone's sweet tooth. It can be enjoyed all year long by using frozen strawberries, but it is especially delicious when it is made with fresh berries in season.

Even though strawberries are now available year-round, locally grown fruit is usually less expensive and better tasting than the fruit flown in from the southern hemisphere. The season for local strawberries is from May through August.

Remember when selecting strawberries that no matter how appealing the big ones look, the medium-sized ones are usually better tasting.

In addition to their distinctive flavor and beautiful appearance, strawberries are quite nutritious. They provide vitamin C and potassium, as well as soluble fiber.

FAT-FREE

Advance Preparation

Day before drain 1 carton (16 ounces) plain, nonfat yogurt to make approximately 1 cup yogurt cheese (see page 129)
Fat-Free Crust (see page 127)

Special Equipment

yogurt cheese funnel or similar device
9-inch nonstick springform pan

Yield

10 servings

Nutrition per Serving

Calories: 191
Carbohydrates: 40 grams
Protein: 8 grams
Fat: Fat-Free*
Cholesterol: 0 milligrams
Sodium: 110 milligrams
Dietary Fiber: 3 grams

*All foods contain some fat. Less than .5 gram of fat per serving is nutritionally insignificant and considered to be "Fat-Free."

frozen strawberry creme tart

ingredients:

1 Fat-Free Crust

2 cups + 1 cup frozen strawberries (defrosted)

4 tablespoons honey

3 tablespoons fruit-juice-sweetened strawberry preserves

2 cups nonfat yogurt cheese

⅓ cup nonfat dry milk solids

½ teaspoon vanilla

1 large ripe banana, sliced

directions:

Prepare crust for 9-inch nonstick springform pan.

For filling, combine 2 cups frozen strawberries, honey, preserves, yogurt cheese, nonfat dry milk solids and vanilla in food processor; puree until smooth. Fold in banana and remaining cup of strawberries into cream mixture. Spoon into prepared crust, and place in freezer for minimum of 45 minutes.

If made well in advance, remove from freezer about 15 minutes before serving for best texture.

Lemon pudding is typical of the kind of dessert that contains "hidden" fat. It doesn't taste like there's any fat in it, yet the traditional recipe calls for three eggs and a half cup of milk. As a result, there can be as much as four grams of fat in a serving. Our version is Fat-Free because we've eliminated the eggs and whole milk. Instead, we use whole wheat flour to thicken the pudding and evaporated skimmed milk for richness.

You can easily turn this versatile pudding/filling into a beautiful parfait. In clear parfait glasses, simply add a tablespoon or so of pudding filling, followed by the same amount of your favorite fruit. Continue the layering until the glass is three-quarters of the way full. For a smoother parfait, layer with our Creamy Berry Topping (see page 153) instead of fresh fruit.

FAT-
FREE

Special Equipment

4 custard cups

Yield

1½ cups (4 servings)

Nutrition per Serving

Calories: 135
Carbohydrates: 26 grams
Protein: 8 grams
Fat: Fat-Free*
Cholesterol: less than 5 milligrams
Sodium: 115 milligrams
Dietary Fiber: 1 gram

*All foods contain some fat. Less than .5 gram of fat per serving is nutritionally insignificant and considered to be "Fat-Free."

lemon pudding/filling

ingredients:

2 tablespoons whole wheat
    pastry flour

1 tablespoon arrowroot

1 can (12 fluid ounces)
    evaporated skimmed milk

3 tablespoons pure maple syrup

½ teaspoon vanilla

2 tablespoons lemon juice

1 teaspoon finely grated lemon peel

directions:

In medium saucepan, over medium-high heat, whisk together flour, arrowroot, evaporated milk and maple syrup. Bring mixture to low boil; reduce heat to low and cook until mixture thickens, approximately 5 minutes. Stir in vanilla, lemon juice and lemon peel. Let cook slightly, approximately 5 minutes.

Pour pudding into 4 custard cups, or use three-quarter cup as filling between 2 9-inch cake layers, and pour remaining pudding into 2 custard cups.

This is not your ordinary pudding recipe. Because of the "crust" on the bottom and fruit garnish on the top, this colorful and festive dessert is really a tropical fruit torte, without all the work and fat. The tropical flavors come from coconut extract that goes into the pudding, and pineapple rings and mandarin oranges placed on the top.

The inspiration for this recipe came from the expensive and rich fruit tortes you often find in specialty bakeries. We wanted to create a new version of these tortes without the fat that you can make even on the busiest of days. It will be our little secret that the recipe is so simple and healthy.

Special Equipment

8 8-ounce glass custard cups

Yield

8 servings

Nutrition per Serving

Calories: 175
Carbohydrates: 40 grams
Protein: 6 grams
Fat: Fat-Free**
Cholesterol: 0 milligrams
Sodium: 70 milligrams
Dietary Fiber: 2 grams

*We developed this recipe using Health Valley Fat-Free Granola with Date and Almond Flavor.
**All foods contain some fat. Less than .5 gram of fat per serving is nutritionally insignificant and considered to be "Fat-Free."

paradise pudding

ingredients:

2 tablespoons whole wheat
   pastry flour

1 tablespoon arrowroot

1 can (12 fluid ounces)
   evaporated skimmed milk

3 tablespoons pure maple syrup

½ teaspoon vanilla

½ teaspoon coconut extract

2 tablespoons lemon juice

1 teaspoon finely grated lemon peel

½ cup fat-free granola
   (without fruit added)*

⅓ cup fruit-juice-sweetened
   strawberry preserves, melted

1 can (8 ounces) juice-packed
   pineapple rings, drained

1 can (10½ ounces) juice-packed
   mandarin oranges, drained

directions:

In medium saucepan, over medium-high heat, whisk together flour, arrowroot, evaporated skimmed milk and maple syrup. Bring mixture to low boil; reduce heat to low and cook until mixture starts to thicken, approximately 10 minutes. Stir in vanilla and coconut extracts, lemon juice and lemon peel. Let pudding cool slightly; pudding will continue to thicken upon cooling.

Pulse granola in food processor into coarse crumbs, approximately 1 minute. In 8 8-ounce glass custard cups, place 1 tablespoon of crumbs per cup.

In each cup, drizzle half tablespoon of melted preserves over crumbs, then divide pudding evenly into each cup over preserves. Cut 8 pineapple rings into tidbits. In each cup, arrange pineapple tidbits and mandarin oranges in spiral design over pudding and place half teaspoon of preserves in center.

Before serving, place custard cups in refrigerator for minimum of 30 minutes.

Bread pudding is a classic "comfort food" that we associate with home cooking. However, it is also a dessert with "hidden" fat because the traditional recipe calls for two eggs and two cups of whole milk, so a serving has six grams of fat.

Our version is just as delicious and soothing, but has one-sixth the fat. Instead of all the fat, this recipe offers you important nutrition, including five grams of fiber from whole wheat bread. You also get beta carotene from the peaches, which are one of the best natural sources of this important antioxidant.

Of course, you probably won't be thinking about nutrition when you taste this recipe because you'll be enjoying the taste too much.

Serving Suggestion:

You might want to serve this pudding with Creamy Maple Sauce (see page 159).

Temperature and Time

Bake at 325°F. for 60-65 minutes

Yield

9 servings

Nutrition per Serving

Calories: 206
Carbohydrates: 43 grams
Protein: 7 grams
Fat: 1 gram
Calories from Fat: 4%
Cholesterol: 0 milligrams
Sodium: 190 milligrams
Dietary Fiber: 3 grams

peach banana bread pudding

ingredients:

8 slices fat-free whole wheat bread, cut into 1-inch cubes (approximately 3½ cups)

1½ cups evaporated skimmed milk

4 egg whites, lightly beaten

½ cup frozen apple juice concentrate (defrosted)

1 can (16 ounces) juice-packed peaches, chopped

2 ripe bananas, sliced

1 teaspoon lemon juice

1¼ teaspoons cinnamon

¼ teaspoon ground nutmeg

⅓ cup pure maple syrup

1 teaspoon vanilla

directions:

Preheat oven to 325°F. In large bowl, add bread cubes, evaporated milk, egg whites, juice concentrate, peaches, bananas, lemon juice, cinnamon, nutmeg, maple syrup and vanilla; mix well.

Pour mixture into 8x11x2-inch ovenproof glass baking dish. Bake at 325°F. for 60-65 minutes, or until knife inserted near center comes out clean. Cool slightly. Serve warm or cold.

H ere is a dessert that is quick and simple to prepare because it is really an "upside down" tart. The crust goes on top instead of at the bottom, and it requires no rolling. All you do is grind some Fat-Free granola in a food processor and add a few other ingredients to make an easy crust that's Fat-Free.

Not only is this dessert a cinch to prepare, it tastes delicious and provides the nutritional benefits of peaches, which are a good source of beta carotene. We recommend using fresh peaches when they're in season, but the recipe works beautifully with canned peaches packed in their own juice with no added sugar.

FAT-FREE   GREAT FOR KIDS

Temperature and Time

Bake at 325°F. for
45 minutes

Yield

8 servings

Nutrition per Serving

Calories: 159
Carbohydrates: 37 grams
Protein: 4 grams
Fat: Fat-Free**
Cholesterol: 0 milligrams
Sodium: 55 milligrams
Dietary Fiber: 3 grams

*We developed this recipe using Health Valley Fat-Free Granola with Date and Almond Flavor.
**All foods contain some fat. Less than .5 gram of fat per serving is nutritionally insignificant and considered to be "Fat-Free."

peach tart

ingredients:

1 bag (16 ounces) frozen peach
  slices (defrosted)

1 cup fat-free granola
  (without fruit added)*

⅓ cup nonfat yogurt

½ cup pure maple syrup

2 egg whites, unbeaten

2 tablespoons arrowroot

½ teaspoon ground ginger

¼ teaspoon ground nutmeg

1 teaspoon vanilla

directions:

Preheat oven to 325°F. Spray 9-inch ovenproof glass pie dish with non-stick cooking spray. Layer peaches in spiral in pie plate.

In food processor, grind granola for 2 minutes; set aside one-third cup ground granola for topping. Add yogurt, maple syrup, egg whites, arrowroot, ginger, nutmeg and vanilla to remaining granola, and process until blended, approximately 30 seconds.

Pour mixture over peaches and sprinkle with reserved granola.

Bake at 325°F. for 45 minutes, or until top is set and lightly browned. Cool on wire rack for 15 minutes. Serve warm or cold.

This truly delicious trifle is an excellent choice to serve at a festive dinner party because it will impress your guests without all of the alcohol and fat usually associated with trifles. Bring it to the table in a clear glass trifle dish to show off the colorful layering of the ingredients.

This dish is also ideal to serve for a dinner party because it can be made ahead of time, and it actually tastes better when you keep it in the refrigerator overnight because the flavors have a chance to blend together. If time is of the essence, at least allow it to rest in the refrigerator for two hours before serving.

Of course, you don't need a special occasion to enjoy this recipe because it's simple to make and very nutritious.

The featured fruit is the peach, which made the Center for Science in the Public Interest's list of fruits with the most nutritional value, because it is a good source of vitamin A and fiber, and it's low in calories.

Here are a few important tips to ensure your trifle looks as good as it tastes: We suggest that you drizzle the jelly mixture for best results; also, the custard must be spread quickly or it will thicken too much to work with easily.

Serving Suggestion:

If desired, garnish the top layer of this trifle with seasonal fruit.

FAT-
FREE

Special Equipment

3-quart trifle dish

Yield

14 servings

Nutrition per Serving

Calories: 211
Carbohydrates: 47 grams
Protein: 7 grams
Fat: Fat-Free**
Cholesterol: 0 milligrams
Sodium: 90 milligrams
Dietary Fiber: 1 gram

**All foods contain some fat. Less than .5 gram of fat per serving is nutritionally insignificant and considered to be "Fat-Free."

peach trifle

ingredients:

¼ cup whole wheat pastry flour

2 tablespoons arrowroot

2 cans (12 fluid ounces each) evaporated skimmed milk

⅓ cup pure maple syrup

2 teaspoons vanilla

1½ teaspoons almond extract

½ angelfood cake, cut into 2-inch squares*

1 jar (10 ounces) fruit-juice-sweetened raspberry preserves, melted

2 cans (16 ounces each) juice-packed peach halves, drained

directions:

In medium saucepan, over medium-high heat, whisk together flour, arrowroot, evaporated milk and maple syrup. Bring mixture to low boil; reduce heat to low and cook until mixture thickens to consistency similar to yogurt, approximately 10 minutes. Stir in vanilla and almond extracts. Let cool slightly, approximately 5 minutes.

In 3-quart or larger trifle dish, assemble 3 layers of cake squares, preserves, pudding and peaches, using one-third of each ingredient per layer.

*note: You can use the Strawberry Angel Food Cake recipe (see page 217). Follow the basic cake recipe, but omit the Fluffy Lemon Frosting and fresh strawberries. The extra cake half can be wrapped in plastic wrap and foil and placed in the freezer for future use.

P ina colada is the classic tropical flavor combination of pineapple and coconut. The only problem with the traditional recipe is that coconuts are high in fat, especially saturated fat. In fact, coconut oil contains more saturated fat than found in lard!

We've captured the distinctive pina colada flavor and texture without the fat, by combining pineapple with a combination of coconut extract for the flavor and grated apples to provide the texture of shredded coconut.

The success of this recipe depends on well-drained pineapple. It's essential to get every last drop of juice out of the crushed pineapple before you use it in the recipe, because excess moisture will make the pudding soggy.

Serving Suggestion:

Try this recipe with La Creme Whipped Topping (see page 175).

GREAT FOR KIDS

Temperature and Time

Bake at 325°F. for 60-65 minutes

Yield

8 servings

Nutrition per Serving

Calories: 186
Carbohydrates: 40 grams
Protein: 7 grams
Fat: 1 gram
Calories from Fat: 5%
Cholesterol: 0 milligrams
Sodium: 180 milligrams
Dietary Fiber: 2 grams

pina colada bread pudding

ingredients:

8 slices fat-free whole wheat bread,
  cut into 1-inch cubes
  (approximately 3½ cups)

1½ cups evaporated skimmed milk

4 egg whites, lightly beaten

½ cup apple juice concentrate
  (defrosted)

1 can (16 ounces) juice-packed
  crushed pineapple, well drained

2 medium apples, peeled, cored and
  grated (approximately 2¼ cups)

1 teaspoon cinnamon

⅓ cup pure maple syrup

1 teaspoon vanilla

½ teaspoon coconut extract

directions:

Preheat oven to 325°F. In large bowl, add bread cubes, evaporated milk, egg whites, juice concentrate, crushed pineapple, apples, cinnamon, maple syrup, vanilla and coconut extracts; mix well.

Pour mixture into 8x11x2-inch ovenproof glass baking dish. Bake at 325°F. for 60-65 minutes or until knife inserted near center comes out clean. Cool slightly. Serve warm or cold.

M any people are intimidated by souffles because they think you need some special skill to get them to rise. The truth is that all that is required to make a successful souffle is a bit of care in handling the ingredients.

One of the keys is simply to be careful in separating the egg whites from the yolks. If you get any of the yolk in with the whites, it becomes very difficult to whip the whites because the fat from the yolks inhibits the aeration process. If you're careful about getting only egg whites together, then start whipping them slowly and gradually increase speed until soft peaks form. The only other mistake you can make is to overwhip the whites. If you follow these simple directions, everything else should go smoothly for you.

In the past, we've stayed away from souffles not because we were afraid they wouldn't rise, but because they can contain so much fat. The classic chocolate souffle recipe calls for four whole eggs, plus three-quarter cup of whole milk, along with butter and chocolate. As a result, a serving contains 24 grams of fat.

Here is a recipe that is every bit as impressive to look at and as exciting to taste as a regular souffle, but without all the fat.

Advance Preparation

Coco Frosting
(see page 151)

Special Equipment

1½-quart souffle dish

Temperature and Time

Bake at 350°F. for
35 minutes

Yield

8 servings

Nutrition per Serving

Calories: 150
Carbohydrates: 36 grams
Protein: 3 grams
Fat: Fat-Free*
Cholesterol: 0 milligrams
Sodium: 40 milligrams
Dietary Fiber: 1 gram

*All foods contain some fat. Less than
.5 gram of fat per serving is nutritionally
insignificant and considered to be
"Fat-Free."

quick raspberry souffle

ingredients:

1 tablespoon whole wheat pastry flour

1 jar (10 ounces) fruit-juice-sweetened raspberry preserves

1-2 tablespoons finely grated orange peel

2 tablespoons hot water

5 egg whites, at room temperature

½ teaspoon cream of tartar

1 recipe Coco Frosting, hot

directions:

Preheat oven to 350°F. Spray 1½ quart souffle dish with nonstick cooking spray. Sprinkle bottom and sides with flour; tap out excess flour.

In medium bowl, mix together raspberry preserves, orange peel and hot water.

In large bowl, combine egg whites and cream of tartar. Using electric mixer, beat egg whites until they hold stiff peaks.

Fold 1 cup of whipped egg whites into preserve mixture; then fold mixture into remaining whipped egg whites. Gently fold mixture into prepared souffle dish and smooth top with spatula.

Place souffle dish in baking pan and surround with hot water to depth of 1½ inches. Bake at 350°F. for 35 minutes, until top is nicely puffed, fairly firm and medium brown.

While souffle is baking, prepare Coco Frosting according to directions, except cook for 3 minutes only and serve warm over individual portions of souffle. Serve immediately.

The traditional rice pudding recipe calls for two eggs and two cups of scalded whole milk. As a result, there are five grams of fat in a single serving.

Our version has the flavor and texture of the classic recipe but it's Fat-Free. It can also be enjoyed even by people who are allergic to milk or who cannot digest lactose, because we've completely eliminated the dairy products. Instead we use our Health Valley Fat-Free Soy Moo® soy drink. In creating this recipe, we discovered that it actually works better than milk because it lends the fragrant aroma of vanilla and it caramelizes on top like creme brulee. Soy Moo is higher in calcium and vitamin D than milk, but is fat free with no cholesterol.

FAT-FREE   DAIRY FREE   WHEAT FREE

GREAT FOR KIDS

Special Equipment

8 2½-inch ovenproof glass dessert cups

Temperature and Time

Bake at 325°F. for 50-60 minutes

Yield

8 servings

Nutrition per Serving

Calories: 186
Carbohydrates: 57 grams
Protein: 5 grams
Fat: Fat-Free***
Cholesterol: 0 milligrams
Sodium: 80 milligrams
Dietary Fiber: 2 grams

*We developed this recipe using Health Valley Fat-Free Soy Moo Soy Drink.
**To make 2 cups, use ⅔ cup raw brown rice and 1⅓ cups water.
***All foods contain some fat. Less than .5 gram of fat per serving is nutritionally insignificant and considered to be "Fat-Free."

rice pudding

ingredients:

1⅓ cups soy beverage*

½ cup honey

3 egg whites

2 teaspoons vanilla

½ teaspoon cinnamon

2 cups cooked brown rice
   (short grain preferred)**

¼ cup raisins

¼ cup chopped dates

pinch of ground nutmeg

directions:

Preheat oven to 325°F. In medium mixing bowl, combine soy beverage, honey, egg whites, vanilla and cinnamon. With electric mixer, beat until smooth. Stir in rice, raisins and dates. Spoon mixture into 8 2½-inch ovenproof glass dessert cups. Sprinkle lightly with nutmeg.

Place cups in baking pan and surround with hot water to depth of 1 inch. Bake at 325°F. for 50-60 minutes, until nicely browned on top. Pudding will appear runny, but will solidify as it cools. Remove from water bath to cool. Serve warm or chilled.

note: As an alternative, spoon mixture into an 8-inch square ovenproof glass baking dish. Sprinkle lightly with nutmeg and bake uncovered (no water bath) at 325°F. about 50-60 minutes or until a knife inserted in center comes out clean.

Vanilla pudding can be enjoyed all by itself, or as an ingredient in everything from parfaits and trifles to cream pies and cakes.

The only drawback to the traditional recipe is the fact that it calls for two egg yolks and two cups of whole milk, so it contains 10 grams of fat in each serving.

We've created a version without the fat by using whole wheat flour to thicken it and evaporated skimmed milk for richness. We use this delicious pudding as a filling for several of our cakes–Banana Cream Cake (see page 185), Boston Cream Cake (see page 191) and Coco Silk Cake (see page 197). You can also create a beautiful, festive dessert quickly and easily by taking a parfait cup, filling it with alternate layers of this pudding and your favorite chopped fruit, and topping it with fat-free granola.

FAT-FREE   GREAT FOR KIDS

Special Equipment
4 custard cups

Yield
1½ cups (4 servings)

Nutrition per Serving

Calories: 127
Carbohydrates: 24 grams
Protein: 7 grams
Fat: Fat-Free*
Cholesterol: less than 5 milligrams
Sodium: 100 milligrams
Dietary Fiber: 0 grams

*All foods contain some fat. Less than .5 gram of fat per serving is nutritionally insignificant and considered to be "Fat-Free."

vanilla pudding/filling

ingredients:

2 tablespoons whole wheat
pastry flour

1 tablespoon arrowroot

1 can (12 fluid ounces)
evaporated skimmed milk

3 tablespoons pure maple syrup

1 teaspoon vanilla

directions:

In medium saucepan, over medium-high heat, whisk together flour, arrowroot, evaporated milk and maple syrup. Bring mixture to low boil; reduce heat to low and cook until mixture thickens, approximately 5 minutes. Stir in vanilla extract. Let cool slightly, approximately 5 minutes.

Pour pudding into 4 custard cups; or use three-quarter cup as filling between 2 9-inch cake layers, and pour remaining pudding into 2 custard cups.

Healthy Five Section

	Calories	Protein g	Carbohydrate g	Fat g	Cholesterol mg	Dietary Fiber g	Vitamin A I.U.	Beta Carotene I.U.	Vitamin C mg	Calcium mg	Sodium mg	Potassium mg	Magnesium mg	Iron mg	Zinc mg	Phosphorus mg	Thiamine mg	Riboflavin mg	Niacin mg	Vitamin B6 mg	Vitamin B12 mcg	Vitamin E I.U.
Aloha Cake	215	4.0	52	FF	0.0	4.0	67.5	15	4.4	25	200	306	38.7	1.2	0.6	74	0.12	0.12	1.6	0.19	0.02	0.8
Carrot Pineapple Cake	199	4.0	47	FF	0.0	3.0	135.7	27	4.7	23	140	286	36.8	1.3	0.7	82	0.13	0.11	1.6	0.13	0.02	0.8
Carrot Raisin Cake	218	4.0	52	FF	0.0	4.0	452.7	75	4.6	24	140	313	37.5	1.4	0.7	89	0.13	0.12	1.7	0.14	0.02	0.9
Citrus Garden Cake	219	4.0	52	FF	0.0	4.0	285.8	54	16.1	22	140	340	38.2	1.2	0.7	88	0.14	0.12	1.7	0.13	0.02	0.8
Coco Garden Cake	198	4.0	47	0.5	0.0	3.0	148.2	27	13.6	21	140	376	47.4	2.1	0.8	98	0.99	0.11	1.6	0.10	0.05	0.8
Harvest Muffins	171	5.0	35	1.5	0.0	1.0	348.3	61	12.2	27	100	266	43.2	1.5	0.8	131	0.20	0.10	0.4	0.08	0.02	0.0
Pumpkin Delight Cake	199	4.0	47	0.5	0.0	2.0	626.2	7	1.8	24	170	294	23.7	2.1	0.4	60	0.19	0.15	1.4	0.07	0.02	0.0
Pumpkin Oat Muffins	197	3.0	47	0.5	0.0	0.4	626.2	7	1.8	24	170	288	23.2	2.1	0.4	60	0.19	0.13	1.4	0.07	0.01	0.0
Pumpkin Pie Bars	116	3.0	27	FF	0.0	3.0	417.2	5	1.0	27	65	191	26.1	1.1	0.4	56	0.09	0.08	1.0	0.07	0.01	0.5
Red Blush Cake	198	4.0	47	FF	0.0	3.0	3.7	1	15.5	18	140	314	38.8	1.1	0.7	80	0.13	0.11	1.7	0.12	0.02	0.8
Southwestern Corn Muffins	140	5.0	29	1.0	0.8	3.0	14.7	3	17.3	33	120	192	27.9	1.2	0.6	80	0.16	0.16	1.5	0.11	0.07	0.6
Spicy Pumpkin Cheesecake	211	7.0	46	FF	2.0	3.0	458.6	5	5.6	209	100	397	17.1	1.0	0.3	42	0.10	0.25	0.5	0.08	0.49	0.2
Spicy Tomato Cake	206	4.0	50	FF	0.0	4.0	28.5	5	4.2	21	180	322	37.3	1.4	0.7	84	0.12	0.11	1.8	0.15	0.01	0.7
Sunshine Cake	218	4.0	53	FF	0.0	4.0	73.7	17	2.4	26	200	256	33.8	1.3	0.6	74	0.11	0.11	1.7	0.10	0.02	0.7
Sweet Carrot Muffins	201	4.0	47	0.5	0.0	3.0	194.4	16	2.1	25	140	257	31.2	1.1	0.6	73	0.12	0.09	1.2	0.09	0.01	0.5
Sweet Potato Muffins	177	5.0	40	FF	0.0	4.0	79.1	15	2.9	63	110	358	46.1	1.4	0.9	112	0.14	0.15	1.9	0.18	0.04	0.9
Sweet Potato Pudding Cups	220	4.0	53	FF	0.0	3.0	79.10	173	11.4	95	75	283	14.8	1.2	0.3	38	0.12	0.23	0.6	0.16	0.05	2.8
Zucchini Bread Ring	130	4.0	29	1.0	0.0	2.0	6.0	5	2.9	19	170	247	35.7	1.2	0.6	87	0.14	0.07	1.0	0.09	0.01	0.5

Cheesecakes

	Calories	Protein g	Carbohydrate g	Fat g	Cholesterol mg	Dietary Fiber g	Vitamin A I.U.	Beta Carotene I.U.	Vitamin C mg	Calcium mg	Sodium mg	Potassium mg	Magnesium mg	Iron mg	Zinc mg	Phosphorus mg	Thiamine mg	Riboflavin mg	Niacin mg	Vitamin B6 mg	Vitamin B12 mcg	Vitamin E I.U.
Apricot Cheesecake	220	8.0	48	FF	2.0	2.0	92.3	11	8.3	238	110	500	18.2	0.8	0.4	53	0.09	0.35	0.6	0.11	0.61	0.7
Blueberry Cheesecake	216	8.0	47	FF	2.0	3.0	18.5	0	19.8	230	110	468	15.9	0.9	0.3	50	0.13	0.35	1.0	0.11	0.61	0.6
Coco Berry Cheesecake	185	7.0	41	FF	1.0	1.0	2.1	0	1.5	160	95	320	18.6	1.0	0.4	38	0.07	0.26	0.7	0.08	0.50	0.3
Fat-Free Crust	629	15.0	145	FF	0.0	17.0	0.0	0	23.5	6	260	627	7.6	0.2	0.0	9	0.00	0.17	0.1	0.02	0.07	0.0
New York Coco Cheesecake	160	7.0	3	FF	0.0	1.0	0.4	0	0.8	184	110	339	7.3	0.5	0.1	10	0.04	0.25	0.2	0.05	0.58	0.0
New York Lemon Cheesecake	211	10.0	43	FF	2.0	2.0	0.0	0	5.5	305	140	505	6.6	0.6	0.2	13	0.13	0.45	0.7	0.10	0.96	0.1
Nonfat Yogurt Cheese	502	52.0	69	FF	17.0	0.0	0.0	0	7.9	1802	690	2309	0.0	0.8	0.0	0	0.44	2.12	1.1	0.48	5.56	0.0
Pear-Bavarian Cheesecake	201	7.0	44	FF	1.0	3.0	0.6	0	7.2	222	100	510	15.4	1.2	0.2	29	0.14	0.30	0.8	0.09	0.58	0.7
Pineapple Cheesecake	189	8.0	40	FF	2.0	2.0	16.6	0	16.2	236	110	538	26.8	1.0	0.4	48	0.20	0.35	1.0	0.16	0.61	0.3
Strawberry Glaze Cheesecake	193	8.0	41	FF	2.0	3.0	16.4	0	35.0	230	110	487	16.9	1.1	0.3	50	0.12	0.36	0.9	0.10	0.61	0.3

Frostings, Sauces, Toppings

	Calories	Protein g	Carbohydrate g	Fat g	Cholesterol mg	Dietary Fiber g	Vitamin A I.U.	Beta Carotene I.U.	Vitamin C mg	Calcium mg	Sodium mg	Potassium mg	Magnesium mg	Iron mg	Zinc mg	Phosphorus mg	Thiamine mg	Riboflavin mg	Niacin mg	Vitamin B6 mg	Vitamin B12 mcg	Vitamin E I.U.
Caramelized Banana Topping	41	0.0	11	FF	0.0	0.0	0.8	0	0.9	14	0	60	3.9	0.2	0.0	3	0.02	0.21	0.1	0.06	0.00	0.0
Coco Frosting	38	1	9	FF	0.0	0.0	10.1	1	0.1	21	10	121	1	0.7	0.0	29	0.00	0.03	0.1	0	0.08	0.0
Creamy Berry Topping	20	0.5	4	FF	0.0	0.0	55.3	2	5.1	654	10	963	30.3	1.9	0.5	92	0.30	0.74	1.3	0.20	1.64	0.0
Creamy Cinnamon Sauce	23	1.0	5	FF	0.0	0.0	13.9	0	3.1	36	0	52	4.1	0.1	0.1	25	0.00	0.04	0.1	0.01	0.03	0.0
Creamy Lemon Frosting	49	2.0	10	FF	0.0	0.0	5.6	0	0.5	79	30	107	2.0	0.2	0.0	9	0.03	0.08	0.1	0.02	0.21	0.0
Creamy Maple Sauce	13	1.0	2	FF	0.0	0.0	13.8	0	0.2	36	15	42	3.6	0.1	0.1	24	0.00	0.04	0.0	0.00	0.03	0.0
Creamy Mocha Frosting	36	1.0	8	FF	0.0	0.0	3.8	0	0.2	54	20	111	5.7	0.4	0.1	13	0.02	0.06	0.1	0.01	0.15	0.0
Creamy Orange Frosting	18	1.0	4	FF	0.0	0.0	2.1	0	1.3	27	10	41	0.9	0.1	0.0	3	0.01	0.03	0.0	0.00	0.07	0.0
Creamy Pineapple Topping	31	1.0	7	FF	0.0	0.0	3.0	0	1.2	42	15	72	3.5	0.1	0.0	5	0.03	0.04	0.1	0.02	0.10	0.0
Creamy Vanilla Frosting	34	1.0	7	FF	0.0	0.0	3.7	0	0.2	52	20	71	1.3	0.1	0.0	6	0.02	0.06	0.0	0.01	0.14	0.0
Fluffy Coco Frosting	28	1	7	FF	0.0	0.0	8.0	1	0.1	15	10	91	8.8	0.5	0.2	22	0.01	0.03	0.1	0.01	0.06	0.0
Fluffy Lemon Frosting	38	1.0	8	FF	0.0	0.0	1.9	0	0.2	31	20	31	1.9	0.2	0.0	5	0.02	0.03	0.0	0.00	0.02	0.0
Fluffy Vanilla Frosting	36	0.0	8	FF	0.0	0.0	0.0	0	0.0	14	10	44	1.6	0.2	0.0	2	0.02	0.03	0.0	0.00	0.00	0.0
La Creme Whipped Topping	43	2.0	8	FF	0.0	0.0	3.0	0	0.0	5	40	10	0.8	0.0	0.0	5	0.00	0.00	0.0	0.00	0.00	0.0
Pineapple Glaze	33	0.0	9	FF	0.0	0.0	1.0	0	2.6	10	0	46	4.5	0.2	0.0	2	0.04	0.00	0.0	0.02	0.00	0.0
Spicy Apple Topping	36	0.0	9	FF	0.0	0.0	0.8	0	0.9	4	0	56	2.0	0.2	0.0	5	0.01	0.00	0.1	0.02	0.00	0.1
Strawberry Glaze	36	0.0	9	FF	0.0	0.0	1.0	0	9.5	9	0	43	3.0	0.2	0.0	3	0.01	0.01	0.1	0.00	0.00	0.1

Cakes

	Calories	Protein g	Carbohydrate g	Fat g	Cholesterol mg	Dietary Fiber g	Vitamin A I.U.	Beta Carotene I.U.	Vitamin C mg	Calcium mg	Sodium mg	Potassium mg	Magnesium mg	Iron mg	Zinc mg	Phosphorus mg	Thiamine mg	Riboflavin mg	Niacin mg	Vitamin B6 mg	Vitamin B12 mcg	Vitamin E I.U.
Banana Cream Cake	151	2.0	37	FF	0.0	2.0	5.1	0	2.1	29	110	212	23.1	0.7	0.4	44	0.07	0.09	0.9	0.17	0.02	0.4
Banana Date Cake	220	4.0	55	FF	0.0	3.0	2.3	0	2.2	21	210	286	36.6	1.1	0.7	72	0.10	0.12	1.5	0.21	0.02	0.8
Black Forest Cake	188	3.0	45	FF	0.0	2.0	7.1	0	0.6	30	80	233	33.3	1.5	0.6	76	0.06	0.10	1.1	0.06	0.05	0.5
Boston Cream Cake	135	3.0	32	FF	0.0	2.0	16.8	1	7.3	31	100	224	28.2	1.1	0.5	71	0.07	0.09	1.0	0.06	0.08	0.5
Chunky Apple Cake	125	4.0	26	1.0	0.0	3.0	9.9	0	9.6	30	170	200	32.2	1.1	0.7	86	0.10	0.11	1.4	0.11	0.05	0.9
Coco-Mo Angel Cake	146	5	32	FF	0	0.0	3.3	0	0.25	81.1	60	302	19.9	1.7	0.2	35	0.11	0.21	0.6	0.01	0.19	0.01
Coco Silk Cake	172	4	41	FF	0	2.0	11.1	0	0.3	35	80	300	39.7	1.8	0.7	90	0.07	0.11	1.1	0.06	0.1	0.5
Honey Lemon Cake	164	3	38	FF	0	3.0	0.4	0	18.3	11	135	216	30.3	0.9	0.5	71	0.08	0.09	1.3	0.08	0.01	0.7
Lemon Cream Cake	169	4	39	FF	0	2.0	28.8	0	13.6	83	120	232	28.1	0.9	0.6	95	0.07	0.14	1	0.07	0.06	0.5
Mandarin Chiffon Cake	134	4.0	30	FF	0.0	2.0	36.6	6	15.2	35	45	202	21.6	0.7	0.4	39	0.10	0.15	0.7	0.04	0.05	0.3
Mocha Mandarin Torte	204	5.0	48	FF	0.0	2.0	23.3	3	7.1	94	100	405	42.1	1.9	0.7	88	0.11	0.17	1.2	0.08	0.25	0.5
Neapolitan Ice Cream Cake	189	6.0	42	FF	0.0	2.0	24.7	0	11.5	177	95	373	24.7	1.2	0.5	70	0.13	0.24	0.8	0.08	0.48	0.4
Orange Cake	193	4.0	46	FF	0.0	3.0	12.2	1	14.5	14	135	231	31.5	1.0	0.7	74	0.12	0.10	1.5	0.09	0.02	0.7
Pineapple Cake	173	4.0	41	FF	0.0	3.0	2.0	0	3.7	15	135	206	32.9	1.0	0.6	70	0.11	0.10	1.4	0.09	0.02	0.9
Sachertorte	197	3.0	48	FF	0.0	2.0	8.2	0	0.5	28	60	268	37.5	1.7	0.7	82	0.06	0.10	1.1	0.06	0.09	0.5
Spice Cake	220	4.0	54	FF	0.0	3.0	4.0	0	10.0	18	140	293	35.2	1.2	0.6	81	0.12	0.11	1.6	0.12	0.02	0.7
Strawberry Angel Food Cake	114	3.0	25	FF	0.0	0.0	0.3	0	6.1	29	45	145	7.8	1.1	0.1	15	0.12	0.17	0.7	0.01	0.05	0.1

Bread, Muffins, Cupcakes

	Calories	Protein g	Carbohydrate g	Fat g	Cholesterol mg	Dietary Fiber g	Vitamin A I.U.	Beta Carotene I.U.	Vitamin C mg	Calcium mg	Sodium mg	Potassium mg	Magnesium mg	Iron mg	Zinc mg	Phosphorus mg	Thiamine mg	Riboflavin mg	Niacin mg	Vitamin B6 mg	Vitamin B12 mcg	Vitamin E I.U.
Apple Raisin Corn Bread	200	5.0	44	1.0	0.0	3.0	12.4	0	1.8	55	220	308	27.4	1.3	0.6	88	0.19	0.22	1.5	0.13	0.11	1.0
Apricot Filled Banana Muffins	144	3.0	31	1.0	0.0	3.0	7.6	0	1.6	21	130	209	7.6	0.7	0.1	16	0.06	0.08	0.9	0.09	0.06	0.1
Blueberry Muffins	99	2.0	22	FF	0.0	2.0	8.0	0	1.8	16	100	91	3.6	0.4	0.1	14	0.03	0.07	0.6	0.02	0.06	0.0
Corn Bread	155	5.0	32	1.0	0.0	2.0	10.9	0	0.3	49	220	203	23.4	1.1	0.5	77	0.17	0.21	1.4	0.09	0.11	0.8
Frosted Coco Cupcakes	164	3.0	39	FF	0.0	2.0	1.9	0	1.1	13	65	253	36.0	1.4	0.6	74	0.07	0.09	1.2	0.12	0.04	0.6
Gingerbread	98	2.0	23	FF	0.0	2.0	2.2	0	1.5	44	55	243	20.4	1.5	0.4	52	0.07	0.07	1.0	0.05	0.01	0.5

Cookies & Bars

	Calories	Protein g	Carbohydrate g	Fat g	Cholesterol mg	Dietary Fiber g	Vitamin A I.U.	Beta Carotene I.U.	Vitamin C mg	Calcium mg	Sodium mg	Potassium mg	Magnesium mg	Iron mg	Zinc mg	Phosphorus mg	Thiamine mg	Riboflavin mg	Niacin mg	Vitamin B6 mg	Vitamin B12 mcg	Vitamin E I.U.
Black & White Brownies	82	2.0	19	FF	0.0	1.0	1.3	0	0.4	36	30	116	12.0	0.6	0.2	25	0.04	0.06	0.4	0.03	0.09	0.2
Brownies	87	2.0	21	FF	0.0	1.0	2.0	0	0.5	7	35	125	18.5	0.8	0.3	38	0.04	0.05	0.6	0.04	0.02	0.3
Chewy Spice Cookies	197	4.0	46	FF	0.0	2.0	0.8	0	6.5	7	25	83	11.7	0.4	0.2	31	0.04	0.02	0.3	0.03	0.00	0.2
Coco Crispy Treats	81	1.0	20	FF	0.0	0.0	0.0	0	0.0	16	10	78	4.6	0.3	0.0	6	0.02	0.03	0.0	0.00	0.00	0.0
Crispy Rice Treats	79	1.0	19	FF	0.0	0.0	0.0	0	0.0	15	10	51	1.7	0.2	0.0	2	0.02	0.03	0.0	0.00	0.00	0.0
Date Filled Cookie Bars	120	2.0	28	FF	0.0	1.0	0.0	0	11.7	8	30	115	21.0	0.7	0.4	57	0.08	0.04	0.6	0.05	0.00	0.3
Date Granola Bars	135	2.0	31	0.5	0.0	2.0	0.8	0	5.3	14	0	176	21.8	0.7	0.4	56	0.09	0.04	0.5	0.05	0.00	0.0
Energy Bars	88	2.0	21	FF	0.0	1.0	63.0	2	0.5	6	35	210	14.8	0.7	0.2	39	0.04	0.05	0.4	0.05	0.00	0.3
Granola Cookies	137	3.0	33	FF	0.0	3.0	43.6	10	1.3	16	75	266	27.5	1.0	0.5	68	0.09	0.08	1.2	0.10	0.01	0.6
Honey Raisin Cookies	187	3.0	43	1.0	0.0	1.0	0.6	0	0.6	17	55	180	26.7	1.0	0.5	83	0.13	0.04	0.3	0.04	0.00	0.0
Oatmeal Date Cookies	158	3.0	37	0.5	0.0	2.0	0.8	0	0.4	14	50	167	27.7	0.9	0.5	72	0.10	0.06	0.9	0.06	0.01	0.3
Oatmeal Raisin Cookies	193	5.0	43	1.0	0.0	2.0	0.3	0	12.9	21	180	222	43.7	1.5	0.9	118	0.16	0.10	1.3	0.10	0.01	0.6
Raisin Grain Bars	126	3.0	29	1.0	0.0	1.0	0.9	0	5.7	18	0	191	24.6	1.0	0.5	74	0.11	0.04	0.6	0.06	0.00	0.0
Raspberry Cookie Bars	149	2.0	35	0.5	0.0	1.0	0.4	0	11.9	10	30	128	23.9	0.8	0.5	64	0.08	0.04	0.8	0.05	0.00	0.3
Thumbprint Cookies	149	3.0	36	FF	0.0	4.0	29.0	6	0.8	16	190	178	18.2	0.7	0.3	46	0.06	0.05	0.8	0.06	0.00	0.4
Tropical Fruit Cookie	195	4.0	44	1.0	0.0	1.0	11.9	1	16.1	18	170	185	29.6	2.1	0.4	70	0.20	0.12	1.3	0.05	0.01	0.0

Fruit Desserts, Puddings, & Pies

	Calories	Protein g	Carbohydrate g	Fat g	Cholesterol mg	Dietary Fiber g	Vitamin A I.U.	Beta Carotene I.U.	Vitamin C mg	Calcium mg	Sodium mg	Potassium mg	Magnesium mg	Iron mg	Zinc mg	Phosphorus mg	Thiamine mg	Riboflavin mg	Niacin mg	Vitamin B6 mg	Vitamin B12 mcg	Vitamin E I.U.
Apple Bread Pudding	163	6.0	35	1.0	0.0	2.0	39.3	0	26.3	126	150	357	28.9	1.1	1.0	121	0.09	0.19	0.7	0.11	0.10	0.3
Apple Crisp	215	2.0	54	FF	0.0	4.0	4.7	1	46.2	19	35	415	13.5	0.7	0.1	26	0.04	0.04	0.3	0.11	0.00	0.7
Apple Rice Pudding	195	4.0	45	FF	0.0	2.0	1.8	0	1.5	24	57	223	29.7	0.6	0.8	74	0.07	0.12	1.0	0.10	0.03	0.2
Blueberry Peach Crisp	190	2.0	46	FF	0.0	4.0	33.3	0	57.6	17	35	371	12.6	0.6	0.2	21	0.03	0.06	0.8	0.08	0.00	0.0
Coco Banana Meringue	196	6.0	44	FF	0.0	2.0	43.6	0	3.0	123	90	375	41.4	1.3	0.8	123	0.10	0.22	1.1	0.20	0.12	0.5
Coco Pudding/Filling	138	5.0	30	FF	0.0	1.0	65.8	0	0.7	198	70	351	35.4	1.3	0.8	144	0.09	0.21	0.5	0.05	0.16	0.2
Coco Raspberry Trifle	209	6.0	48	FF	0.0	3.0	39.8	0	20.0	121	85	309	22.4	2.0	0.5	88	0.05	0.16	0.7	0.03	0.10	0.1
Crustless Apple Pie	133	3.0	32	FF	0.0	2.0	1.5	0	2.2	26	110	159	11.7	0.4	0.3	36	0.03	0.09	0.5	0.04	0.04	0.4
Frozen Fruit Creme	80	4.0	17	FF	0.0	1.0	29.3	1	21.2	132	50	243	10.8	0.5	0.2	45	0.04	0.17	0.3	0.04	0.38	0.2
Frozen Strawberry Creme Tart	191	8.0	40	FF	0.0	3.0	21.3	0	25.4	243	110	503	13.9	0.7	0.2	36	0.08	0.34	0.5	0.16	0.73	0.2
Lemon Pudding/Filling	135	8.0	26	FF	0.3	1.0	111.2	0	5.3	294	115	369	34.1	0.6	1.0	201	0.08	0.32	0.4	0.07	0.22	0.1
Paradise Pudding	175	6.0	40	FF	0.0	2.0	88.9	5	18.5	159	70	306	27.1	0.7	0.7	108	0.10	0.18	0.5	0.08	0.11	0.1
Peach Banana Bread Pudding	206	7.0	43	1.0	0.0	3.0	65.4	3	26.9	164	190	496	43.4	1.4	0.8	154	0.12	0.28	1.4	0.25	0.13	0.0
Peach Tart	159	4.0	37	FF	0.0	3.0	43.5	7	4.0	60	55	281	14.8	0.6	0.3	48	0.04	0.13	0.7	0.03	0.07	0.0
Peach Trifle	211	7.0	47	FF	0.0	1.0	88.8	4	3.3	187	90	363	29.0	1.2	0.7	134	0.11	0.28	1.0	0.06	0.16	0.1
Pina Colada Bread Pudding	186	7.0	40	1.0	0.0	2.0	45.9	0	26.4	153	180	374	38.2	1.3	0.7	137	0.15	0.24	0.9	0.13	0.12	0.2
Quick Raspberry Souffle	150	3.0	36	FF	0.0	1.0	8.7	0	0.9	26	40	166	15.9	0.9	0.2	31	0.01	0.11	0.2	0.02	0.10	0.0
Rice Pudding	186	5.0	57	FF	0.0	2.0	0.5	0	0.3	33	80	192	39.5	1.0	1.1	100	0.09	0.15	1.2	0.13	0.04	0.0
Vanilla Pudding/Filling	127	7.0	24	FF	2.6	0.0	98.7	0	1.1	262	100	323	30.5	0.6	0.9	180	0.07	0.28	0.4	0.06	0.20	0.1

Bibliography

Food, by Waverly Root, Simon and Schuster, N.Y., 1980

Foods That Heal, by Maureen Salaman, Statford Publishing, Menlo Park, Calif, 1989

The Healing Foods, by Patricia Hausman and Judith Benn Hurley, Rodale Press, Emmaus, Penn., 1989

The Healing Herbs, by Michael Castleman, Rodale Press, Menlo Park, Calif., 1991

Heinerman's Encyclopedia of Fruits, Vegetables and Herbs, by John Heinerman, Parker Publishing Co., West Nyack, N.Y., 1988

Joy of Cooking, by Irma S. Rombauer and Marion Rombauer Becker, The Bobbs-Merrill Co., N.Y., 1975

The Juiceman's Power of Juicing, by Jay Kordich, William Morrow and Co., Inc., N.Y., 1992

The New Doubleday Cookbook, by Jean Anderson and Elaine Hanna, Doubleday, N.Y., 1985

The New LaRousse Gastronomique, by Prosper Montagne, Crown Publishers, N.Y., 1977

Notes From an Ecological Kitchen, by Lorna Sass, Workman Press, N.Y., 1993

On Food and Cooking: The Science and Lore of the Kitchen, by Harold McGee, Scribners, N.Y., 1984

Raw Energy, by Leslie and Susannah Kenton, Warner Books, N.Y., 1984

Index

**BAKING
without
FAT**

Cookbook Reorder Form

I would like to order_____ additional copies of *Baking Without Fat* under your money-back guarantee.

The price is $12.95 each. California residents must add $1.07 sales tax for a total price of $14.02 per book.

Mail to:

Health Valley Foods Cookbook Offer
16100 Foothill Boulevard
Irwindale, CA 91706-7811

_____
NAME (Please print or type)

_____
STREET

_____
CITY   STATE   ZIP

Offer void where prohibited. Please allow 2-4 weeks delivery.
State tax will be billed where applicable.

❑ My check for the total amount of
    $_____ is enclosed.

❑ Charge it to my
    ❑ Visa or ❑ MasterCard

Card Number_____

Expiration Date_____

Signature_____

To order additional copies, use photocopies of this form or a plain sheet of paper.

BB94 REORDER

FREE! *With Your Purchase*

Annual Membership in Health Valley's Preferred Customer Club

For a limited time, when you purchase *Baking Withou Fat,* you'll receive a FREE one year membership in the **Health Valley Preferred Customer Club.**

You'll enjoy all the membership benefits and privileges, including:

- Quarterly newsletter filled with valuable information and healthy recipes
- Exclusive toll-free 800 hotline that puts you in touch with the dietitian/nutritionist
- New product announcements and samples
- Special offers on featured products – each issue of the newsletter will contain a coupon for a featured product that offers 50% or more off the retail price

Complete & return this card to Health Valley. We will enroll you in our Preferred Customer Club and send you membership materials.

_____
NAME

_____
ADDRESS

_____
CITY   STATE   ZIP

_____
TELEPHONE

ACB   Limit: one membership for each book published.   P1010394